300 slow cooker favorites

300 slow cooker favorites

Donna-Marie Pye

For complete cataloguing information, see page 367.

Disclaimers

The recipes in this book have been carefully tested by our kitchen and our tasters. To the best of our knowledge, they are safe and nutritious for ordinary use and users. For those people with food or other allergies, or who have special food requirements or health issues, please read the suggested contents of each recipe carefully and determine whether or not they may create a problem for you. All recipes are used at the risk of the consumer.

We cannot be responsible for any hazards, loss or damage that may occur as a result of any recipe use.

For those with special needs, allergies, requirements or health problems, in the event of any doubt, please contact your medical adviser prior to the use of any recipe.

Editor: Sue Sumeraj
Proofreader: Sheila Wawanash
Indexer: Gillian Watts
Design and Production: Kevin Cockburn/PageWave Graphics Inc.
Cover Photography: Colin Erricson
Interior Photography: Mark T. Shapiro
Food Styling: Kate Bush
Prop Styling: Charlene Erricson

Cover image: Spicy Cuban Turkey Stew (page 118)

We acknowledge the financial support of the Government of Canada through the Book Publishing Industry Development Program (BPIDP) for our publishing activities.

Published by Robert Rose Inc.
120 Eglinton Avenue East, Suite 800,
Toronto, Ontario, Canada M4P 1E2
Tel: (416) 322-6552 Fax: (416) 322-6936

Printed in Canada

1 2 3 4 5 6 7 8 9 CPL 15 14 13 12 11 10 09 08 07

Contents

Acknowledgments

It's hard for me to believe that almost 40 years after the first slow cooker was introduced, consumers still have a love of cooking with this appliance. As calendars fill up, it gets harder and harder to find the time to enjoy family meals together. This collection for *300 Slow Cooker Favorites* can help you ease that dinnertime crunch. Each one of the recipes in this consolidated collection has been tested to guarantee it works perfectly and is practical for today's families.

Many thanks to the readers of both of my previous books, *Best Slow Cooker Recipes* and *The Best Family Slow Cooker Recipes*; I very much appreciate all your letters, emails and comments, and especially your questions, as they gave me a clear idea of what you were looking for in a slow cooker cookbook.

Once again, thanks go to the entire Robert Rose creative team, especially Bob Dees and Marian Jarkovich, who have produced another great-looking, exceptionally edited cookbook; Jennifer MacKenzie for her impeccable recipe standards and fine-tuned palate, and for ensuring that everything was tested-till-perfect; Sue Sumeraj for her superb editing on this book; Kevin Cockburn at PageWave Graphics for turning type into beautiful design; and Kate Bush, Mark Shapiro, Colin Erricson and Charlene Erricson, the picture experts who worked their magic and made everything look so good. Many thanks to fellow home economists and colleagues Barb Holland and Wendy Heibert for their meticulous proofreading and editing assistance with the original manuscripts.

Thanks also to the countless family members, neighbors and friends who gave me encouragement, suggestions and writing and testing assistance. I cannot begin to thank those who offered to sample the recipes and gave me ideas and recipes for this book. I have tried to incorporate as many as possible and give credit where credit is due.

In the end, I have to thank my husband, Lawrence Greaves, and children, Darcy and Jack, who supported me whenever I needed to sit at my computer and retype or retest any recipe from this collection. They have been the best family any wife and mother could have — quietly patient while I was writing, and uncomplaining when I placed yet another slow cooker meal in front of them.

With the creative ideas in *300 Slow Cooker Favorites*, you will always have the help and inspiration you need to fit satisfying home-cooked meals into your busy family routine. Enjoy!

Introduction

My love affair with the slow cooker began many years ago when I commuted to a job that was a lengthy drive from my home. In order to have a tasty home-cooked meal on the dinner table, I would use my slow cooker at least once a week. Now, after many years of using it, I have become even more convinced of the wonderful benefits of the slow cooker.

Today, though I no longer commute, I am a freelance home economist, busy wife and mother to two children. With their array of after-school activities, I continue to use my slow cooker, looking for new and creative ways to feed my on-the-go family.

While most of us like to eat, we are all challenged by the stress of thinking about what to make for dinner every night. That's why more and more people are once again discovering the benefits of slow cookers. Introduced more than thirty years ago as a device for cooking dried beans, today's slow cooker has undergone various improvements and innovations. However, it continues to be an effective time-management tool no kitchen should be without. After all, who doesn't want to come home to a hot home-cooked meal at the end of the day?

When putting together this collection of recipes, my goal was to keep it family-friendly, to cook with ingredients and use recipes that would appeal to a busy household like mine. Some require longer slow cooking than others, but I think you will be quite surprised by how many different dishes can be prepared in the slow cooker. The recipes include traditional family favorites, as well as dishes that reflect our ever-expanding multicultural world. I still love a simple meatloaf (page 266) or macaroni and cheese (page 186). However, I can also travel to all corners of the globe — to China for saucy shredded pork flavored with hoisin and ginger (page 301), to India for a savory mulligatawny soup (page 90) or to Russia for a bowl of bubbling borscht (page 71). I have included some of my favorite desserts here too, such as an unbelievable slow cooker cheesecake (page 338) and a decadent bread pudding (page 363), along with a few appetizers, condiments and snacks that store well.

Slow cooker dishes have always been ideal for social gatherings and a great way to share food with friends. They are perfect for toting to potlucks, work functions and church events. With more than six million slow cookers being sold in North America every year, consumers are finding more ways to use this handy household appliance. For this reason, I have included a section called Entertaining with Your Slow Cooker (page 19), designed especially for those occasions when you are faced with the question, "What should I take to ...?"

I hope you enjoy this collection of slow cooker recipes and will come to rely on your slow cooker to help you create stress-free home-cooked meals.

— Donna-Marie Pye

Using Your Slow Cooker

Slow cooking is for everyone — families, couples, singles, first-time cooks and seniors. Whether you are on a tight schedule or love leisurely cooking, slow cookers can provide good, healthy food without requiring you to spend hours over a hot stove.

The basic premise is simple. Assemble and prepare the ingredients at your convenience — whether it's the night before or earlier in the day — place them in the slow cooker stoneware, turn it on and let the food cook while you walk away. Delicious aromas greet you when you return at the end of the day. Toss a salad, pour the drinks, and a delicious, home-prepared meal is ready for you to serve and savor.

Benefits of Slow Cooking

Slow cookers are ideally suited to meeting the needs of today's busy families. Their advantages include:

Convenience

Because the appliance cooks with such low heat, food won't scorch (and therefore, it does not need tending). Once you add the ingredients to the slow cooker and turn it on, you can forget about it and devote your time to other activities. At the end of the day, you can enjoy a hot, nutritious, home-cooked meal with minimal effort. Most recipes can be assembled the night before, refrigerated overnight and cooked the following day. The slow cooker is especially handy when you're entertaining or cooking for a large crowd, as it frees you from the kitchen and allows you to spend time with your guests. And because you can use your slow cooker as a serving bowl, there's one less dish to clean.

Economy

Basically, the slow cooker works by simmering food at a constant low temperature, which enhances the flavor and texture of some ingredients. Slow cooking tenderizes less expensive cuts of meat, such as beef brisket, stewing beef and pork, pork shoulder roasts and chops. The lengthy cooking time also allows flavors to blend, resulting in the tastiest soups, stews, chilies and pot roasts.

Dried beans, peas and lentils are an economical alternative to canned and can be cooked very easily in the slow cooker. Once they're cooked, simply add them to the recipe for a delicious one-pot meal.

Practicality

Because it cooks primarily with moisture, there is virtually no sticking with the slow cooker. (For some dishes, such as desserts, puddings and custards, I recommend that you lightly grease the bowl first, to make cleaning even easier). The appliance also runs on very little electricity. And it's perfect for warm-weather months, when using a conventional oven would make the kitchen uncomfortably warm. The slow cooker also frees up valuable oven space when you're entertaining or cooking for a crowd and is ideally suited to cooking holiday side dishes (see Entertaining with Your Slow Cooker, page 19).

How Does It Work?

The slow cooker is a simple appliance that is relatively low-tech. The appliance consists of a metal casing, stoneware insert and tight-fitting glass or plastic lid. The low-wattage metal casing houses electric heating elements between the inner and outer sides. As the elements heat up, they warm the insulated air trapped between the metal walls, ultimately heating the metal. Heat is then transferred to the cushion of air between the inner metal wall and the stoneware. Because the heating elements never make direct contact with the stoneware, there are no hot spots, eliminating the need for constant stirring. Slow cookers use about the same amount of energy as a 100-watt light bulb — substantially less than a conventional oven.

Types of Slow Cookers

The first slow cooker was introduced in 1971 as the Rival Company's Crock-Pot. While the original slow cooker came in only one size, today's models come in a variety of sizes, from tiny 1-quart to large 7-quart capacity. The smaller sizes are ideal for sauces and dips, while the larger ones are good for whole roasts and desserts. For convenience and ease of cleaning, look for a model with a removable stoneware insert.

Many people own more than one slow cooker. Our two-person household outgrew our original 3½-quart size as our family expanded. I now rely on larger slow cookers to feed my busy family of four. Most of the recipes in this book have been developed using a 4- and 6-quart size — the most popular models on the market today — but many can be made in a range of sizes. Check the guidelines at the beginning of each recipe for the suggested slow cooker size. The size and shape of the dish are likely to affect the cooking times; in general, the smaller the slow cooker, the shorter the cooking time.

Some manufacturers sell a multipurpose cooker, which can fulfill a variety of functions, such as browning, sautéing, boiling, braising, simmering and deep-frying. While these can be used for certain types of slow cooking, they are not suited to all slow cooker recipes. In these models, the heating element is located in the base of the housing unit, so the appliance cooks with direct heat. Unlike slow cookers, multipurpose cookers require supervision and stirring, as foods tend to stick to the bottom. When used for slow cooking, these cookers are best suited to soups and stews. Because of the direct heat, liquids tend to evaporate quickly, and foods can't always endure the long hours that slow cooking requires.

Your manufacturer's instruction booklet will give you further information on how best to care for and clean your slow cooker. Read these instructions carefully before embarking on your first recipe. Other variables that can affect the cooking time are extreme humidity, power fluctuations and high altitudes. Caution should be taken if these factors affect you.

Adapting Recipes

You can convert a favorite recipe from conventional directions to a slow-cooking method by following these simple guidelines:

- Select a recipe that uses a less-tender meat, such as pork shoulder or beef roast, which usually requires long cooking.
- You'll need to experiment with recipes that use dairy products because they can break down during extended cooking. Stir in cream, sour cream or cheese just before serving.
- Find a slow cooker recipe that's similar to your recipe to use as a sample. It will give you a feel for quantities and liquid amounts.
- Since there is little evaporation in a slow cooker, reduce liquid by about half when adapting a conventional recipe.
- Vegetables tend to cook more slowly than meat. To avoid undercooked vegetables, place vegetables on the bottom and around the sides of the cooker and place the meat on top. Since smaller pieces cook faster than large chunks, cut carrots, potatoes and turnips into small, bite-size portions and keep them submerged in the cooking liquid to ensure uniform cooking. Potatoes can be scrubbed, but it is not necessary to peel them; leaving them unpeeled helps them retain their shape and color in the cooking liquid.
- Add tender vegetables (such as peas and snow peas) and strongly flavored vegetables (broccoli, Brussels sprouts, cauliflower and greens such as kale and chard) in the last 15 to 60 minutes. Frozen

vegetables such as peas and corn should be added during the last 15 to 30 minutes. Eggplant should be parboiled or sautéed first to eliminate any bitter flavor.

- Dried beans must be softened completely before they are added to any recipe. Sugar and acid have a hardening effect on beans and will prevent softening. See additional information about cooking with dried beans on page 146.
- Some recipe ingredients — such as pasta and seafood — are not suited for extended cooking in the slow cooker. They should be added during the last hour of cooking time.
- Cook pasta to the tender-but-firm stage before adding to the slow cooker.
- Uncooked rice can be added to the slow cooker, but you'll want to add ¼ cup (50 mL) extra liquid per ¼ cup (50 mL) rice. Use long-grain parboiled (converted) rice for the best results in all-day cooking. The process by which converted rice is made helps keep the kernels from sticking together, resulting in an evenly cooked product.

Following is a chart that will help you adapt some of your favorite recipes to the slow cooker. Keep in mind that these times are approximate; you will be the best judge of when your food is tender and completely cooked.

If recipe says	Cook in slow cooker
15 to 30 minutes	1½ to 2 hours on **High** 4 to 6 hours on **Low**
25 to 45 minutes	3 to 4 hours on **High** 6 to 10 hours on **Low**
50 minutes to 3 hours	4 to 6 hours on **High** 8 to 18 hours on **Low**

Tips for Successful Slow Cooking

The slow cooker can save you precious time while creating delicious and nutritious dishes. However, there are tips that will help you use the appliance to its best advantage.

Brown Meats and Poultry and Sauté Vegetables First

In general, it is a good idea to brown meats before adding them to the slow cooker. Although this step may add a few extra minutes in preparation time, browning dramatically improves the end result. Not only does it improve the color by caramelizing the meat, it also breaks down the natural sugars and releases their flavors. Sautéing vegetables with spices and dried herbs before slow cooking also produces a richer, more intense sauce.

To brown meats and sauté vegetables, add a small amount of oil to a large nonstick skillet or Dutch oven. Heat over medium-high heat, then add the food. It is best to brown meat in small batches, ensuring that the meat will brown rather than steam. Stir or turn frequently to brown evenly on all sides, then transfer to the slow cooker. Dredge meat in seasoned flour before cooking rather than after to reduce the chance of lumpy gravy.

To maximize flavor, deglaze the pan with either wine or broth after browning. Simply pour a small amount of liquid into the skillet, stirring to remove the caramelized juices and cooked-on food particles. Bring to a boil, reduce heat and simmer for 1 to 2 minutes while stirring. Pour this liquid over the meat in the slow cooker.

Don't Overdo the Liquid

One of the first things you will notice about slow cooking is the amount of liquid that accumulates inside the pot. Because the slow cooker cooks at low heat, liquid doesn't evaporate as it does in dry heat cooking. Since the steam cannot escape as it rises, it collects under the lid, dripping back down into the cooking liquid. This can make the cooking juices more watery. For this reason, most slow cooker recipes, with the exception of soups, stews and sauces, call for about half as much liquid as conventional recipes.

If there is too much liquid at the end of the cooking time, remove the lid, increase the temperature to **High** and cook uncovered for 30 to 45 minutes to reduce the liquid. Alternatively, remove the solid contents with a slotted spoon and cover to keep warm. Pour the cooking liquid into a saucepan and reduce on the stovetop over high heat until the sauce cooks down to the desired consistency.

Always Cook Covered

Always cook with the slow cooker lid on. Most slow cookers have a heavy glass or plastic lid to trap the heat as it rises and convert it into steam. This is, in fact, what cooks the food. Removing the lid will result in major heat losses (which the slow cooker can't quickly recover), ultimately affecting the cooking time. Lift the lid only when it is time to check for doneness, when adding ingredients or when stirring is recommended.

Cut Vegetables into Same-Sized Pieces

Raw vegetables often take longer to cook in a slow cooker than meat and poultry. Root vegetables such as carrots, parsnips, turnips and potatoes simmer rather than boil in the cooking liquid. For this reason, food should be cut into uniform pieces no larger than 1-inch (2.5 cm) cubes. It is best to place them as close as possible to the bottom and sides of the stoneware bowl, so that they benefit from proximity to the heat source.

Observe Recommended Cooking Temperatures and Times

The slow cooker works by simmering food at a constant low temperature. The **Low** setting cooks food at about 200°F (100°C), and the **High** setting cooks food at about 300°F (150°C). However, the cooking temperatures of different makes and models can vary. When you first start to use your slow cooker, check foods after the minimum recommended cooking time. You will soon find out how fast your slow cooker operates, and you can adjust the cooking times if necessary.

In recipes where only one temperature is given, cook on that temperature. This is especially important for appetizers and desserts, where overcooking or undercooking can affect the quality of the finished dish. For the most tender results, tougher cuts of meat, such as pot roasts and stewing meat, are often best cooked on the **Low** setting.

Many people want to turn on their slow cooker early in the day and return 9 or 10 hours later to a hot, ready-to-eat meal. Many of the main-course dishes and soups in this book can be cooked this long at **Low**, although they may also be ready to eat several hours earlier (in these cases, a wide range of cooking times may be indicated). However, some foods, such as chicken and pork chops, do not stand up to longer cooking times. Bean dishes may also become very soft if cooked for a long time. You will soon find out how to achieve the best results cooked to your own taste.

Season Liberally

Because slow cooker foods cook longer than they do using conventional methods, it is best to use dried herb leaves and whole or crushed spices rather than ground herbs and spices. In general, fresh herbs such as basil and cilantro should be added during the last hour of cooking. Always taste the finished dish before serving and adjust the seasoning as needed.

Using Additional Dishes and Pans

In conventional cooking, foods such as custards, puddings and cheesecakes are often baked in a hot water bath, or bain-marie. This involves placing the filled baking dish in another pan filled with hot water. Heat is transferred from the hot water to the custard, cooking it gently and slowly so that it doesn't curdle or form a crust.

The water bath technique works beautifully in the slow cooker. Custards, puddings and cheesecakes stay creamy and smooth, and cheesecakes do not crack.

The challenge is finding a dish that will fit properly in the slow cooker. First, you will need a large round or oval slow cooker. Smaller cookers will usually accommodate only a dish or pan purchased from the slow cooker manufacturer or an old-fashioned pudding mold with a lid. Standard 4-cup (1 L) or 6-cup (1.5 L) ovenproof baking bowls work well in most larger slow cookers. If you are making a cheesecake, a 7- or 8-inch (18 or 20 cm) springform pan should fit nicely.

To easily remove a pan from the slow cooker, make foil handles. Cut a 2-foot (60 cm) piece of foil in half lengthwise. Fold each strip in half lengthwise and crisscross the strips under the pan. Bring the strips up the sides of the pan and tuck the ends inside the lid. Use the foil handles as lifters to remove the pan from the slow cooker. You can also line the slow cooker with a double thickness of cheesecloth to help you lift. Both of these methods will save you from having to awkwardly remove the dish using spatulas or oven mitts.

Make Ahead

The biggest challenge to slow cooking is being organized enough to have everything ready in advance. If you need to start your slow cooker early in the day, try preparing a few things the night before:

- Pre-chop carrots, celery and other ingredients and refrigerate until the next day.
- Defrost frozen vegetables overnight in the refrigerator.
- Trim and cut (but do not brown) meat and poultry.
- Assemble non-perishable ingredients and cooking utensils in a convenient spot for a quick start.

In this book, recipes that lend themselves to some advance preparation or cooking are accompanied by Make Ahead instructions. Many recipes can also be completely cooked in advance and stored in the refrigerator or freezer for future use.

Food Safety

According to the U.S. Department of Agriculture, bacteria is killed at a temperature of 165°F (74°C). In a slow cooker that is used properly (i.e., the lid is left on and food is cooked at the appropriate heat level for the appropriate length of time), foods will reach their safe internal cooked temperature quickly enough to inhibit bacterial growth. To make sure the slow cooker can effectively transfer heat from the metal walls to the stoneware insert and then to the food, do not fill the cooker more than three-quarters full, and always cook with the lid on.

Safety Tips

- Always start with fresh or thawed meat and poultry. Using frozen or partially frozen meat will increase the time required for the temperature to reach the "safe zone" where bacteria growth is inhibited.
- In general, defrost frozen vegetables, such as peas and corn, before adding them to the slow cooker, to prevent them from slowing the cooking process. Defrost in the refrigerator overnight or place under cold running water to thaw and separate.
- Cook all ground meat and ground poultry completely before adding it to the slow cooker. (The exception to this is for meatloaf, and proper cooking directions are given for this in the individual recipes.) If you are cooking the ground meat the night before, chill it separately before combining it with other ingredients in the slow cooker.
- Do not refrigerate uncooked or partially cooked meat or poultry in the slow cooker stoneware, as the insert will become very cold and will slow the cooking process. Partially cook meat or poultry only when adding immediately to the slow cooker. Do not refrigerate for later cooking.
- Meats and vegetables that have been pre-cut should be stored separately in the refrigerator. After cutting uncooked meat, never use the same cutting board or knife for other foods without thoroughly washing them with soap and hot water between uses.
- When cooking whole poultry and meatloaf, use a meat thermometer to accurately test doneness. Insert the thermometer into the thickest part of the thigh or loaf. The U.S. Department of Agriculture recommends cooking to an internal temperature of 165°F (74°C); Health Canada recommends ensuring that the temperature has reached 170°F (77°C).
- Do not lift the lid of the slow cooker while the food is cooking. Every time you remove the lid, the slow cooker takes about 20 minutes to recover its cooking temperature.
- Remove leftovers from the stoneware and refrigerate in small portions as quickly as possible.
- Do not reheat cooked food in the slow cooker. Leftovers can be thawed in the refrigerator or microwave and then reheated in a conventional oven, microwave oven or a saucepan on the stove.

Entertaining with Your Slow Cooker

You're heading off to a special get-together and you've volunteered to bring something yummy for the buffet table. But it has been a busy week, and you haven't had time to really think about it. What are you going to do?

While most of us have a hard time trying to figure out what we're going to have for dinner every night, choosing the perfect dish to offer to friends and company can be even more difficult.

Enter your lifesaver, the slow cooker. Potlucks provide the perfect opportunity to use your slow cooker. It is a great time saver, and it will free up important oven space that is needed for other dishes. And, of course, you can serve directly from your slow cooker, which saves on extra dishes and eases cleanup.

Tips for Transporting Your Slow Cooker

- Wrap the slow cooker in a towel or in newspapers for insulation, then place in a box (or other container) that will stay flat in your vehicle. Some slow cooker manufacturers sell insulated totes that perfectly hold a slow cooker. You may want to consider investing in one if you transport your slow cooker frequently.
- Attach rubber bands around the handles and lid to secure the lid.
- Serve the food within an hour or plug in the slow cooker and set on **Low** or **Keep Warm** so it will stay warm.

What Should I Take To . . . ?

Here are a few popular situations for which your slow cooker could come in handy, along with suggestions for recipes suited to the occasion, whether you are the host or have to tote along.

Super Bowl Party

What would a football party be without a big pot of simmering chili? Prepare it early in the day so it is ready for the halftime show. Be sure to include some crusty rolls, or make a batch of cornbread the day before. Include some dips and appetizers for snacking on during the game (some of which can be made up to a week in advance). And, of course, don't forget to provide a good selection of beer!

- Johnnycake Cornbread (page 34)
- Bourbon Bangers (page 48)
- Hot Corn Dip (page 56)
- Nacho Cheese Dip (page 57)
- Bacon-Onion Chip Dip (page 58)
- Best Beer Nuts (page 63)
- Vegetable Chili with Sour Cream Topping (page 148)
- Football Sunday Chili (page 151)
- Rock'n and Roast'n Chili (page 153)
- Party Pleas'n Chili (page 158)
- Tailgating Four-Bean Hot Dish (page 191)
- Easy-on-Ya Lasagna (page 244)
- Southern Barbecued Pork on a Bun (page 300)
- Upside-Down Fudge Brownie Pudding (page 362)

Winter Warm-up

Nothing warms those cold feet and hands after a day of winter activities like a piping hot bowl of soup or a thick, hearty stew. Prepare it in the morning and let it cook while you are out having fun. When you return, serve it with a green salad and a crusty loaf of bread for an easy one-pot meal. Add some excitement for the kids with a delicious and fun fondue. Or walk in the door to a welcoming hot drink or warm dessert.

- Mulled Raspberry Tea (page 37)
- Caramel Hot Chocolate (page 39)
- Hot Buttered Rum (page 40)
- Tangy Winterberry Warmers (page 42)
- Winter Trail Mix (page 67)
- Cabbage Roll Soup (page 73)
- Hearty Beef Goulash (page 98)
- That's-a-Lotta-Beans Soup (page 103)
- Chicken Stew with Rosemary Dumplings (page 110)
- Mahogany Beef Stew (page 124)
- Cider Pork Stew (page 136)
- Stratford's Sweet Chili (page 149)
- Winter Chicken and Corn Chili (page 161)
- Pizza Fondue (page 181)
- Rhubarb-Blueberry Pudding Cake (page 340)
- Double Berry Maple Crumble (page 345)
- Apricot Croissant Pudding with Caramel Sauce (page 360)
- Double Chocolate Caramel Bread Pudding (page 363)

Aces Are Wild

Everyone is a winner when friends and family come together for games and good food, whether you're playing billiards, cards, board games or hamming it up with a karaoke machine. Keep the food simple with a buffet of tasty appetizers that you can eat with toothpicks and napkins.

- Bourbon Bangers (page 48)
- Fruity Glazed Meatballs (page 49)
- Turkish Winglets (page 53)
- Peking Pork Bites (page 54)
- Roadhouse-Style Spinach and Artichoke Dip (page 55)
- Nacho Cheese Dip (page 57)
- Bacon-Onion Chip Dip (page 58)
- Warm-and-Wonderful Seafood Dip (page 60)
- Best Beer Nuts (page 63)
- Spicy Popcorn with Nuts (page 66)
- Pizza Fondue (page 181)
- Very Adult Rice Pudding (page 366)

Summer Celebrations

Summer is always a popular time to reconnect with young and old, whether it's a family reunion, a Father's Day celebration or visiting a friend's summer cottage. While barbecuing is popular, some days can be too hot for you to stand over a sweltering grill, so slow cookers can be the answer. Ingredients are farm fresh and perfect for delicious slow-cooked one-dish meals and desserts. Be sure to serve lots of coleslaw (page 115) and jugs of lemonade.

- Best-Ever Baked Beans (page 167)
- Cowpoke Baked Beans (page 169)
- Slow-Cooked Macaroni and Cheese (page 186)
- Cheesy Tortellini Bake (page 187)
- Comforting Shredded Beef (page 256)
- Philly Beef Wraps (page 257)
- Texas-Style Barbecued Brisket Sandwiches (page 276)
- Country-Style Honey Garlic Ribs (page 291)
- Slow Cooker-to-Grill Sticky Ribs (page 294)
- Pulled Pork Fajitas (page 298)
- Southern Barbecued Pork on a Bun (page 300)
- Pineapple Upside-Down Cake (page 336)
- Plum Cobbler (page 343)
- Aunt Beatty's Betty (page 344)

Book Club Night

Make use of your slow cooker at your monthly book club meetings. That way, you can spend more time enjoying the discussion instead of being in the kitchen preparing the meal.

- Chocolate Chai Tea (page 36)
- Mulled Raspberry Tea (page 37)
- Sun-Dried Tomato Appetizer Cheesecake (page 46)
- Roadhouse-Style Spinach and Artichoke Dip (page 55)
- Novel Curried Walnuts (page 64)
- Roasted Red Pepper and Tomato Soup (page 80)
- Potato-Leek Soup with Stilton (page 85)
- Perfectly Poached Salmon (page 174)
- Black Bean Moussaka (page 192)
- Chicken with Orange Gremolata (page 206)
- Chicken in Honey-Mustard Sauce (page 212)
- Vegetable-Stuffed Chicken with Mushroom Sauce (page 213)
- Spinach Turkey Rolls (page 235)
- Oxford Beef with Mushrooms (page 259)
- Coconut Beef Curry (page 262)
- Osso Buco with Lemon Gremolata (page 278)
- Honey-Lemon Beets (page 311)
- Sweet Potato Custard (page 322)
- Barley Mushroom "Risotto" (page 326)
- Middle Eastern Pilaf (page 327)
- Pecan Mushroom Wild Rice (page 328)
- Wild Rice Stuffing with Almonds and Cranberries (page 330)
- Basic-But-Beautiful Slow Cooker Cheesecake (page 338)
- Bananas with Honey-Roasted Nuts (page 347)
- Baked Lemon Sponge (page 352)
- Bayou Bread Pudding with Rum Sauce and Lazy Cream (page 364)

Especially for Kids

Whether you are throwing a back-to-school brunch for your children and their friends, looking for perfect party food for a group of teens or serving a Friday night meal to the family, here are some kid-friendly recipes everyone will enjoy, from make-ahead foods that can be packed into lunch boxes to keep-warm main dishes for families on the fly.

- Good Morning Granola (page 28)
- Maple Pecan Multigrain Porridge (page 30)
- Banana Walnut French Toast (page 31)
- Johnnycake Cornbread (page 34)
- Caramel Hot Chocolate (page 39)

- Savory Meatballs with Cranberry Sauce (page 50)
- Hot Corn Dip (page 56)
- Nacho Cheese Dip (page 57)
- Winter Trail Mix (page 67)
- Harvest Corn Chowder with Bacon and Cheddar (page 76)
- I'd-Swear-It-Was-Pizza Soup (page 97)
- Easy Wieners and Beaners Soup (page 102)
- PBJ Chicken Stew (page 113)
- Mom's Old-Fashioned Beef Stew (page 120)
- Simple Salmon Pie with Creamy Dill Sauce (page 176)
- Pizza Fondue (page 181)
- Fia's Favorite Pasta Sauce (page 182)
- Basic Spaghetti Sauce Italiano (page 241)
- Slow-Cooked Macaroni and Cheese (page 186)
- Kids' Favorite Tuna Noodle Casserole (page 188)
- Veggie-Stuffed Baked Potatoes (page 201)
- Chicken-in-a-Pot (page 210)
- Plum-Good Chicken (page 216)
- Clubhouse Chicken (page 218)
- Polynesian Chicken (page 225)
- Anthony's Big Ragu (page 240)
- Easy-on-Ya Lasagna (page 244)
- Three-Cheese Meatloaf (page 269)
- Cheeseburger Sloppy Joes (page 271)
- Tortilla Stack (page 272)
- Beef and Bean Burritos (page 274)
- Slow Cooker-to-Grill Sticky Ribs (page 294)
- Pulled Pork Fajitas (page 298)
- Double-Decker Spicy Pork Tacos (page 299)
- Ginger Pork Wraps (page 301)
- Cheddar Scalloped Potatoes (page 323)
- Mashed Potato Soufflé (page 324)
- Aunt Beatty's Betty (page 344)
- Caramel Peaches (page 348)

The Perfect Potluck

Community potlucks and church suppers give everyone a chance to show off their talents, and many recipes have been exchanged and passed down through generations as a result of such occasions. The most popular, of course, is the classic casserole, and the slow cooker makes toting these a breeze.

- Mexican Weekend Brunch Bake (page 32)
- Bourbon Bangers (page 48)

- Fruity Glazed Meatballs (page 49)
- Savory Meatballs with Cranberry Sauce (page 50)
- Oriental Chicken Wings (page 52)
- Turkish Winglets (page 53)
- Peking Pork Bites (page 54)
- Sauerbraten Beef Stew (page 125)
- Adobe Pork and Bean Chili (page 157)
- Shredded White Chicken Chili (page 162)
- Best-Ever Baked Beans (page 167)
- Molasses Baked Beans (page 168)
- Cowpoke Baked Beans (page 169)
- Pizza Fondue (page 181)
- Creamy Spinach Ricotta Noodles (page 183)
- Vegetable Pastitsio (page 184)
- Black Bean Moussaka (page 192)
- Corn and Green Chili Tamale Casserole (page 199)
- Cheesy Pesto Pasta (page 228)
- Polenta Tamale Pie (page 229)
- Turkey Tetrazzini (page 234)
- Easy-on-Ya Lasagna (page 244)
- Nancy's Rouladen (page 254)
- Old-Fashioned Gingerbread with Lemon Sauce (page 334)
- Rhubarb Blueberry Pudding Cake (page 340)
- Plum Cobbler (page 343)
- Apricot Croissant Pudding with Caramel Sauce (page 360)
- Upside-Down Fudge Brownie Pudding (page 362)

Holiday Specials

Holiday celebrations mean lots of friends, family, fun and food. The turkey and stuffing are a given, but oven space is always at a premium. Take advantage of your slow cooker to prepare a few appetizers or condiments a day or two ahead, make the stuffing in the morning and have it warming during the day or keep a hot drink simmering. Have a Tourtière Shepherd's Pie (page 297) waiting at home after church on Christmas Eve. Or use your slow cooker to serve up a soup for starters, to prepare an extra dessert or a separate entrée for vegetarians, or to use as an extra server for a delicious array of side dishes.

Beverages, Appetizers and Condiments

- Mulled Raspberry Tea (page 37)
- Tangy Winterberry Warmers (page 42)
- Sun-Dried Tomato Appetizer Cheesecake (page 46)
- Savory Meatballs with Cranberry Sauce (page 50)
- Olives in Red Wine (page 62)
- Winter Trail Mix (page 67)
- Rhubarb Apple Sauce (page 331)

Soups

- Autumn Celebration Soup (page 72)
- Roasted Pear and Parsnip Soup (page 79)
- Southwestern Pumpkin Soup (page 82)
- Squash and Apple Soup (page 83)
- Spicy Sweet Potato Soup (page 86)

Side Dishes and Stuffings

- Lisa's Classic Green Beans (page 310)
- Braised Cabbage and Raspberries (page 312)
- Tangy Red Cabbage with Apples (page 313)
- Scalloped Corn (page 315)
- Scalloped Sweet Potatoes and Parsnips (page 321)
- Sweet Potato Custard (page 322)
- Mashed Potato Soufflé (page 324)
- Oktoberfest Hot Potato Salad (page 325)
- Country-Style Sage and Bread Stuffing (page 329)
- Wild Rice Stuffing with Almonds and Cranberries (page 330)

Desserts

- Basic-But-Beautiful Slow Cooker Cheesecake (page 338)
- Amaretti Pear Crisp (page 341)
- Maple-Sauced Pears (page 349)
- Pumpkin Pie Custard Dessert (page 353)
- Almond-Pear Steamed Pudding with Coconut-Lime Sauce (page 354)
- Steamed Cranberry Pudding with Grand Marnier Sauce (page 356)
- Carrot Marmalade Pudding with Lemon Sauce (page 358)
- Double Chocolate Caramel Bread Pudding (page 363)

Breakfasts, Breads and Beverages

Good Morning Granola

Makes about 4 cups (1 L)

This crunchy mix is a perfect topping on hot cereal or yogurt. It also tastes great served on its own with milk.

• • •

Tips

If your liquid honey has crystallized or if, like me, you use solid creamed honey, place the jar (or as much as you need in a small bowl) in a saucepan of hot water, heating gently until melted. Or heat in microwave until melted.

When measuring honey, rub measuring cup with a little vegetable oil, then measure honey. It will easily pour out, with no sticky mess!

Use dried fruit such as cranberries, cherries or chopped apricots.

- Slow cooker size: 5 to 6 quart

2 cups	large-flake rolled oats	500 mL
1/4 cup	raw wheat germ	50 mL
2 tbsp	sesame seeds	25 mL
1/2 cup	chopped almonds or pecans	125 mL
1/2 cup	flaked sweetened coconut	125 mL
1/2 cup	liquid honey	125 mL
1/4 cup	frozen cranberry juice cocktail concentrate, thawed	50 mL
1/4 cup	butter, melted	50 mL
2 tbsp	packed brown sugar	25 mL
1 1/2 tsp	vanilla	7 mL
1 cup	dried fruit (see tip, at left)	250 mL
1/2 cup	raisins	125 mL

1. In a slow cooker stoneware, combine oats, wheat germ, sesame seeds, almonds and coconut.
2. In a bowl, combine honey, cranberry juice concentrate, melted butter, brown sugar and vanilla. Mix well and pour over oat mixture. Stir to combine.
3. Cook, uncovered, on **High** for 2 to 3 hours, or until most of liquid has evaporated. Stir every 30 minutes during cooking time.
4. Reduce heat to **Low**, cover and cook for 3 to 4 hours longer, or until granola is dry and crisp. Stir frequently to prevent over-browning.

5. Spread granola over a foil-lined baking sheet and cool to room temperature. Mix in dried fruit and raisins and store in an airtight container at room temperature for up to 1 month.

No-Bake Granola Crunchies

In a double boiler over hot (not boiling) water, melt 1 cup (250 mL) peanut butter, 1 cup (250 mL) milk chocolate chips and ½ cup (125 mL) butter. Stir in 3 cups (750 mL) dry chow mein noodles and 1½ cups (375 mL) granola. Drop by heaping teaspoons onto waxed paper-lined baking sheets. Chill until firm. Store in an airtight container, placing waxed paper between each layer. Refrigerate or freeze for up to 2 weeks. *Makes about 4 dozen cookies.*

Variation

You can replace the cranberry cocktail with an equal amount of frozen apple juice concentrate.

Maple Pecan Multigrain Porridge

Serves 4

Kick-start your morning with a bowl of this stick-to-your ribs cereal served with milk. Prepare and start cooking the night before, so a bowl of hot porridge is waiting for those early risers.

Tips

A sure-fire way to get kids to eat this nutritious cereal is to serve it with a scoop of vanilla ice cream.

Use an uncooked multigrain porridge cereal that contains whole grains such as cracked wheat, rye and flax.

Make Ahead

Assemble ingredients and begin cooking the night before; the porridge will be hot and ready to eat in the morning.

- Slow cooker size: 3½ to 6 quart

3 cups	water	750 mL
1 cup	uncooked multigrain cereal	250 mL
2 tbsp	maple syrup	25 mL
½ tsp	salt	2 mL
1½ tsp	vanilla	7 mL
½ cup	chopped toasted pecans or almonds (optional)	125 mL

1. In slow cooker stoneware, combine water, cereal, maple syrup, salt and vanilla.
2. Cover and cook on **Low** for 8 to 10 hours, or until thickened.
3. Spoon into individual serving bowls and sprinkle with chopped nuts, if using.

Toasting Nuts

Toasting nuts enhances their flavor and texture. Spread nuts on a baking sheet. Toast in a 350°F (160°C) oven for 5 to 7 minutes, or until golden brown, stirring occasionally.

Banana Walnut French Toast

Serves 8

Serve this make-ahead French toast with maple syrup as a light lunch or brunch dish.

• • •

Tip

Evaporated milk holds up extremely well in slow cookers and will not curdle. Don't confuse this milk with the sweetened condensed milk used in desserts and candies.

Make Ahead

Assemble ingredients in slow cooker up to 24 hours before cooking.

- Slow cooker size: 5 to 6 quart

2	ripe bananas, cut into ¼-inch (5 mm) slices	2
2 tbsp	freshly squeezed lemon juice	25 mL
1	loaf day-old French bread, crust removed, cut into ½-inch (1 cm) cubes (about 10 cups/2.5 L)	1
3	eggs, lightly beaten	3
1	can (13 oz/385 mL) evaporated milk	1
3 tbsp	liquid honey	45 mL
1 tsp	vanilla	5 mL
½ tsp	ground cinnamon	2 mL
1 cup	chopped toasted walnuts (see box, page 30)	250 mL
1 tsp	granulated sugar	5 mL

1. In a bowl, gently toss bananas with lemon juice.
2. Arrange half the bread cubes in bottom of lightly greased slow cooker stoneware. Top bread with bananas. Add remaining bread cubes.
3. In a blender or food processor, combine eggs, evaporated milk, honey, vanilla and cinnamon. Slowly pour egg mixture over bread to coat evenly. Press down lightly with the back of a spoon to moisten all bread.
4. Cover and refrigerate for 8 hours or overnight.
5. Sprinkle bread with walnuts and sugar. Cover and cook on **Low** for 5 to 7 hours or on **High** for 2½ to 3½ hours, until golden brown and slightly puffed.

Mexican Weekend Brunch Bake

Serves 6 to 8

This is an ideal brunch or light supper idea — sausage and eggs with a Mexican twist. All the work is done the night before. Invite company after church and the food is ready. Olé!

• • •

Tips

Mild green chilies are found in the Mexican foods section of the supermarket. They are sold whole or chopped.

Look for corn tortillas in the deli department of the supermarket or where flour tortillas are sold. If you have difficulty finding them, substitute tortilla chips. Don't use flour tortillas, since they will become soggy.

- Slow cooker size: 3½ to 6 quart

2 lbs	hot or mild Italian sausage, casings removed	1 kg
2	cans (each 4½ oz/128 g) chopped green chilies	2
4	corn tortillas, cut into 1-inch (2.5 cm) strips	4
2 cups	shredded Monterey Jack or Mexican-style cheese combination	500 mL
½ cup	milk	125 mL
8	eggs	8
½ tsp	ground cumin	2 mL
	Paprika	
1	tomato, thinly sliced	1
	Salsa	
	Sour cream	

1. In a large nonstick skillet, cook sausage over medium-high heat, breaking up with a spoon. Drain well.
2. In lightly greased slow cooker stoneware, layer half the green chilies, half the tortilla strips, half the sausage and then half the cheese. Repeat the layers.
3. In a bowl, beat together milk, eggs and cumin. Pour over sausage mixture. Sprinkle with paprika. Cover and refrigerate overnight.
4. The next day, set insert in slow cooker. Top with tomato slices. Cover and cook on **Low** for 7 to 9 hours or on **High** for 3 to 4 hours. Skim off any accumulated fat. Serve topped with salsa and sour cream.

Boston Brown Bread

Makes 3 loaves

This traditional steamed bread is a sweet, harmonious blend of grains and molasses. Serve it warm with any meal.

Tip

The bread can be baked in three 19-oz (540 mL) vegetable cans or a 1-lb (500 g) coffee can. An old-fashioned pudding bowl with a lid or a 6-cup (1.5 L) heavy glass mixing bowl will also work well.

- Slow cooker size: 5 to 6 quart

½ cup	rye flour	125 mL
½ cup	yellow cornmeal	125 mL
½ cup	whole wheat flour	125 mL
3 tbsp	granulated sugar	45 mL
1 tsp	baking soda	5 mL
¾ tsp	salt	4 mL
½ cup	chopped walnuts	125 mL
½ cup	raisins	125 mL
1 cup	buttermilk or sour milk (see tips, pages 336–37)	250 mL
⅓ cup	fancy molasses	75 mL

1. In a large bowl, sift together rye flour, cornmeal, whole wheat flour, sugar, baking soda and salt. Stir in walnuts and raisins.
2. In a small bowl, whisk together buttermilk and molasses. Add buttermilk mixture to dry ingredients. Stir until well blended.
3. Spoon mixture evenly into 3 lightly greased 19-oz (540 mL) cans. Lightly grease three 6-inch (15 cm) pieces of foil. Place a piece of foil, greased side down, on top of each can. Secure foil with elastic bands or string.
4. Place cans in slow cooker stoneware. Add enough boiling water to come halfway up sides of cans. Make sure foil does not touch the water.
5. Cover and cook on **Low** for 3 to 4 hours, or until a tester inserted in center of loaves comes out clean.
6. Remove cans from slow cooker and let cool for 5 minutes. Lay cans on their sides. Roll and tap gently on all sides until bread releases. Remove loaves from cans and cool completely on wire racks.

Johnnycake Cornbread

Serves 8

This is one of my husband's absolute favorites. Serve it as a side dish with chili or stew, or serve thick slices with warm maple syrup for a dessert treat.

• • •

Tip

You may wish to cook the cornbread with the slow cooker lid slightly ajar to allow any condensation to escape.

- Slow cooker size: 5 to 6 quart

1 1/4 cups	all-purpose flour	300 mL
3/4 cup	yellow cornmeal	175 mL
1/4 cup	granulated sugar	50 mL
1 tsp	baking powder	5 mL
1 tsp	baking soda	5 mL
1 tsp	salt	5 mL
1	egg, lightly beaten	1
1 cup	buttermilk or sour milk (see tips, pages 336–37)	250 mL
1/4 cup	vegetable oil	50 mL

1. Turn slow cooker to **Low** to preheat stoneware.
2. In a large bowl, combine flour, cornmeal, sugar, baking powder, baking soda and salt.
3. In a small bowl, whisk together egg, buttermilk and oil.
4. Make a well in center of dry ingredients and pour in liquid ingredients. Mix together just until moistened.
5. Pour batter into a lightly greased 8-cup (2 L) soufflé dish or 2-lb (1 kg) coffee can and cover with foil. (There is no need to secure the foil with an elastic band or string since there is no water in the bottom of the slow cooker.) Place in bottom of preheated slow cooker stoneware.
6. Cover and cook on **Low** for 3 to 4 hours or on **High** for 1 1/2 to 2 hours, until edges of cornbread are golden and a knife inserted in center comes out clean.

Steamed Pumpkin Date Cornbread

Makes 1 loaf

I love to make a batch of this ahead and have it on hand to serve it with coffee. Believe it or not, it also makes a superb accompaniment to Vegetable Chili with Sour Cream Topping (page 148).

• • •

Tip

Make sure the soufflé dish will fit in your slow cooker before you start to make the recipe.

Make Ahead

This steamed bread can be made up to 24 hours before serving. Cool completely. Return bread to soufflé dish. Cover tightly with foil and secure with a string or elastic band. Store at room temperature. Bread can be resteamed on a rack set in a saucepan filled with about 1 inch (2.5 cm) simmering water. Cover and steam until heated through, about 15 minutes.

- Slow cooker size: 5 to 6 quart

½ cup	all-purpose flour	125 mL
½ cup	whole wheat flour	125 mL
½ cup	yellow cornmeal	125 mL
1 tsp	baking soda	5 mL
½ tsp	salt	2 mL
¼ cup	chopped dates	50 mL
¼ cup	chopped walnuts or pecans	50 mL
⅔ cup	buttermilk or sour milk (see tips, pages 336–37)	150 mL
½ cup	pumpkin purée (not pie filling)	125 mL
½ cup	liquid honey	125 mL
1	egg yolk	1

1. In a large bowl, combine all-purpose and whole wheat flours, cornmeal, baking soda and salt. Stir in dates and walnuts.
2. In a separate bowl, whisk together buttermilk, pumpkin, honey and egg yolk.
3. Make a well in the center of dry ingredients. Pour in liquid ingredients and stir just until blended.
4. Spoon batter into a well-greased 6-cup (1.5 L) soufflé dish. Cover dish with foil. Secure foil with an elastic band or string and place in bottom of slow cooker stoneware lined with foil strips or cheesecloth (see page 16). Pour in enough boiling water to come 1 inch (2.5 cm) up sides of soufflé dish. (If soufflé dish fits snugly in slow cooker, add water before placing dish in cooker.)
5. Cover and cook on **High** for 3 to 4 hours, or until a tester inserted in center of bread comes out clean.
6. Remove bread from slow cooker and allow to cool slightly. Remove foil. Run knife around sides of bread and remove from soufflé dish. Serve warm.

Chocolate Chai Tea

Serves 10 to 12

Chai is an Indian spiced tea that can be enjoyed hot or cold. Here it is mixed with cocoa to make a very creamy spiced hot chocolate — perfect after a day of outdoor winter activities. Ladle the tea into mugs and serve garnished with a cinnamon stick.

• • •

Tips

For added orange flavor, float a long strip of orange zest in the tea mix while it is in the slow cooker. Remove before serving so it doesn't impart a bitter aftertaste.

For a more authentic flavor, brew tea with black tea leaves such as Darjeeling. Strain before adding to the slow cooker.

- Slow cooker size: 3½ to 6 quart

1¾ cups	skim milk powder	425 mL
¾ cup	powdered non-dairy creamer	175 mL
¾ cup	granulated sugar	175 mL
½ cup	unsweetened cocoa powder	125 mL
2 tsp	ground cinnamon	10 mL
1 tsp	ground nutmeg	5 mL
12 cups	brewed black tea	3 L

1. In a bowl, combine skim milk powder, powdered creamer, sugar, cocoa, cinnamon and nutmeg.
2. Transfer mixture to slow cooker stoneware. Slowly whisk in tea until mixture is smooth and no lumps remain.
3. Cover and cook on **Low** for 4 to 5 hours, or until hot. Stir well before serving.

Mulled Raspberry Tea

Serves 6

This beautiful lemony ruby-red drink sparkles and tastes delicious. Serve it at winter gatherings. The recipe can easily be doubled and cooked in a large slow cooker. Double all ingredients except for the raspberries.

- **Slow cooker size: 3½ to 6 quart**

3	whole allspice berries	3
1	cinnamon stick	1
1 tsp	whole cloves	5 mL
2 cups	brewed black tea	500 mL
2 cups	cranberry raspberry cocktail	500 mL
1 cup	frozen lemonade concentrate	250 mL
½ cup	water	125 mL
1	package (13½-oz/400 g) frozen raspberries in syrup, thawed	1

1. Wrap allspice, cinnamon stick and cloves in a double thickness of cheesecloth and tie with kitchen twine to form a bag.
2. In slow cooker stoneware, combine tea, cranberry raspberry cocktail, lemonade concentrate, water and raspberries. Add spice bag.
3. Cover and cook on **Low** for 2 to 5 hours, or until hot and fragrant. Remove spice bag before serving.

Apple Cinnamon Sippers

Serves 8 to 10

As this punch heats up, it fills the house with a spicy welcoming scent. For a colorful presentation, serve in a mug with a red cinnamon-candy swizzle stick for stirring.

- Slow cooker size: 6 to 7 quart

2	cinnamon sticks	2
1 tsp	whole cloves	5 mL
1 tsp	whole allspice berries	5 mL
8 cups	apple cider	2 L
½ cup	packed brown sugar	125 mL
1	orange, sliced	1
3	large baking apples, cored (optional)	3

1. Place cinnamon sticks, cloves and allspice on a double thickness of cheesecloth. Bring up corners of cloth and tie with an elastic band or kitchen twine to form a bag.
2. In slow cooker stoneware, combine cider and brown sugar, stirring until sugar dissolves. Add spice bag. Place orange slices on top.
3. Cover and cook on **Low** for 2 to 5 hours, or until hot. Remove spice bag and discard.
4. *Optional:* For a decorative touch, cut apples in half crosswise and place cut side down in a 13- by 9-inch (3 L) baking dish. Bake in a 350°F (180°C) oven for 25 minutes, or until apple halves are fork-tender. Place apples in punch, floating skin side up.

Caramel Hot Chocolate

Serves 10 to 12

A sip or two of this cold-weather favorite is bound to produce warm smiles, especially when its secret ingredient — the chocolate caramel candy bar — is dissolved.

Tip

I use dry skim milk powder in this recipe because it doesn't curdle and holds up well during long cooking. You will be surprised at how creamy this beverage is.

Variation

You can substitute mini marshmallows for the whipped cream. For an adult version, try adding a shot of Irish Cream liqueur or brandy to the mug.

- **Slow cooker size: 6 to 7 quart**

4 cups	dry skim milk powder	1 L
¾ cup	unsweetened cocoa powder	75 mL
½ cup	granulated sugar	125 mL
8 cups	water	2 L
1	chocolate-covered caramel-filled candy bar (about 2 oz/50 g)	1
	Whipped cream	
	Grated chocolate (optional)	

1. In slow cooker stoneware, combine skim milk powder, cocoa and sugar. Slowly add water, whisking constantly to avoid lumps.
2. Cover and cook on **Low** for 4 to 5 hours, or until hot.
3. Break chocolate bar into pieces and add to hot chocolate, stirring until completely melted. To serve, ladle into mugs and garnish with whipped cream and grated chocolate, if desired.

Hot Buttered Rum

Serves 6 to 8

After a day on the icy slopes this drink is sure to warm everyone to their toes. Serve in mugs garnished with whole cinnamon sticks.

• • •

Tip

Amber or dark rum is the best choice for this winter warmer; white rum tends to give it a metallic flavor.

- **Slow cooker size: 6 to 7 quart**

2 cups	packed brown sugar	500 mL
½ cup	butter	125 mL
Pinch	salt	Pinch
½ tsp	ground nutmeg	2 mL
6 cups	hot water	1.5 L
3 or 4	whole cloves	3 or 4
3	cinnamon sticks	3
2 cups	amber or dark rum	500 mL

1. In slow cooker stoneware, combine brown sugar, butter, salt and nutmeg. Pour in hot water, stirring until butter is melted and sugar dissolved.
2. Wrap cloves and cinnamon sticks in a cheesecloth bag, secure with an elastic band and place in slow cooker.
3. Cover and cook on **Low** for 4 to 10 hours. Add rum just before serving.

Mulled Red Wine

Serves 12

Any time you are feeling a chill, there's nothing better than a warm mug of mulled red wine.

• • •

Tip

Don't let the citrus peel float in the wine longer than 4 hours or it will impart a bitter taste to the beverage.

- Slow cooker size: 6 to 7 quart

2	bottles (each 25 oz/750 mL) red wine	2
2 cups	orange juice	500 mL
2 cups	pineapple juice	500 mL
½ cup	granulated sugar	125 mL
1	lemon, sliced	1
1	orange, sliced	1
2	cinnamon sticks	2
4	whole cloves	4
4	whole allspice berries	4

1. In slow cooker stoneware, combine wine, orange juice, pineapple juice, sugar, lemon slices and orange slices. Wrap cinnamon sticks, cloves and allspice in a piece of cheesecloth and secure with an elastic band. Float in wine mixture.
2. Cover and cook on **Low** for 4 hours or until hot. Remove cheesecloth packet and citrus slices. Leave temperature set on **Low**. Slow cooker will keep punch at proper serving temperature for up to 4 hours.

Tangy Winterberry Warmers

Serves 12 to 14

This non-alcoholic winter warmer is perfect after a family day outdoors.

• • •

Tips

For a fruity alcoholic version, add a shot of peach or apple schnapps to your mug.

Spice sachets are a perfect holiday gift that even the kids can make. Inside squares of cheesecloth place 2 cinnamon sticks about 4 inches (10 cm) long, 15 allspice berries, and 2 tsp (10 mL) whole cloves. Secure with an elastic band. Attach a handwritten recipe card and tie it up with a pretty red satin ribbon. (Don't forget to make one for yourself!) Use this packet in teas or punches that call for a spice sachet.

- Slow cooker size: 6 to 7 quart

6 cups	cranberry juice	1.5 L
2	cans (each 12½ oz/355 mL) frozen lemonade concentrate, thawed	2
2 cups	water	500 mL
2	cinnamon sticks	2
½ tsp	ground allspice	2 mL
1	lemon, cut into thick slices	1

1. In slow cooker stoneware, combine cranberry juice, lemonade concentrate and water.
2. Wrap cinnamon sticks and allspice in a cheesecloth bag and secure with elastic band. Add to juice mixture. Float lemon slices in juice.
3. Cover and cook on **Low** for 4 hours or until hot. Remove cheesecloth packet. Leave temperature set on **Low**. Slow cooker will keep punch at the proper serving temperature for up to 4 hours.

Hot 'n' Spicy Winter Punch

Serves 6 to 8

Tip

If you have difficulty finding cranberry-apple cocktail, use 6 cups (1.5 L) apple juice and 2 cups (500 mL) cranberry cocktail.

- Slow cooker size: 6 to 7 quart

8 cups	cranberry-apple cocktail	2 L
1 tsp	freshly squeezed lemon juice	5 mL
4 oz	cinnamon red hots or cinnamon heart candy	125 g
2	cinnamon sticks	2
16	whole cloves	16
1 cup	white rum	250 mL

1. In slow cooker stoneware, combine cranberry-apple cocktail, lemon juice and cinnamon red hots.
2. Wrap cinnamon sticks and cloves in a cheesecloth bag; secure with an elastic band and place in slow cooker. Cover and heat on **Low** for 4 to 6 hours or on **High** for 1 to 2 hours.
3. Stir in rum just before serving.

Appetizers, Dips and Snacks

Sun-Dried Tomato Appetizer Cheesecake

Serves 8 to 10 as an appetizer

Holiday entertaining just got easier! This fabulous savory cheesecake can be made the day before your party.

• • •

Tips

You will need to use a large round or oval slow cooker. Make sure your slow cooker is big enough to hold the springform pan. A 7- or 8-inch (17 or 20 cm) springform pan should fit in nicely.

Cheesecakes cook beautifully in the slow cooker. Because of the moist heat, cracks do not appear and a silky top is the result.

Be sure to crumble the rosemary between your fingers before adding it. This helps to release the full aromatic flavor of the herb.

- Slow cooker size: 5 to 7 quart

Crust

¾ cup	crushed buttery-type cracker crumbs	175 mL
3 tbsp	butter, melted	45 mL

Filling

¼ cup	sliced oil-packed sun-dried tomatoes	50 mL
2	packages (each 8 oz/250 g) cream cheese, softened	2
2	eggs, lightly beaten	2
¼ cup	whipping (35%) cream	50 mL
¾ cup	shredded Havarti cheese	175 mL
4	green onions, chopped	4
½ tsp	dried rosemary, crumbled	2 mL

1. *Crust:* In a bowl, combine cracker crumbs and melted butter. Press mixture into bottom of a well-greased 7- or 8-inch (18 or 20 cm) springform pan (or another pan that will fit in slow cooker). Place in freezer until ready to use.
2. *Filling:* Drain oil from tomatoes, reserving 1 tbsp (15 mL). In a large bowl, using an electric mixer, beat cream cheese and reserved oil until smooth. Beat in eggs one at a time until incorporated. Beat in whipping cream.
3. Gently fold in Havarti, sun-dried tomatoes, green onions and rosemary. Spoon filling over prepared crust and wrap entire pan tightly with foil, securing with string or elastic bands.

4. Place pan in slow cooker stoneware lined with cheesecloth or foil strips (see page 16). Pour in enough boiling water to come 1 inch (2.5 cm) up sides of springform pan (if pan fits snugly in slow cooker, you can add water before inserting pan).
5. Cover and cook on **High** for 3 to 4 hours, or until edges are set and center is just slightly jiggly. Remove pan from slow cooker and chill for 2 hours or overnight in refrigerator.

Tip

For an added touch, you can sprinkle chopped toasted pine nuts (see box, page 326) over the cooked cheesecake.

Bourbon Bangers

Serves 10 to 12 as an appetizer

Sometimes a party just doesn't seem like a party without cocktail franks. Serve them straight from the slow cooker with lots of napkins or small plates to catch the drips.

• • •

Tip

This recipe can easily be doubled and made in a large slow cooker.

- Slow cooker size: 3½ quart

1¼ cups	ketchup	300 mL
½ cup	packed brown sugar	125 mL
1	small onion, finely chopped	1
2 tsp	prepared mustard	10 mL
¼ cup	bourbon whiskey or orange juice	50 mL
1 lb	smoked cocktail sausages, separated if attached	500 g

1. In a bowl, combine ketchup, brown sugar, onion, mustard and bourbon.
2. Place sausages in slow cooker stoneware and pour sauce over top.
3. Cover and cook on **Low** for 3 to 4 hours, or until sauce is hot and sausages are heated through.

Fruity Glazed Meatballs

Serves 10 to 12 as an appetizer (about 30 meatballs)

People just can't seem to get enough of this slow cooker party classic with its tangy sweet-and-sour sauce.

• • •

Tip

If you are short of time, you can make the meatballs ahead or substitute store-bought precooked frozen meatballs. Defrost for about 30 minutes at room temperature before adding them to the slow cooker.

Make Ahead

Meatballs can be made ahead and frozen. Bake meatballs, allow to cool and then freeze for up to a month. Before adding to slow cooker, allow meatballs to defrost for about 30 minutes at room temperature.

- Slow cooker size: 3½ quart

Meatballs

1 lb	lean ground pork, turkey or chicken	500 g
1	egg, lightly beaten	1
½ cup	dry bread crumbs	125 mL
3 tbsp	finely chopped fresh parsley	45 mL
2	green onions, finely chopped	2
1 tsp	soy sauce	5 mL
½ tsp	salt	2 mL
¼ tsp	freshly ground black pepper	1 mL

Grape Chili Sauce

1 cup	chili sauce	250 mL
1 cup	grape jelly	250 mL
1 tsp	freshly squeezed lemon juice	5 mL
2 tbsp	packed brown sugar	25 mL
1 tbsp	soy sauce	15 mL

1. *Meatballs:* In a large bowl, combine ground pork, egg, bread crumbs, parsley, green onions, soy sauce, salt and pepper. Mix well and shape into 1-inch (2.5 cm) balls.
2. Arrange meatballs in a single layer on a foil-lined baking sheet and bake in a preheated 400°F (200°C) oven for 10 to 12 minutes, or until no longer pink inside. Drain off any accumulated juices and transfer to slow cooker stoneware.
3. *Grape chili sauce:* In a bowl, combine chili sauce, grape jelly, lemon juice, brown sugar and soy sauce; mix well and pour over meatballs.
4. Cover and cook on **High** for 3 to 4 hours, or until sauce is bubbly and meatballs are hot.

Savory Meatballs with Cranberry Sauce

Serves 10 to 15 as an appetizer or 6 to 8 as a main dish

Portable and delicious, meatballs make the perfect party food. This dish can be prepared, brought to the party, and ultimately served in the slow cooker.

• • •

Tip

Meatballs can be served directly from the slow cooker or transferred to a bowl and garnished with freshly chopped parsley. If serving as a main dish, serve over hot buttered noodles.

- Slow cooker size: 3½ quart

Meatballs

2 lbs	lean ground beef or pork	1 kg
2	eggs, lightly beaten	2
1 cup	fine dry bread crumbs	250 mL
½ tsp	salt	2 mL
½ tsp	freshly ground black pepper	2 mL
½ tsp	garlic powder	2 mL
½ tsp	paprika	2 mL

Cranberry Sauce

1 cup	ketchup	250 mL
1 cup	tomato juice	250 mL
1	can (14 oz/398 mL) whole-berry cranberry sauce (or 1½ cups/375 mL homemade cranberry sauce)	1
1	onion, finely chopped	1
1 tbsp	packed brown sugar	15 mL
1 tsp	ground ginger	5 mL

1. *Meatballs:* In a large bowl, combine beef, eggs, bread crumbs, salt, pepper, garlic powder and paprika. Mix well and shape into 1-inch (2.5 cm) balls.
2. Arrange meatballs in a single layer on a foil-lined baking sheet and bake in a preheated 400°F (200°C) oven for 10 to 12 minutes, or until no longer pink inside. Drain off any accumulated juices and transfer to slow cooker stoneware.

3. *Cranberry sauce:* In a bowl, combine ketchup, tomato juice, cranberry sauce, onion, brown sugar and ginger; mix well and pour over meatballs.
4. Cover and cook on Low for 6 to 10 hours or on **High** for 3 to 4 hours.

Dry Bread Crumbs

To make your own dry bread crumbs, spread bread slices on a flat surface and let stand overnight, until completely dry and brittle. Break bread into pieces and place in a food processor or blender. Process until bread is in fine crumbs.

Make Ahead

These meatballs can be made up to 1 day ahead and stored in the refrigerator or frozen for up to 2 months. To freeze, place meatballs in a single layer on baking sheet. When frozen, place in a storage container. To assemble dish, place meatballs in slow cooker. Add sauce and heat on Low for 6 to 10 hours.

Oriental Chicken Wings

Serves 8 to 10 as an appetizer or 4 to 6 as a main course

This is one of my favorite dishes for the buffet table. But you can also enjoy it as a main course served over steamed rice.

• • •

Tips

Buy pre-separated wings for faster preparation.

This recipe can easily be doubled for a larger crowd.

Wings are also tasty cold, so refrigerate any leftovers to enjoy the next day as a snack.

- **Slow cooker size: 3½ to 6 quart**

½ cup	cider vinegar	125 mL
½ cup	packed brown sugar	125 mL
¼ cup	soy sauce	50 mL
¼ cup	water	50 mL
4	cloves garlic, minced	4
1 tsp	freshly squeezed lemon juice	5 mL
1 tsp	ground ginger	5 mL
½ tsp	dry mustard	2 mL
2 lbs	chicken wings, tips removed and split in half at joint	1 kg
	Sesame seeds (optional)	

1. In a bowl, combine vinegar, brown sugar, soy sauce, water, garlic, lemon juice, ginger and dry mustard; mix well and set aside.
2. Arrange split chicken wings on foil-lined baking pan. Broil wings under preheated broiler (6 inches/15 cm from heat) for 15 to 20 minutes, or until golden, turning wings once during cooking. Transfer wings to slow cooker stoneware and discard foil and drippings. Pour reserved sauce over wings and gently stir to coat.
3. Cover and cook on **Low** for 4 to 5 hours or on **High** for 2 to 3 hours, turning 2 or 3 times during cooking.
4. Wings can be served directly from the slow cooker or arranged on a serving platter. If desired, garnish with a sprinkling of sesame seeds.

Turkish Winglets

Serves 4 to 6 as an appetizer

These Middle Eastern inspired chicken wings, smothered in a tasty mixture of chutney and spices, are finger-licking good. You may want to serve them as a main course with steamed rice (page 163) and green beans.

Tips

Try to buy extra-large chicken wings that have already been separated at the joint. They are perfect for these appetizers as they are exceptionally meaty. Broiling the wings before slow cooking helps to remove excess fat from the skin.

To toast sesame seeds, place in a dry skillet over medium-high heat and cook, stirring, for 4 to 6 minutes, or until golden.

- Slow cooker size: 3½ to 6 quart

⅓ cup	mango chutney	75 mL
1 tbsp	liquid honey	15 mL
1 tbsp	freshly squeezed lime juice	15 mL
2 tsp	Dijon mustard	10 mL
1½ tsp	grated gingerroot	7 mL
¼ tsp	five-spice powder	1 mL
2 lbs	chicken wings, tips removed, and split in half at joint	1 kg

Topping (optional)

1 tbsp	chopped fresh parsley	15 mL
1 tbsp	sesame seeds, toasted (see tip, at left)	15 mL
2 tsp	grated orange zest	10 mL

1. Chop any large pieces of fruit in chutney. In a small bowl, combine chutney, honey, lime juice, mustard, ginger and five-spice powder; set aside.
2. Arrange chicken wings on a foil-lined baking sheet in a single layer. Broil under preheated broiler (6 inches/ 15 cm from heat), for 15 to 20 minutes, or until golden, turning wings once during cooking. Transfer wings to slow cooker stoneware and discard foil and drippings. Pour reserved sauce over wings and gently stir to coat.
3. Cover and cook on **Low** for 3 to 4 hours, or until wings are glazed and no longer pink inside. Turn twice during cooking time.
4. *Topping (if using):* In a small bowl, combine parsley, sesame seeds and orange zest. Sprinkle wings with parsley mixture before serving.

Five-Spice Powder

You can find five-spice powder at any Asian market. Or make your own by combining equal parts ground cinnamon, cloves, fennel seeds, star anise and Szechwan peppercorns.

Peking Pork Bites

Makes about 24

You won't be able to stop at just a few of these tasty bites. The sauce makes them irresistible.

• • •

Tip

Hoisin sauce is a kind of Chinese "ketchup." It has a sweet but tangy flavor and is available in the Oriental foods section of the supermarket.

Make Ahead

Pork bites can be cooked up to a day ahead and stored in the refrigerator (or frozen for up to 2 months). To freeze, place in a single layer on a baking sheet and place in the freezer. When frozen, transfer to covered containers or resealable freezer bags. Thaw before placing in sauce.

- Slow cooker size: 3½ quart

Pork Bites

1 lb	lean ground pork	500 g
½ cup	fine dry bread crumbs	125 mL
2 tbsp	hoisin sauce	25 mL
2	cloves garlic, minced	2
1	green onion, minced	1
1	egg, lightly beaten	1

Peking Sauce

¾ cup	hoisin sauce	175 mL
¾ cup	red currant jelly	175 mL
1 tbsp	freshly squeezed lemon juice	15 mL
2	cloves garlic, minced	2
1 tbsp	grated gingerroot (or 1 tsp/5 mL ground ginger)	15 mL
	Sesame seeds	

1. *Pork Bites:* In a bowl, combine ground pork, bread crumbs, hoisin sauce, garlic, green onion and egg; mix well. Shape into 1-inch (2.5 cm) balls.
2. Arrange meatballs in a single layer on a foil-lined baking sheet and bake in a preheated 350°F (180°C) oven for 20 minutes or until browned. Drain off any accumulated juices and transfer to slow cooker. Discard foil and drippings.
3. *Peking Sauce:* In a 4-cup (1 L) measure or bowl, combine hoisin sauce, red currant jelly, lemon juice, garlic and ginger; mix well and pour over meatballs. Cover and cook on **Low** for 5 to 6 hours or on **High** for 2 to 3 hours.
4. Meatballs can be served directly from the slow cooker or arranged on a serving platter and sprinkled with sesame seeds.

Roadhouse-Style Spinach and Artichoke Dip

Makes about 3 cups (750 mL)

This is one of my favorite appetizers when we have games nights with friends. It tastes just like the dip served in roadhouse-style restaurants. Serve with warm pita triangles, tortilla chips, breadsticks, pretzels or slices of crusty baguette.

Tip

Different brands of artichoke hearts have different flavors, which will affect the taste of this dip (some taste more vinegary than others). Use your favorite brand; you could also use marinated artichokes.

Variation

Roasted Red Pepper and Artichoke Dip: Use Asiago cheese in place of Parmesan. Omit spinach and Cheddar. Add 2 chopped roasted red bell peppers (see box, page 310) with artichokes.

- Slow cooker size: 3½ to 6 quart

2	cloves garlic, minced	2
2	packages (each 8 oz/250 g) cream cheese, softened	2
¼ cup	mayonnaise	50 mL
⅓ cup	freshly grated Parmesan cheese	75 mL
1	package (10 oz/300 g) frozen chopped spinach, thawed and squeezed dry	1
1	can (14 oz/398 mL) artichoke hearts, rinsed, drained and coarsely chopped	1
⅔ cup	shredded Cheddar cheese	150 mL

1. In a food processor or bowl, combine garlic, cream cheese, mayonnaise and Parmesan. Process until smooth and creamy.
2. Add spinach and artichokes and combine. Spoon mixture into slow cooker stoneware.
3. Cover and cook on **Low** for 2 to 3 hours or on **High** for 1½ to 2 hours, until heated through.
4. Sprinkle with Cheddar, cover and cook on **High** for 15 to 20 minutes longer, or until cheese melts.

Hot Corn Dip

Makes about 6 cups (1.5 L)

The inspiration for this recipe hails from the Deep South. The jalapeño pepper adds a definite spicy nip.

• • •

Tips

There are a variety of pre-shredded cheeses available in the supermarket. If you wish, you can substitute a Mexican blend or hot pepper Monterey Jack in place of the Cheddar.

Enjoy with tortilla chips and a Mexican beer.

- Slow cooker size: 3½ to 4 quart

1 tbsp	butter	15 mL
3½ cups	fresh or frozen corn kernels (thawed if frozen)	875 mL
1	onion, finely chopped	1
½ tsp	salt	2 mL
¼ tsp	freshly ground black pepper	1 mL
2	cloves garlic, minced	2
1	green onion, finely chopped	1
1	jalapeño pepper, seeded and finely chopped	1
½	red bell pepper, finely chopped	½
1 cup	mayonnaise	250 mL
1½ cups	shredded Cheddar cheese	375 mL

1. In a large nonstick skillet, melt butter over medium-high heat. Add corn, onion, salt and pepper. Cook, stirring occasionally, until kernels turn a deep golden brown, about 5 minutes. Transfer to a bowl.
2. Add garlic, green onion, jalapeño, red pepper, mayonnaise and cheese to corn. Mix well. Spoon into lightly greased slow cooker stoneware.
3. Cover and cook on **Low** for 3 to 4 hours or on **High** for 1 to 2 hours, until bubbly. Serve hot.

Handling Hot Peppers

When chopping and seeding jalapeños or other hot peppers, make sure you keep your hands away from your eyes. Better yet, wear rubber or latex gloves and wash your hands, cutting board and utensils thoroughly in hot soapy water after handling peppers.

Nacho Cheese Dip

Makes about 4 cups (1 L)

This dip is sure to be a hit during football playoffs; serve it with lots of tortilla chips for scooping.

• • •

Tip

While many North Americans prefer Cheddar cheese, the key to this creamy dip is the processed cheese loaf, which will not curdle when heated. Enjoy the indulgence!

- Slow cooker size: 3½ to 6 quart

½ cup	beer	125 mL
1 tsp	ground cumin	5 mL
½ tsp	dried oregano	2 mL
½ tsp	garlic powder	2 mL
1	can (14 oz/398 mL) refried beans	1
½ cup	salsa	125 mL
1	processed cheese loaf (1 lb/500 g), cut into ½-inch (1 cm) cubes	1
¼ cup	chopped fresh cilantro	50 mL

1. In a small saucepan, combine beer, cumin, oregano and garlic powder. Bring to a boil, reduce heat and simmer for 2 minutes.
2. In a bowl, combine beans, salsa, cheese cubes and beer mixture. Spoon into lightly greased slow cooker stoneware.
3. Cover and cook on **Low** for 3 to 4 hours or on **High** for 1 to 2 hours, until bubbly and cheese has melted. Sprinkle with cilantro before serving.

Cilantro

Fresh cilantro, also known as coriander or Chinese parsley, has a very distinctive smell and flavor that suits many chilies, as well as Asian and Indian dishes.

To maximize its fairly short refrigerator shelf life, wash the leaves well, spin-dry and wrap in paper towels. Store in a plastic bag in the fridge. If the cilantro has roots attached, leave them on — it helps keep the leaves fresh.

Bacon-Onion Chip Dip

Makes about 3 cups (750 mL)

Why serve the store-bought variety when you can put out a pot of this warm dip? Try it with potato chips or, for a change, crunchy pretzels or sesame sticks. Everyone will be looking for more.

• • •

Tip

A mini (1-quart) slow cooker is ideal for entertaining. It is inexpensive and handy to have on hand for warm dips and spreads.

Make Ahead

The ingredients for this dip can be prepared up to 24 hours in advance and refrigerated. Spoon into prepared slow cooker and heat as directed. To reheat leftovers, microwave at Medium for 2 to 3 minutes. Stir before serving.

- **Slow cooker size: 1 to 3½ quart**

6	slices bacon, finely chopped	6
1	package (8 oz/250 g) light cream cheese, softened	1
1 cup	light sour cream	250 mL
½ cup	shredded old Cheddar cheese	125 mL
2	green onions, finely chopped	2
	Potato chips or crackers	

1. In a nonstick skillet over medium-high heat, cook bacon 7 to 8 minutes, or until crisp. Transfer to a paper towel–lined plate to drain.
2. In a bowl, combine cream cheese, sour cream, Cheddar cheese, green onions and cooked bacon. Mix well and transfer to lightly greased slow cooker stoneware.
3. Cover and cook on **High** for 1 hour, or until cheese is melted (do not stir). Reduce heat to **Low** until ready to serve.
4. Transfer to a bowl and serve with plain potato chips or as a spread on crackers. Dip will keep well in the refrigerator for several days.

Just-Like-Refried Frijoles Dip

Serves 8 to 10

Contrary to popular belief, refried beans aren't actually fried twice — they're first boiled in a pot of water, then fried in a skillet. And in fact, this "refried" bean dip isn't even fried once, but the slow cooker brings out a great "refried" flavor.

• • •

Tip

Use any leftover dip to make a delicious burrito: Spread dip on a warm tortilla shell; add seasoned ground beef, chopped lettuce, tomato, salsa and sour cream; roll up and serve with extra salsa.

- Slow cooker size: 3½ to 6 quart

2 tsp	vegetable oil	10 mL
1	onion, finely chopped	1
4	cloves garlic, minced	4
1½ tbsp	chili powder	20 mL
1 tsp	ground cumin	5 mL
2	cans (each 19 oz/540 mL) pinto or Romano beans, drained and rinsed	2
¾ cup	hot water	175 mL
½ tsp	salt	2 mL
1 cup	shredded Cheddar cheese	250 mL
½ cup	light sour cream	125 mL
	Chopped green onions	
	Tortilla chips	

1. In a small skillet, heat oil over medium heat. Add onion, garlic, chili powder and cumin; sauté for 5 minutes, or until onion is translucent and tender. Set aside.
2. In a bowl, with a potato masher (or in a blender or food processor), combine beans and hot water until smooth. Add seasoned onion mixture and salt; mix well. Transfer to lightly greased slow cooker stoneware.
3. Cover and cook on **Low** for 3 to 4 hours or on **High** for 1 to 2 hours. Reduce heat to **Low**. Sprinkle with Cheddar cheese and spoon sour cream in center of dip. Cover and cook for 20 minutes longer, or until cheese has melted. Set slow cooker to **Low** to keep dip warm until ready to serve. Garnish dip with chopped green onions and serve with tortilla chips.

Warm-and-Wonderful Seafood Dip

Serves 4 to 6

Less than 5 minutes to prepare the ingredients, then a few hours of unattended cooking — that's all you need to make this wonderful dip for vegetables, crackers or thin slices of baguette.

• • •

Tips

A mini (1-quart) slow cooker is ideal for this recipe; it's just the right size and will keep its contents at the right temperature for serving your guests.

In the unlikely event that you have any leftover dip, don't let it go to waste. It can be refrigerated, then enjoyed the next day; just reheat in the microwave at Medium for 2 to 2½ minutes or until warm. Or, for a tasty lunchtime treat, make a hot seafood wrap: Spread leftover dip on a soft flour tortilla; add sliced red bell pepper and cucumber, and sprinkle with alfalfa sprouts; roll up the tortilla and serve.

- **Slow cooker size: 1 to 3½ quart**

1	package (8 oz/250 g) cream cheese, softened	1
½ cup	mayonnaise	125 mL
3	green onions, chopped	3
2	cloves garlic, minced	2
2 tbsp	freshly squeezed lemon juice	25 mL
¼ cup	tomato paste	50 mL
2	cans (each 4 oz/113 g) tiny shrimp or 2 cans (each 6 oz/170 g) crabmeat, drained	2
	Salt and freshly ground black pepper	

1. In a bowl, blend together cream cheese, mayonnaise, green onions, garlic, lemon juice and tomato paste. Blend in seafood, mashing with a fork. Season to taste with salt and pepper. (Alternatively, place all ingredients except shrimp in a food processor; pulse 2 or 3 times, until mixture is smooth and well blended; add shrimp and pulse once or twice more.) Transfer mixture to slow cooker stoneware.
2. Cover and cook on **Low** for 2 to 3 hours or on **High** for 1 to 1½ hours. Set slow cooker to **Low** to keep dip warm until ready to serve with assorted vegetable dippers or crackers.

Hot Crab, Artichoke and Jalapeño Spread

Makes about 3 cups (750 mL)

This spread is the ultimate winter treat — warm and creamy, with just a nip of spicy heat from the jalapeño peppers. Serve it after skiing, with a basket of breadsticks or crackers.

• • •

Tips

Both light and regular mayonnaise work well in this recipe. Just be sure that it's real mayonnaise — not whipped-style salad dressing.

You can substitute a well-drained 4-oz (113 g) can of shrimp for crabmeat.

- Slow cooker size: 1 to 3½ quart

1 tsp	vegetable oil	5 mL
1	jalapeño pepper, seeded and finely chopped	1
½	red bell pepper, finely chopped	½
1	can (14 oz/398 mL) artichokes, drained and finely chopped	1
1 cup	mayonnaise	250 mL
¼ cup	freshly grated Parmesan cheese	50 mL
2	green onions, finely chopped	2
2 tsp	freshly squeezed lemon juice	10 mL
2 tsp	Worcestershire sauce	10 mL
½ tsp	celery seed	2 mL
1	can (6 oz/170 g) crabmeat, drained	1

1. In a nonstick skillet, heat oil over medium heat. Add jalapeño and red pepper; sauté for 5 minutes, or until tender.
2. In a bowl, combine artichokes, mayonnaise, Parmesan, green onions, lemon juice, Worcestershire sauce, celery seed, crabmeat and sautéed peppers. Mix well and spoon into lightly greased slow cooker stoneware.
3. Cover and cook on **Low** for 4 to 6 hours or on **High** for 2 to 2½ hours. Do not stir. Alternatively, cook on **High** for 1½ to 2 hours and then reduce to **Low** to keep warm until ready to serve.

Olives in Red Wine

Serves 6 as an appetizer

Black olives absorb the flavor of red wine and fennel in this warm appetizer. Be sure to provide toothpicks as well as a dish for the olive pits.

• • •

Tips

A mini (1 qt) slow cooker is ideal for this recipe. It's just the right size and will keep the olives at the right temperature.

Buy Kalamata olives if you can find them. They are assertively flavored ripe Greek olives marinated in wine vinegar or olive oil. Be sure to use the brine-cured variety in this recipe.

- **Slow cooker size: 1 to 3½ quart**

1 cup	unpitted brine-cured black olives	250 mL
½ cup	dry red wine	125 mL
¼ tsp	fennel seeds, coarsely crushed	1 mL
1	clove garlic, peeled and thinly sliced	1
2 tsp	olive oil	10 mL

1. Combine olives, wine, fennel seeds, garlic and olive oil in slow cooker stoneware
2. Cover and cook on **Low** for 3 to 4 hours, or until olives are heated through. Serve warm.

Best Beer Nuts

Makes about 2½ cups (625 mL)

Who would have thought that these favorite stadium nibblers could be made in the slow cooker? You won't believe the rave reviews you will get, and the cleanup is a lot easier than making them in the oven. Of course, drinking a beer with them is a must!

• • •

Tip

Keep these delicious nuts on hand as extra nibbles for parties. They will keep in an airtight container at room temperature for up to a month. They also make a perfect hostess gift packaged in an attractive container with ribbon tied around it.

- Slow cooker size: 3½ to 6 quart

1 cup	granulated sugar	250 mL
¼ cup	water	50 mL
2 cups	peanuts, preferably unsalted	500 mL

1. In a small bowl, combine sugar and water.
2. Place peanuts in slow cooker stoneware. Pour sugar mixture over nuts and toss to coat.
3. Cover and cook on **High**, stirring frequently, for 2 to 3 hours, or until sugar mixture is golden brown and peanuts are toasted.
4. Turn out onto a foil-lined baking sheet and set aside to cool.

Novel Curried Walnuts

Makes about 4 cups (1 L)

These little nibblers have an exotic spicy flavor. I like to snack on them as I read a novel — hence the name! You can't stop at one.

- **Slow cooker size: 3½ to 6 quart**

¼ cup	melted butter or margarine	50 mL
2 tbsp	curry powder	25 mL
2 tbsp	Worcestershire sauce	25 mL
2 tsp	salt	10 mL
1 tsp	onion powder	5 mL
4 cups	walnut halves	1 L

1. In a 1-cup (250 mL) measure, combine butter, curry powder, Worcestershire sauce, salt and onion powder; mix well. Place walnuts in slow cooker stoneware and pour in butter mixture; toss nuts to coat.
2. Cover and cook on **High**, stirring 2 or 3 times during cooking, for 2 hours or until nuts are browned and fragrant.
3. Cool and store in a tightly sealed container for up to 3 weeks.

Storing Nuts

Because of their high fat content, nuts (and particularly walnuts) will quickly become rancid unless kept in the refrigerator or freezer. If possible, taste before buying. If you do store them in the freezer, there's no need to defrost before use.

Zesty Nuts and Birdseed

Makes about 2½ cups (625 mL)

This tasty snack is definitely not for the birds! It will keep in an airtight container for up to 2 weeks.

• • •

Variation

Sunflower seeds can be replaced with pumpkin seeds or dried soybeans. Look for them in the bulk-food department of supermarkets or in health food stores.

- Slow cooker size: 3½ quart

2 cups	unsalted cashews, pecans or almonds	500 mL
½ cup	unsalted sunflower seeds	125 mL
2 tbsp	melted butter or margarine	25 mL
¼ cup	soy sauce	50 mL
½ tsp	salt	2 mL
¼ tsp	hot pepper sauce	1 mL

1. Place nuts and sunflower seeds in slow cooker stoneware. Add melted butter, soy sauce, salt and hot pepper sauce; toss nuts to coat with butter mixture.
2. Cover and cook on **High** for 2 hours, stirring frequently (about 4 or 5 times). Allow to cool before nibbling.

Spicy Popcorn with Nuts

Makes about 3 cups (750 mL)

If you are anything like me, there's nothing quite so satisfying as a little snack at about 8:00 at night, after the children have gone to bed. My husband and I enjoy this tasty mixture, which combines crunchy popcorn and savory spiced nuts.

• • •

Tips

Enjoy with a cold beer or herbal tea.

This mixture stores well in a tightly-sealed plastic container for up to 1 week.

- Slow cooker size: 3½ to 6 quart

¼ cup	popping corn	50 mL
½ cup	peanuts, salted or unsalted	125 mL
½ cup	pecan halves	125 mL
2 tbsp	melted butter	25 mL
2 tsp	chili powder	10 mL
1 tsp	garlic powder	5 mL
½ tsp	ground cumin	2 mL
½ tsp	salt	2 mL

1. In a hot-air popper or large saucepan with a tight-fitting lid, pop corn. Place in a large bowl with peanuts and pecans.
2. In a small bowl, combine butter, chili powder, garlic powder, cumin and salt; mix well. Drizzle over popcorn and nuts, tossing to coat well. Transfer mixture to slow cooker stoneware.
3. Cover and cook on **High** for 2 hours, stirring once or twice during cooking time. Allow to cool slightly before serving.

Winter Trail Mix

Makes about 6 cups (1.5 L)

Chunks of caramelized pecan crunch combine with dried apricots and cherries to make an irresistible tote-along snack. You can toss together a batch in no time. Store in a tightly sealed plastic container and it will keep fresh for up to 1 week.

• • •

Variation

For a delicious bridge mix, try adding chocolate-covered cherries or blueberries to the cooked, cooled mixture.

- Slow cooker size: 1½ to 3½ quart

½ cup	granulated sugar	125 mL
2 tbsp	melted butter or margarine	25 mL
1½ tbsp	water	20 mL
½ tsp	vanilla	2 mL
1½ cups	pecan halves	375 mL
1 cup	whole almonds	250 mL
2 tsp	finely grated orange zest	10 mL
1½ cups	sesame sticks or pretzel sticks	375 mL
1 cup	dried apricots	250 mL
1 cup	dried cherries or dried cranberries	250 mL

1. In a small glass measure, combine sugar, butter, water and vanilla. Place pecans and almonds in slow cooker stoneware; pour butter mixture over nuts and toss to coat.
2. Cover and cook on **High**, stirring frequently, for 2 to 3 hours, or until sugar mixture is golden brown and nuts are toasted. Stir in orange zest; toss to coat and turn out onto foil-lined baking sheet. Set aside to cool.
3. In a large bowl or airtight storage container, combine nut mixture with sesame sticks, apricots and cherries.

Soups

No-Fuss Chicken or Turkey Stock

Makes 6 cups (1.5 L)

Nothing could be easier than this homemade stock. Put all the ingredients in the slow cooker and let it simmer all day or overnight. Then make the tastiest soup ever!

• • •

Tip

You can use this stock for a variety of soups and recipes in this book, but it works especially well with Royal Chicken Soup (see recipe, page 89) or Boxing Day Turkey Soup (see recipe, page 92).

- Slow cooker size: 6 to 7 quart

3 lbs	chicken leg quarters, separated into drumsticks and thighs, or 2 turkey thighs, skin on	1.5 kg
1	onion, quartered	1
1	carrot	1
1	celery stalk, with leaves	1
8 to 10	whole peppercorns	8 to 10
1	bay leaf	1
2 tsp	salt	10 mL
	Water (about 6 to 8 cups/1.5 to 2 L)	

1. Place chicken pieces, onion, carrot, celery stalk, peppercorns, bay leaf and salt in slow cooker stoneware; cover with water.
2. Cover and cook on **Low** for 8 to 10 hours or on **High** for 4 to 6 hours.
3. Strain broth through cheesecloth-lined sieve into a large bowl, pressing vegetables to extract as much liquid as possible. Discard vegetables, reserving chicken.
4. Cover and refrigerate broth overnight; remove congealed fat from surface. Remove meat from bones and discard bones and skin. Refrigerate stock and chicken for up to 3 days or freeze for up to 4 months.

Springtime Russian Borscht

Serves 6 to 8

No slow cooker cookbook is complete without a good long-cooked borscht. Chock full of vegetables, this glorious ruby-red soup will brighten up even the gloomiest of days.

Tip

When beets with tops are not available, substitute additional shredded cabbage or Swiss chard for the beet greens.

Make Ahead

This soup can be assembled up to 24 hours before cooking. Combine ingredients and refrigerate overnight in the slow cooker stoneware. The next day, place stoneware in slow cooker and continue to cook as directed.

- Slow cooker size: 3½ to 6 quart

4	beets, including tops	4
1 cup	shredded cabbage	250 mL
1 cup	finely chopped turnip	250 mL
1	large potato, peeled and finely chopped	1
1	carrot, peeled and shredded or finely chopped	1
1	stalk celery, finely chopped	1
4 cups	vegetable or chicken stock	1 L
¼ cup	ketchup	50 mL
1 tsp	paprika	5 mL
¼ cup	chopped fresh dill, divided	50 mL
2 tbsp	red wine vinegar	25 mL
	Salt and freshly ground black pepper	
¼ cup	sour cream	50 mL

1. Peel beets and reserve tops. Chop or shred beets.
2. Combine beets, cabbage, turnip, potato, carrot, celery, stock, ketchup, paprika and 2 tbsp (25 mL) dill in slow cooker stoneware.
3. Cover and cook on **Low** for 8 to 10 hours or on **High** for 4 to 6 hours, until vegetables are tender.
4. Finely chop beet tops. Stir tops and vinegar into slow cooker and season with salt and pepper. Cover and let sit for 5 minutes, or just until beet greens wilt.
5. Spoon soup into individual serving bowls and serve with a dollop of sour cream. Sprinkle soup with remaining dill.

Autumn Celebration Soup

Serves 4 to 6

Here's a flavorful harvest soup that makes a great starter for Thanksgiving or Christmas dinner — or, served with crusty bread, a hearty lunch on its own.

• • •

Tips

For a decorative touch, use a skewer to draw a design through the sour cream on the surface of the soup.

Rutabagas are a yellow-fleshed relative of the turnip — although they are larger and slightly sweeter. Rutabagas and turnips (you can use either in this recipe) will keep all winter in a cold cellar. Remember to remove the waxy outer skin before cooking.

Make Ahead

The purée and vegetable stock can be prepared in advance and refrigerated for up to 3 days or frozen for up to 1 month. Reheat previously thawed purée in slow cooker and add thawed stock and cream as directed.

- Slow cooker size: 3½ to 6 quart

1 lb	rutabaga, peeled and cut into 1-inch (2.5 cm) cubes (about 4 cups/1 L)	500 g
1	onion, chopped	1
1	potato, peeled and cubed	1
2	carrots, peeled and chopped	2
1 cup	chicken stock	250 mL
½ cup	dry white wine	125 mL
2 cups	water	500 mL
2 tbsp	packed brown sugar	25 mL
2 tsp	caraway seeds	10 mL
1 tbsp	paprika	15 mL
2 cups	milk or light (5%) cream	500 mL
	Sour cream	
	Crisp bacon bits (optional)	

1. In slow cooker stoneware, combine rutabaga, onion, potato, carrots, stock, wine, water, brown sugar, caraway seeds and paprika.
2. Cover and cook on **Low** for 10 to 12 hours or on **High** for 6 to 8 hours, until vegetables are tender.
3. Strain the vegetables, reserving stock. In a blender or food processor, purée vegetables in batches. Transfer back to slow cooker; add reserved stock and milk. Heat on **Low** for 25 to 30 minutes, or until warmed through.
4. Spoon soup into individual bowls and garnish with dollops of sour cream and a sprinkle of bacon bits.

Cabbage Roll Soup

Serves 6 to 8

This cabbage roll soup is hearty enough to be a meal by itself — perfect for warding off winter's chill. Garnish each serving with a dollop of sour cream.

• • •

Tips

Look for a small cabbage for this soup or, to save time, buy packaged pre-shredded coleslaw cabbage.

There is no need to pre-cook the rice in this recipe. As the meatballs simmer in the broth, the liquid cooks the rice, resulting in a tender, tasty meatball.

Make an extra batch of meatballs to have on hand for the next time you want to make this soup. They freeze well and will keep in the freezer for up to 1 month.

- Slow cooker size: 5 to 6 quart

½ lb	lean ground beef	250 g
½ lb	lean ground pork	250 g
1	egg, lightly beaten	1
¾ cup	uncooked long-grain parboiled (converted) white rice	175 mL
1	small onion, finely chopped	1
2	cloves garlic, minced	2
½ tsp	salt	2 mL
¼ tsp	freshly ground black pepper	1 mL
3 cups	chicken stock	750 mL
1	can (28 oz/796 mL) diced tomatoes, with juices	1
1	can (10 oz/284 mL) condensed tomato soup, undiluted	1
4 cups	shredded cabbage	1 L
¼ cup	chopped fresh parsley	50 mL

1. In a bowl, combine ground beef, ground pork, egg, rice, onion, garlic, salt and pepper. Mix well and shape into 1-inch (2.5 cm) balls.
2. Arrange meatballs in a single layer on a foil-lined baking sheet and bake in a preheated 350°F (180°C) oven for 20 minutes, or until no longer pink inside.
3. In slow cooker stoneware, combine stock, tomatoes, tomato soup and cabbage. Add meatballs and stir gently to combine.
4. Cover and cook on **Low** for 8 to 10 hours or on **High** for 4 to 6 hours, until hot and bubbling. Stir in parsley.

Carrot Orange Bisque

Serves 4

This is a wonderful starter for an elegant meal — or it can be a meal on its own.

Tips

This recipe can easily be doubled, but don't change the quantity of orange zest: it will be too overpowering.

To extract the most juice from oranges, use fruit that has been sitting at room temperature. Roll firmly on a flat surface using the palm of your hand. Or microwave a whole orange on High for 30 seconds, and then roll. Juice can be frozen in ice cube trays, then stored in recloseable plastic bags for later use. Peel can also be wrapped and frozen for later use.

To zest an orange, use the fine edge of a cheese grater, ensuring you don't grate the white pith underneath. Or use a zester to remove the zest, then finely chop. Zesters are inexpensive and widely available at specialty kitchen shops.

- **Slow cooker size: 3½ to 5 quart**

1	onion, finely chopped	1
1½ lbs	carrots, cut into 1-inch (2.5 cm) chunks (about 5 cups/1.25 L)	750 g
3 cups	chicken stock	750 mL
	Grated zest and juice of 1 orange	
½ cup	whipping (35%) cream	125 mL
	Salt and freshly ground black pepper	

1. In slow cooker stoneware, combine onion, carrots, stock and orange juice.
2. Cover and cook on **Low** for 8 to 10 hours or on **High** for 4 to 6 hours, until carrots are fork-tender.
3. Strain vegetables, reserving stock. In a blender or food processor, purée vegetables until smooth. Transfer back to slow cooker and add zest and cream. Season to taste with salt and pepper. Reheat on **High** for 15 minutes.

French Onion Soup

Serves 6

In restaurants, bowls of onion soup are served capped with toasted French bread sprinkled with cheese and broiled to melt the cheese. For this version, broil the cheese on the bread first, then place in the bottom of the serving bowls.

• • •

Tip

Aside from using sweet onions, the key to making a great onion soup is the stock (see box, page 95). Use the best-quality stock you can.

- Slow cooker size: 3½ to 6 quart

¼ cup	butter	50 mL
4	large sweet onions, sliced	4
2	cloves garlic, minced	2
2 tbsp	all-purpose flour	25 mL
6 cups	beef stock	1.5 L
¼ cup	dry sherry or dry red wine	50 mL
1 tbsp	Worcestershire sauce	15 mL
1 tsp	granulated sugar	5 mL
½ tsp	salt	2 mL
¼ tsp	dried thyme	1 mL
1	bay leaf	1
½ tsp	freshly ground black pepper	2 mL

Croutons

6	slices French bread (½ inch/1 cm thick)	6
1 cup	shredded Swiss cheese	250 mL

1. In slow cooker stoneware, combine butter, onions and garlic.
2. Cover and cook on **High** for 40 to 60 minutes, or until onions begin to brown slightly around edges.
3. Sprinkle onions with flour and stir to combine. Add stock, sherry, Worcestershire sauce, sugar, salt, thyme, bay leaf and pepper. Cover and cook on **Low** for 6 to 8 hours or on **High** for 3 to 4 hours, until onions are tender and soup is bubbling. Discard bay leaf.
4. *Croutons:* Place bread slices on a baking sheet. Place under preheated broiler about 6 inches (15 cm) from the element and broil for about 2 minutes, or until browned. Turn bread, sprinkle with cheese and continue to broil until cheese is bubbling, about 1 minute.
5. Place bread croutons in bottom of individual serving bowls and spoon soup over top.

Harvest Corn Chowder with Bacon and Cheddar

Serves 8 to 10

The slow cooker isn't just for wintertime fare. I love to make this soup when the harvest of fresh corn appears in late July and August.

• • •

Tips

To use fresh sweet corn in this recipe, remove the husks and stand cobs on end. Use a sharp knife and cut kernels off cobs.

Serve with a hearty multigrain bread or bagels and glasses of ice-cold lemonade.

For a meatless version, omit bacon and add all ingredients to slow cooker. Cook as directed.

- Slow cooker size: 3½ to 6 quart

4	slices bacon, chopped	4
2	onions, chopped	2
2	stalks celery, chopped	2
2	potatoes, chopped	2
4 cups	corn kernels, fresh or frozen	1 L
4 cups	chicken stock	1 L
1	bay leaf	1
1 tsp	salt	5 mL
½ tsp	freshly ground black pepper	2 mL
2 tbsp	butter or margarine	25 mL
2 tbsp	all-purpose flour	25 mL
1	can (13 oz/385 mL) evaporated milk or 1½ cups (375 mL) whipping (35%) cream	1
1 cup	shredded Cheddar cheese	250 mL
	Additional shredded Cheddar cheese	
	Chopped fresh parsley	

1. In a large nonstick skillet, over medium heat, cook bacon, onions and celery for 5 minutes, or until onions are translucent. With a slotted spoon, transfer mixture to slow cooker stoneware. Add potatoes, corn, stock, bay leaf, salt and pepper; stir to combine.
2. Cover and cook on **Low** for 8 to 10 hours or on **High** for 4 to 6 hours, until vegetables are tender and soup is bubbling. Remove bay leaf and discard.

3. In a saucepan, over medium-high heat, melt butter. Add flour and stir to make a smooth paste. Slowly add milk, whisking constantly to combine. Bring mixture to a boil, whisking constantly until thickened. Remove from heat and stir in cheese until completely melted. Gradually stir milk sauce mixture into slow cooker.
4. Cover and cook on **High** for 20 to 30 minutes longer. Serve garnished with additional Cheddar cheese and chopped fresh parsley.

Evaporated Milk

Evaporated milk holds up extremely well in slow cookers and will not curdle. Don't confuse this milk with the sweetened condensed milk used in desserts and candies.

Make Ahead

This soup can be made up to the point of thickening. Refrigerate for 3 days or freeze up to 3 months. To reheat, thaw first, place soup in slow cooker with ½ cup (125 mL) water, cover and reheat on High for 2 to 3 hours or on Low for 4 to 6 hours. Continue with Step 3 as directed.

French Canadian Split Pea Soup

Serves 6 to 8

Making a pot of hearty pea soup to enjoy after outdoor activities is a wonderful winter tradition.

• • •

Tips

A thick, crusty bun and warm tea or glass of crisp white wine is all that's needed for a tasty meal.

Split peas will be very tough unless they are soaked before making the soup. They can either be left to stand in water overnight or boiled for 2 minutes and left to stand for 1 hour.

Make Ahead

It is best to start making this soup 12 to 24 hours in advance — in fact, all the ingredients can be assembled in the slow cooker stoneware and refrigerated overnight. The next day, place stoneware in slow cooker and cook as directed.

- **Slow cooker size: 6 to 7 quart**

1 lb	yellow split peas	500 g
8 oz	smoked pork hock, skin removed	250 g
3	carrots, diced	3
1	large potato, peeled and diced	1
1	stalk celery, finely chopped	1
1	bay leaf	1
1/4 tsp	dried thyme	1 mL
1/4 tsp	dried basil	1 mL
1/4 tsp	dried oregano	1 mL
	Salt and freshly ground black pepper	

1. Place peas in a bowl and add enough cold water to cover; soak peas for at least 12 hours (Alternatively, place peas in a pot, cover with water, bring to a boil, remove from heat and let stand for 1 hour.). Drain, rinse well and place in slow cooker stoneware. Add 7 cups (1.75 L) water, smoked pork hock, carrots, potato, celery, bay leaf, thyme, basil and oregano.
2. Cover and cook on **Low** for 10 to 12 hours or on **High** for 6 to 8 hours, until soup is thick and bubbling.
3. With a slotted spoon, gently remove pork hock from soup. Remove meat from bone, cut into chunks and return to pot. Remove bay leaf and discard. Serve immediately and season to taste with salt and pepper.

Roasted Pear and Parsnip Soup

Serves 4 to 6

Parsnips "roasted" in the slow cooker give a smoky taste to this hearty winter soup. Serve it garnished with fresh thyme sprigs.

• • •

Tip

The best pears to choose for this soup are Bartlett or Bosc.

Make Ahead

This soup can be prepared up to the purée and then refrigerated or frozen. Defrost purée before placing in slow cooker.

- Slow cooker size: 3½ to 6 quart

2 cups	chopped peeled parsnips	500 mL
1	slightly underripe pear, peeled and chopped	1
1	onion, chopped	1
2	cloves garlic, minced	2
1	yellow bell pepper, chopped	1
1 tbsp	butter, melted	15 mL
1 tbsp	packed brown sugar	15 mL
1 tbsp	balsamic vinegar	15 mL
½ tsp	dried thyme	2 mL
4 cups	vegetable or chicken stock, divided	1 L

1. Place parsnips, pear, onion, garlic and yellow pepper in slow cooker stoneware.
2. In a small bowl, combine melted butter, brown sugar, vinegar and thyme. Pour over vegetables and toss to coat.
3. Cover and cook on **Low** for 4 to 6 hours or on **High** for 2 to 3 hours, until vegetables are tender.
4. In a blender or food processor, purée vegetable mixture with 1 cup (250 mL) stock until smooth. Return mixture to slow cooker and add remaining stock.
5. Cover and cook on **Low** for 4 to 6 hours or on **High** for 3 to 4 hours longer, until bubbling.

Roasted Red Pepper and Tomato Soup

Serves 4 to 6

When I walk through our local farmers' market in August and September, I am overcome with an incredible urge to make as many dishes as I can with the bountiful display of lush, ripe tomatoes and red peppers. This is one of my favorites.

• • •

Tips

In season, red bell peppers are very inexpensive, so I broil or grill extra and keep them in the freezer to have on hand during the winter months.

If you make this soup in the winter, use vine-ripened tomatoes for best flavor. Add an extra tablespoon (15 mL) of tomato paste after the mixture is puréed.

To ripen tomatoes, place in a paper bag and leave on the counter at room temperature. Never store tomatoes in the refrigerator; it dulls their delicate flavor.

- Slow cooker size: 3½ to 5 quart

4	large red bell peppers	4
5	large tomatoes, peeled, seeded and chopped or 1 can (28 oz/796 mL) Italian-style stewed tomatoes, with juices (see box, page 97)	5
1	onion, finely chopped	1
1	stalk celery, finely chopped	1
2	fresh basil leaves (or ½ tsp/2 mL dried)	2
2 cups	chicken stock	500 mL
1 tbsp	tomato paste	15 mL
2 tsp	granulated sugar	10 mL
	Juice of ½ lemon	
	Salt and freshly ground black pepper	
	Fresh basil	
	Whipping (35%) cream (optional)	

1. Cut peppers in half and remove seeds. Place cut side down on a baking sheet. Broil or grill until skins are blackened and puffed. Remove from oven and place in a paper bag to steam. When cooled, peel off and discard skins; cut pepper into chunks.
2. Transfer peppers to slow cooker stoneware. Add tomatoes, onion, celery, basil, stock and tomato paste.
3. Cover and cook on **Low** for 4 to 6 hours or on **High** for 2 to 3 hours.
4. Transfer soup, in batches, to a blender or food processor and process until smooth.

5. Return mixture to slow cooker. Stir in sugar, lemon juice and salt and pepper to taste. Serve hot or refrigerate and serve cold. Garnish with snips of fresh basil. For a richer soup, drizzle 1 to 2 tbsp (15 to 25 mL) whipping cream into soup bowl before serving.

Tomato Paste

Tomato paste is made from tomatoes that have been cooked for several hours until the sauce has thickened and has a rich, concentrated flavor and color. Look for tomato paste in squeezable tubes rather than cans. It is especially easy to use when a recipe calls for smaller quantities. The tubes can be found in Italian grocery stores and some supermarkets. Refrigerate after opening.

Tip

An immersion blender is ideal for puréeing the soup right in the slow cooker without having to transfer it to a blender or food processor.

Southwestern Pumpkin Soup

Serves 4 to 6

This easy-to-make soup is flavored with cumin and chili powder. Make sure you buy a can of pumpkin purée, not pumpkin pie filling.

• • •

Tips

To get the most juice from a lime, leave at room temperature and roll on counter, pressing down with the palm of your hand, before squeezing.

To zest a lime, use the fine edge of a cheese grater, ensuring you don't grate the white pith underneath. Or use a zester to remove the zest, then finely chop. Zesters are inexpensive and widely available at specialty kitchen shops.

- **Slow cooker size: 3½ to 6 quart**

3 cups	vegetable or chicken stock	750 mL
1	can (28 oz/796 mL) pumpkin purée (not pie filling)	1
1 tbsp	packed brown sugar	15 mL
1 tsp	ground cumin	5 mL
½ tsp	chili powder	2 mL
Pinch	ground nutmeg	Pinch
1	can (14 oz/400 mL) coconut milk	1
½ tsp	grated lime zest	2 mL
2 tsp	freshly squeezed lime juice	10 mL
½ cup	shredded Cheddar cheese	125 mL
1 tbsp	chopped fresh cilantro	15 mL

1. In slow cooker stoneware, combine stock, pumpkin purée, brown sugar, cumin, chili powder and nutmeg.
2. Cover and cook on **Low** for 4 to 6 hours or on **High** for 2 to 3 hours, until hot and bubbling.
3. Stir in coconut milk, lime zest and juice. Spoon soup into individual serving bowls and top with grated Cheddar and cilantro.

Coconut Milk

Canned coconut milk is made from grated and soaked coconut pulp, not (as you might expect) from the liquid inside the coconut. It can be found in the Asian or canned milk section of most supermarkets or in Asian food stores. Make sure you don't buy coconut cream, which is used to make tropical drinks such as piña coladas.

Squash and Apple Soup

Serves 4 to 6

Of all the vegetables I serve my children, squash is their least favorite. However, they love this soup and always ask for more.

• • •

Tip
This recipe can easily be doubled and it freezes well.

• • •

Variation
Any buttery squash, such as Hubbard or Acorn, can be used in this recipe. You can also substitute 1 can (28 oz/796 mL) canned pumpkin purée (not pie filling) for the squash.

Make Ahead
This soup can be assembled 12 to 24 hours in advance of cooking (but without adding the cheese). Prepare ingredients as directed in slow cooker stoneware and refrigerate overnight. The next day, place stoneware in slow cooker and cook as directed.

- Slow cooker size: 3½ to 5 quart

1	butternut squash (about 3 lbs/1.5 kg), peeled and cut into 1-inch (2.5 cm) cubes	1
2	apples, peeled and chopped	2
1	onion, chopped	1
3 cups	chicken stock	750 mL
1 cup	apple juice	250 mL
½ tsp	dried marjoram	2 mL
½ tsp	dried thyme	2 mL
½ tsp	salt	2 mL
½ tsp	freshly ground black pepper	2 mL
½ cup	shredded Swiss cheese	125 mL

1. In slow cooker stoneware, combine squash, apples, onion, stock, juice, marjoram, thyme, salt and pepper.
2. Cover and cook on **Low** for 8 to 10 hours or on **High** for 4 to 6 hours, until squash is tender.
3. In a colander, strain soup, reserving liquid. Transfer mixture to a blender or food processor. Add 1 cup (250 mL) reserved liquid and process until smooth.
4. Return soup to the slow cooker along with remaining stock. Season to taste with additional salt and pepper.
5. Spoon into serving bowls and top each with grated Swiss cheese.

Mexican Squash Soup

Serves 6 to 8

This easy-to-make soup is fun for a party because the guests can help themselves to a variety of colorful garnishes. Along with the toppings, be sure to pass a basket of tortilla chips.

Make Ahead

This soup can be prepared up to 24 hours before cooking. Combine ingredients in slow cooker stoneware and refrigerate overnight. The next day, place stoneware in slow cooker and continue to cook as directed.

- Slow cooker size: 3½ to 6 quart

2	onions, finely chopped	2
2	cloves garlic, minced	2
4 cups	diced squash	1 L
1 tsp	ground cumin	5 mL
1 tsp	salt	5 mL
½ tsp	dried oregano	2 mL
½ tsp	hot pepper flakes	2 mL
½ tsp	freshly ground black pepper	2 mL
4 cups	vegetable or chicken stock	1 L
3 cups	fresh or frozen corn kernels (thawed if frozen)	750 mL
½	red bell pepper, finely chopped	½
½ cup	chopped fresh cilantro	125 mL

Toppings

½ cup	shredded Cheddar or Monterey Jack cheese	125 mL
½ cup	pine nuts, toasted (see box, page 326)	125 mL
½ cup	walnut halves, toasted (see box, page 30)	125 mL
2	jalapeño peppers, seeded and chopped	2

1. In slow cooker stoneware, combine onions, garlic, squash, cumin, salt, oregano, hot pepper flakes, black pepper and stock.
2. Cover and cook on **Low** for 8 to 10 hours or on **High** for 4 to 6 hours, until vegetables are tender and soup is bubbling.
3. Stir in corn, red pepper and cilantro. Cover and cook on **High** for 15 to 20 minutes longer, or until heated through.
4. Spoon into individual bowls and sprinkle with cheese, pine nuts, walnuts and jalapeños.

Potato-Leek Soup with Stilton

Serves 4 to 6

This is a classic French soup with an English twist — Stilton cheese has been one of our family favorites for years!

• • •

Tips

Serve with lots of crumbled Stilton cheese and a loaf of French bread.

Blue cheese or Roquefort cheese can be substituted for Stilton, but the flavor won't be the same.

An immersion blender is ideal for puréeing the soup right in the slow cooker without having to transfer it to a blender or food processor.

Make Ahead

This soup can be prepared up to the point before adding cream. It can be refrigerated up to 2 days or frozen for up to 3 months. To reheat, add 1 cup (250 mL) water and heat until piping hot.

- Slow cooker size: 3½ to 5 quart

2 tbsp	butter or margarine	25 mL
3	leeks (white parts only), trimmed, well rinsed (see tip, page 89) and sliced	3
1	onion, chopped	1
4	potatoes, peeled and chopped	4
6 cups	chicken stock	1.5 L
1 tsp	salt	5 mL
½ tsp	freshly ground black pepper	2 mL
Pinch	ground nutmeg	Pinch
1 cup	whipping (35%) cream	250 mL
	Crumbled Stilton cheese	
	Salt and freshly ground black pepper	

1. In a large pot, heat butter over medium-high heat. Add leeks and onion; cover, reduce heat to medium-low and cook for 10 minutes, or until tender. Transfer to slow cooker stoneware. Add potatoes, stock, salt, pepper and nutmeg.
2. Cover and cook on **Low** for 8 to 10 hours or on **High** for 4 to 6 hours, until vegetables are tender.
3. Transfer soup, in batches, to a blender or food processor and process until smooth. Season to taste with salt and pepper.
4. Return soup to slow cooker; stir in cream. Cover and cook on **High** for 15 to 20 minutes longer, or until heated through.
5. Crumble cheese into bottom of individual serving bowls and ladle in soup. If desired, sprinkle with additional Stilton. Season to taste with salt and pepper.

Spicy Sweet Potato Soup

Serves 6

See if your guests can guess the secret ingredient in this soup (peanut butter).

• • •

Tips

Be sure to grate the zest before juicing the lime when you are preparing the ingredients for this recipe.

An immersion blender is ideal for puréeing the soup right in the slow cooker without having to transfer it to a blender or food processor.

This soup's exotic flavors suit a spicy wine such as a Gewürztraminer. Serve it with crusty European-style bread.

Make Ahead

The purée can be prepared in advance (up to the end of Step 3) and refrigerated for up to 3 days or frozen for up to 1 month. Reheat purée with remaining stock in a saucepan on the stove.

- Slow cooker size: 3½ to 6 quart

2	large sweet potatoes, peeled and chopped (about 1½ to 2 lbs/750 g to 1 kg)	2
1	onion, chopped	1
2	cloves garlic, peeled and sliced	2
4 cups	vegetable or chicken stock	1 L
½ tsp	ground cumin	2 mL
¼ tsp	hot pepper flakes	1 mL
1 tsp	ground ginger	5 mL
¼ cup	crunchy or smooth peanut butter	50 mL
	Juice of 1 lime	
	Salt and freshly ground black pepper	
1 tbsp	chopped fresh cilantro	15 mL
½ cup	sour cream	125 mL
1 tsp	grated lime zest	5 mL
¼ cup	finely chopped red bell pepper	50 mL

1. In slow cooker stoneware, combine sweet potatoes, onion, garlic, stock, cumin, hot pepper flakes and ginger.
2. Cover and cook on **Low** for 8 to 10 hours or on **High** for 4 to 6 hours, until sweet potatoes are tender.
3. In a colander, strain soup, reserving liquid. Transfer sweet potato mixture to a blender or food processor. Add 1 cup (250 mL) reserved liquid, peanut butter and lime juice. Process until smooth.
4. Return soup to slow cooker along with remaining liquid. Season to taste with salt and pepper. Stir in cilantro. Cover and cook on **High** for 10 minutes longer, or until heated through.
5. In a small bowl, combine sour cream and lime zest.
6. Spoon soup into serving bowls. Add a dollop of sour cream mixture and garnish with chopped red pepper.

New England–Style Clam Chowder

Serves 6 to 8

Every restaurant in Boston claims to serve "the best" clam chowder. I think this one rates right up there too!

• • •

Tips

Remember not to add the clams until the end; they will get tough if cooked too long.

For a meatless version, omit bacon. Add onion, celery and green pepper directly to the slow cooker. Continue cooking as directed.

To avoid lumps in soups and stews, place liquid and flour in a jar with a tight-fitting lid. Shake well and pour into hot stock mixture.

• **Slow cooker size: 3½ to 6 quart**

6	strips bacon, finely chopped	6
1	onion, finely chopped	1
3	stalks celery, finely chopped	3
2	cans (each 5 oz/142 g) whole baby clams	2
1 cup	water	250 mL
3 cups	diced peeled potatoes	750 mL
1 tsp	Worcestershire sauce	5 mL
½ tsp	salt	2 mL
¼ tsp	freshly ground black pepper	1 mL
1	bay leaf	1
¼ cup	all-purpose flour	50 mL
2 cups	light (5%) cream or half-and-half (10%) cream or 1 can (13 oz/385 mL) evaporated milk	250 mL
½	green bell pepper, finely chopped	½

1. In a large nonstick skillet, sauté bacon, onion and celery for 5 minutes or until vegetables are softened and onion is translucent. With a slotted spoon, transfer mixture to slow cooker stoneware.
2. Drain clam liquid into slow cooker; set aside whole clams. Add water, potatoes, Worcestershire sauce, salt, pepper and bay leaf.
3. Cover and cook on **High** for 3 to 4 hours or on **Low** for 6 to 10 hours, until potatoes are tender and soup is bubbling. Remove bay leaf and discard.
4. In a bowl, combine flour and ¼ cup (50 mL) cream; mix well to dissolve lumps. Add to slow cooker along with reserved whole clams, green pepper and remaining cream. Cover and cook on **High** for 25 to 30 minutes longer, or until thickened.

Curried Cream of Chicken Soup

Serves 4 to 6

Tips

To eliminate the raw taste of curry powder and sweeten the spice, sauté it in a dry skillet before using. Cook for about 30 seconds, or just until fragrant.

An immersion blender is ideal for puréeing the soup right in the slow cooker without having to transfer it to a blender or food processor.

- Slow cooker size: 3½ to 6 quart

1	large onion, chopped	1
2	carrots, chopped	2
1½ tbsp	curry powder	22 mL
5 cups	chicken stock	1.25 L
¼ cup	parsley	50 mL
1	chicken (about 2 to 3 lbs/1 to 1.5 kg), quartered	1
½ cup	long-grain rice	125 mL
1 cup	half-and-half (10%) cream or light (5%) cream	250 mL
1 cup	frozen peas	250 mL
	Salt and freshly ground black pepper	

1. In slow cooker stoneware, combine onion, carrots, curry powder, stock, parsley, chicken pieces and rice; stir to mix well.
2. Cover and cook on **Low** for 8 to 10 hours or on **High** for 4 to 6 hours.
3. With a slotted spoon, gently remove chicken pieces from stock. Set aside to cool slightly. Remove meat from bones; dice chicken and reserve. Discard bones and skin.
4. Transfer vegetables and stock, in batches, to a blender or food processor and process until smooth.
5. Return soup to slow cooker. Add cream, reserved chicken and peas. Adjust seasoning, adding more curry powder if desired. Heat on **Low** for 15 to 20 minutes. Season to taste with salt and pepper.

Royal Chicken Soup

Serves 6 to 8

With so many fresh root vegetables on hand, the home economists at the Royal Agricultural Winter Fair (held annually in Toronto) always whip up a batch of this soup for the media. Its wonderful flavor keeps them coming back for more. Now you can enjoy it too!

• • •

Tips

If time won't allow you to make homemade chicken stock, use the next best thing — canned. Avoid using bouillon mix or cubes, since these can be extremely salty and don't give the same rich taste.

Leeks must be cleaned carefully, since they contain a lot of sand. Remove most of the green part and cut the white part into halves lengthwise. Rinse thoroughly under cold running water and drain in a colander.

- **Slow cooker size: 5 to 6 quart**

6 cups	No-Fuss Chicken Stock (see recipe, page 70) or 3 cans (each 10 oz/284 mL) chicken broth, diluted with an equal amount of water	1.5 L
3	leeks (white parts only), chopped	3
4	carrots, sliced	4
2	stalks celery, finely chopped	2
2	parsnips, diced	2
2 cups	diced cooked chicken	500 mL
1/4 cup	chopped fresh parsley	50 mL
1/2 tsp	paprika	2 mL
2 cups	egg noodles	500 mL
	Salt and freshly ground black pepper	

1. In slow cooker stoneware, combine stock, leeks, carrots, celery, parsnips, chicken, parsley and paprika.
2. Cover and cook on **Low** for 8 to 10 hours or on **High** for 4 to 6 hours, until vegetables are tender and soup is bubbling.
3. In a large pot of boiling salted water, cook noodles according to package directions. Drain well. Add to slow cooker; stir to combine. Season to taste with salt and pepper.

Mulligatawny Soup

Serves 6 to 8

This famous Indian soup was originally developed by cooks who served in English homes during the colonization of India in the 18th century. It is based on chicken and vegetables cooked in a rich stock that has been seasoned with curry. Serve topped with toasted shredded coconut if you wish. For a heartier meal, serve it over steamed basmati rice (see box, page 163).

• • •

Tip

Purchase chicken thighs in economical family packs. Divide into meal-sized portions, wrap in plastic wrap and freeze in freezer bags.

- **Slow cooker size: 3½ to 6 quart**

1 tbsp	all-purpose flour	15 mL
1 lb	boneless skinless chicken thighs, cut into 1-inch (2.5 cm) pieces	500 g
1 tbsp	vegetable oil	15 mL
1 tbsp	curry powder	15 mL
1 tsp	ground ginger	5 mL
½ tsp	hot pepper flakes	2 mL
¼ tsp	ground cloves	1 mL
4 cups	chicken stock, divided	1 L
2	carrots, peeled and finely chopped	2
1	onion, finely chopped	1
2	stalks celery, finely chopped	2
2	cloves garlic, minced	2
½ cup	diced turnip	125 mL
1	Granny Smith apple, unpeeled, chopped	1
1	can (19 oz/540 mL) chickpeas, drained and rinsed, or 2 cups (500 mL) home-cooked chickpeas (page 146)	1
1 tbsp	grated lemon zest	15 mL
	Juice of 1 lemon	
1 tbsp	chopped fresh cilantro	15 mL

1. Place flour in a large heavy-duty plastic bag. In batches, toss chicken in flour to coat.
2. In a large nonstick skillet, heat oil over medium-high heat. Add chicken, curry powder, ginger, hot pepper flakes and cloves. Cook, stirring occasionally, for 5 to 7 minutes, or until chicken is browned on all sides. With a slotted spoon, transfer chicken to slow cooker stoneware.

3. Add 1 cup (250 mL) stock to skillet. Bring to a boil and stir to scrape up any brown bits. Transfer stock mixture to slow cooker.
4. Add carrots, onion, celery, garlic, turnip, apple, chickpeas and remaining stock to slow cooker. Mix well to combine.
5. Cover and cook on **Low** for 6 to 8 hours or on **High** for 3 to 4 hours, until vegetables are tender and soup is bubbling.
6. Stir in lemon zest, lemon juice and cilantro.

Curry Powder

Curry powder, a blend of more than 20 herbs, seeds and spices, is integral to Indian cuisine (in India, most cooks blend their own mixtures). Cardamom, chilies, cinnamon, coriander, cumin, fennel, mace, pepper, poppy and sesame seeds and saffron are common curry seasonings. Turmeric gives curry its distinctive yellow color.

Curry paste can be used instead of curry powder. It comes in different heat levels, so buy a mild version if you don't like your curry too hot.

To eliminate the raw taste of curry powder and sweeten the spice, sauté it in a dry skillet before using. Cook for about 30 seconds, or just until fragrant.

Tip

Hot pepper flakes: This fiery flavor booster can be found in the spice section of the supermarket. Leave on the table for a great seasoning alternative to salt and pepper.

Boxing Day Turkey Soup

Serves 4 to 6

Here's a rich and delicious solution to an age-old post-Christmas problem — What to do with the leftover turkey?

• • •

Tips

For a creamier version, omit the tomatoes and add 1 can (14 oz/398 mL) cream-style corn.

For best results with all-day cooking, use long-grain parboiled (converted) rice.

Make Ahead

You don't have to wait until Boxing Day to try this delicious soup. I often make stock and freeze it for later use. The meat, removed from the bones, can also be wrapped and frozen for later use. Thaw frozen stock and meat first; add to slow cooker and continue as directed.

- **Slow cooker size: 6 to 7 quart**

6 cups	No-Fuss Turkey Stock (see recipe, page 70) or 3 cans (each 10 oz/284 mL) chicken broth, diluted with equal parts water	1.5 L
2 cups	chopped cooked turkey	500 mL
1	can (19 oz/540 mL) diced tomatoes, with juices	1
2	carrots, chopped	2
2	stalks celery, chopped	2
1	onion, chopped	1
1/4 cup	long-grain parboiled (converted) rice	50 mL
2 tbsp	chopped fresh parsley (or 2 tsp/10 mL dried)	25 mL
1/2 tsp	dried thyme	2 mL
1 1/2 cups	frozen corn kernels	375 mL
	Salt and freshly ground black pepper	

1. In slow cooker stoneware, combine stock, turkey, tomatoes, carrots, celery, onion, rice, parsley and thyme.
2. Cover and cook on **Low** for 8 to 10 hours or on **High** for 4 to 6 hours, until vegetables are tender and soup is bubbling.
3. Add corn; cover and cook on **High** for 20 minutes longer. Season to taste with salt and pepper.

Rich Vegetable Broth with Meatballs

Serves 4 to 6

This is a perfect soup to serve guests after a day of winter activities.

• • •

Tips

If you need a few more servings, this soup can be extended by adding pasta such as fusilli or rotini.

Serve with warm foccacia bread or a thick Italian loaf to soak up the sauce.

I like to make an extra batch of the meatballs used in this soup. They're great to have on hand to use in quick appetizers or pasta sauces. They freeze well and keep in the freezer for up to 3 months.

- Slow cooker size: 3½ to 6 quart

Meatballs

1 lb	lean ground beef	500 g
½ cup	fine dry bread crumbs	125 mL
1 tbsp	chopped fresh parsley	15 mL
1 tsp	salt	5 mL
¼ tsp	freshly ground black pepper	1 mL
1	egg, lightly beaten	1

Vegetable Broth

2	onions, finely chopped	2
2	carrots, finely chopped	2
1	stalk celery, finely chopped	1
1	can (19 oz/540 mL) Italian-style tomatoes, with juices (see box, page 97)	1
2 cups	beef stock	500 mL
¼ tsp	dried oregano	1 mL
¼ tsp	dried basil	1 mL
1	bay leaf	1
	Freshly grated Parmesan cheese	

1. *Meatballs:* In a large bowl, combine ground beef, bread crumbs, parsley, salt, pepper and egg. Mix well and shape into ½-inch (1 cm) balls.
2. Arrange meatballs in a single layer on a foil-lined baking sheet and bake in a preheated 400°F (200°C) oven for 10 to 12 minutes, or until no longer pink inside.
3. *Vegetable broth:* In slow cooker stoneware, combine onions, carrots, celery, tomatoes, stock, oregano, basil, and bay leaf. Add cooked meatballs.
4. Cover and cook on **Low** for 8 to 10 hours or on **High** for 4 to 6 hours, until hot and bubbling. Discard bay leaf.
5. Spoon into bowls and sprinkle with Parmesan.

Meaty Minestrone

Serves 6 to 8

Minestrone means "big soup" in Italian and refers to a thick soup full of vegetables and pasta. This meaty version makes a hearty meal.

• • •

Tips

Select lean stewing beef or trim the excess fat from the meat before using. (Trimming may take a little extra time, but the result will be worth it.)

Chopped garlic in the jar is a convenient alternative to fresh garlic. It's easy to use and will keep in the refrigerator for up to 6 months.

- Slow cooker size: 5 to 6 quart

1 tbsp	vegetable oil	15 mL
1 lb	stewing beef, cut into 1-inch (2.5 cm) cubes	500 g
3/4 tsp	dried Italian seasoning (see box, page 105)	4 mL
1 tsp	salt	5 mL
1/2 tsp	freshly ground black pepper	2 mL
3 cups	beef stock, divided	750 mL
1	can (19 oz/540 mL) diced tomatoes, with juices	1
2	cloves garlic, minced	2
2	carrots, peeled and finely chopped	2
1	stalk celery, finely chopped	1
1 cup	shredded cabbage	250 mL
1	bay leaf	1
1	can (12 oz/355 mL) cola	1
1	can (19 oz/540 mL) white kidney beans, drained and rinsed, or 2 cups (500 mL) home-cooked beans (page 146)	1
1	piece (1 inch/2.5 cm) Parmesan cheese rind	1
1 cup	diced green beans	250 mL
1	small zucchini, cut in half lengthwise and chopped	1
1 cup	cooked macaroni or other small pasta	250 mL
2 tbsp	freshly grated Parmesan cheese	25 mL

1. In a large nonstick skillet, heat oil over medium-high heat. Add beef cubes, Italian seasoning, salt and pepper and cook, stirring, for 8 to 10 minutes, or until meat is browned on all sides. With a slotted spoon, transfer meat to slow cooker stoneware.
2. Add 1 cup (250 mL) stock to skillet and bring to a boil, scraping up any browned bits from bottom of pan. Add to meat in slow cooker.

3. Add remaining stock, tomatoes, garlic, carrots, celery, cabbage, bay leaf, cola and kidney beans to slow cooker. Stir to combine. Immerse Parmesan cheese rind in soup mixture.
4. Cover and cook on **Low** for 8 to 10 hours or on **High** for 4 to 6 hours, until meat and vegetables are tender and soup is bubbling.
5. Stir in green beans, zucchini and macaroni. Cover and cook on **High** for 20 to 25 minutes longer, or until hot and bubbly. Discard Parmesan rind and bay leaf.
6. Spoon soup into individual bowls and sprinkle with grated Parmesan cheese.

Tip

When you purchase a piece of real Parmesan cheese (e.g., Parmigiano Reggiano), it usually comes with the rind. The rind is too tough to grate or eat, so add it to this soup for extra flavor. (Be sure to discard it before serving the soup.)

Stock

"Stock" refers to the strained liquid that results from cooking poultry, meat or vegetables and seasonings in water. Other terms for this include "broth" and "bouillon." The best stock is homemade, but if time won't allow, use canned stock (dilute as directed) or refrigerated stocks sold in tetra paks. Try to avoid using bouillon powder or cubes since these tend to be quite salty and don't give the same rich taste. If you do use powdered stock or cubes, add salt to taste at the end of the cooking.

Taco Beef Soup

Serves 4 to 6

This soup can be put together quickly, and it will satisfy a hungry family at the end of the day. Spoon the soup into individual serving bowls and pass toppings such as grated Cheddar, sour cream or crushed tortilla chips.

Make Ahead

This soup can be assembled up to 24 hours before cooking. Complete Step 1 and chill meat mixture completely. Then combine all ingredients in slow cooker stoneware and refrigerate overnight. The next day, place stoneware in slow cooker and continue to cook as directed.

- **Slow cooker size: 3½ to 6 quart**

1½ lbs	lean ground beef	750 g
½ cup	chopped green onions (about 4)	125 mL
2	cloves garlic, minced	2
1 tsp	ground cumin	5 mL
1 tsp	chili powder	5 mL
¼ tsp	dried oregano	1 mL
2 cups	beef stock	500 mL
1	can (19 oz/540 mL) diced tomatoes, with juices	1
1	can (7½ oz/213 mL) tomato sauce	1
1	can (4½ oz/127 mL) chopped mild green chilies, drained	1
1	can (19 oz/540 mL) pinto or red kidney beans, drained and rinsed, or 2 cups (500 mL) home-cooked beans (page 146)	1
½ tsp	salt	2 mL
¼ tsp	freshly ground black pepper	1 mL

1. In a large nonstick skillet, over medium-high heat, cook ground beef, green onions and garlic, breaking up meat as it cooks, for 5 to 7 minutes, or until meat is no longer pink. Add cumin, chili powder and oregano. Cook for 1 minute. With a slotted spoon, transfer mixture to slow cooker stoneware.
2. Add stock, tomatoes, tomato sauce, chilies, beans, salt and pepper to slow cooker. Stir to combine.
3. Cover and cook on **Low** for 6 to 10 hours or on **High** for 3 to 4 hours, until soup is bubbling.

Mexican Weekend Brunch Bake (page 32)

Fruity Glazed Meatballs (page 49)

Winter Trail Mix (page 67) and
Tangy Winterberry Warmers (page 42)

Turkish Winglets (page 53)

Carrot Orange Bisque (page 74)

Italian Sausage and Tortellini Soup (page 101)

Chicken Stew with Rosemary Dumplings (page 110)

I'd-Swear-It-Was-Pizza Soup

Serves 4 to 6

Your kids will love this soup, because it tastes like really good pizza. But I've found that its simple and delicious flavors are equally popular with adults.

• • •

Tips

The croutons in the bottom of each serving bowl are my substitute for a crunchy pizza crust.

If your kids dislike chunks in their food (as mine do), purée the tomatoes before adding them to the slow cooker.

• • •

Variation

You can substitute your favorite pizza meat topping for the pepperoni in this soup. Try cooked sweet or hot Italian sausage, ham or cooked ground beef.

- Slow cooker size: 3½ to 6 quart

1	onion, chopped	1
1 cup	sliced mushrooms (about 5 or 6 medium)	250 mL
1	can (28 oz/796 mL) Italian-style stewed tomatoes, with juices	1
1 cup	beef stock	250 mL
1 cup	thinly sliced pepperoni	250 mL
1	green bell pepper, chopped	1
½ cup	croutons	125 mL
1 cup	shredded mozzarella cheese	250 mL

1. In slow cooker stoneware, combine onion, mushrooms, tomatoes and stock; stir to mix well.
2. Cover and cook on **Low** for 5 to 6 hours or on **High** for 3 to 4 hours. Add pepperoni and green pepper during last 30 minutes of cooking.
3. Divide croutons equally between individual bowls. Spoon soup over croutons and top each with grated mozzarella cheese.

Italian-Style Tomatoes

In place of one 28-oz (796 mL) can Italian-style stewed tomatoes, use regular stewed tomatoes and add 1 tsp (5 mL) dried Italian seasoning or a combination of dried basil, marjoram, thyme and oregano (see box, page 105). If using a 19-oz (540 mL) can, add ½ tsp (2 mL) Italian seasoning.

Hearty Beef Goulash

Serves 6 to 8

This is one of those soups that some might call a stew. Its rich, beefy taste has lots of old-fashioned appeal.

Tips

For a great light meal, serve with thick crusty rolls and a tossed salad.

This soup makes enough for leftovers. It will freeze well, so ladle into freezer-safe containers, label and store up to 3 months. Add ½ cup (125 mL) water to soup when reheating.

- Slow cooker size: 3½ to 6 quart

¼ cup	all-purpose flour	50 mL
2 tsp	paprika	10 mL
1 tsp	salt	5 mL
½ tsp	freshly ground black pepper	2 mL
½ tsp	dried thyme	2 mL
2 lbs	stewing beef, cut into 1-inch (2.5 cm) cubes	1 kg
1 tbsp	vegetable oil	15 mL
3 cups	beef stock	750 mL
1	can (7½ oz/213 mL) tomato sauce	1
2	onions, chopped	2
2	cloves garlic	2
1 cup	diced carrots (about 2 medium)	250 mL
1 cup	chopped celery (about 2 stalks)	250 mL
2	potatoes, peeled and diced	2
1	bay leaf	1

1. In a bowl or plastic bag, combine flour, paprika, salt, pepper and thyme. In batches, add beef to flour mixture and toss to coat.
2. In a large skillet, heat half the oil over medium-high heat. Add beef in batches and cook, adding more oil as needed, until browned all over. With a slotted spoon, transfer beef to slow cooker stoneware.
3. Add stock, tomato sauce, onions, garlic, carrots, celery, potatoes and bay leaf to slow cooker.
4. Cover and cook on **Low** for 8 to 10 hours or on **High** for 4 to 6 hours, until vegetables are tender. Remove and discard bay leaf before serving.

Caribbean Pepper Pot Soup

Serves 4 to 6

This delectable soup, almost a meal in itself, brings home a touch of the West Indies. Make it the centerpiece of a "beat the winter blahs" party: Invite friends over, put on some calypso music, and serve a few tropical drinks to start, then bring on the soup.

• • •

Tips

Scotch bonnet peppers are available in supermarkets where West Indian produce is sold. They are reputed to be the hottest peppers in the world — so be sure to wear gloves when chopping and seeding.

If the soup is ready before you are, reduce the slow cooker temperature to Low. This will keep the food warm without overcooking.

- Slow cooker size: 3½ to 6 quart

1 tbsp	vegetable oil	15 mL
2 lbs	stewing beef, cut into 1-inch (2.5 cm) cubes	1 kg
1	Scotch bonnet pepper, seeded and finely chopped (or 1 tsp/5 mL hot pepper sauce)	1
4	cloves garlic, minced	4
3	sweet potatoes, peeled and cut into 1-inch (2.5 cm) cubes	3
2	onions, finely chopped	2
4 cups	beef stock	1 L
1 cup	water	250 mL
¼ cup	tomato paste	50 mL
1 tsp	dried thyme	5 mL
1 tsp	salt	5 mL
½ tsp	freshly ground black pepper	2 mL
1	red bell pepper, diced	1
1	green bell pepper, diced	1

1. In a large nonstick skillet, heat oil over medium-high heat. Add beef cubes and Scotch bonnet pepper and cook until meat is brown on all sides. (If using hot sauce, this is added in Step 4.) With a slotted spoon, transfer meat and pepper to slow cooker stoneware.
2. Add garlic, sweet potatoes, onions, stock, water, tomato paste, thyme, salt and pepper to slow cooker; stir to combine.
3. Cover and cook on **Low** for 8 to 10 hours or on **High** for 4 to 6 hours, until vegetables are tender and soup is bubbling.
4. Add red pepper, green pepper and, if using, hot pepper sauce; stir to mix well. Cover and cook on **High** for 20 to 25 minutes longer.

BLT Soup

Serves 6

This fun soup was inspired by my husband's favorite sandwich. It includes all the BLT ingredients, even the shredded lettuce. Serve it with white bread that has been lightly spread with mayonnaise.

• • •

Tip

For a smoother, creamier consistency, this soup can be puréed. After the soup has cooked, transfer to a blender or food processor and, in batches, purée until smooth. Return to slow cooker and season to taste with salt and pepper.

Make Ahead

This soup can be assembled up to 24 hours before cooking. Prepare ingredients as directed, assemble in slow cooker stoneware and refrigerate overnight. The next day, place stoneware in slow cooker and continue to cook as directed.

- **Slow cooker size: 3½ to 6 quart**

½ lb	bacon (6 to 8 slices), finely chopped	250 g
1	large onion, finely chopped	1
2	cloves garlic, minced	2
1	can (19 oz/540 mL) Italian-style stewed tomatoes, with juices (see box, page 97)	1
4 cups	chicken stock	1 L
1 tsp	dried basil	5 mL
1 tbsp	tomato paste	15 mL
½ tsp	granulated sugar	2 mL
	Salt and freshly ground black pepper	
1 cup	finely shredded lettuce	250 mL

1. In a large nonstick skillet, on medium-high heat, cook bacon, onion and garlic, stirring occasionally, for 5 minutes, or until onion is translucent. With a slotted spoon, transfer mixture to slow cooker stoneware.
2. Add tomatoes, stock, basil, tomato paste and sugar to slow cooker.
3. Cover and cook on **Low** for 6 to 10 hours or on **High** for 3 to 4 hours, until soup is bubbling. Season with salt and pepper.
4. Spoon into individual serving bowls and sprinkle with shredded lettuce.

Italian Sausage and Tortellini Soup

Serves 4 to 6

Serve this soup after a football game, accompanied by big bowls of chips and dip.

• • •

Tip

Italian sausage is highly seasoned and adds a wallop of great flavor. For less heat, stick to the mild variety.

• Slow cooker size: 3½ to 6 quart

1 lb	mild or hot Italian sausages, casings removed	500 g
1	large onion, chopped	1
2	carrots, peeled and chopped	2
4 cups	beef or chicken stock	1 L
½ tsp	dried Italian seasoning (see box, page 105)	2 mL
½ tsp	salt	2 mL
¼ tsp	freshly ground black pepper	1 mL
1	can (7½ oz/213 mL) tomato sauce	1
1	can (19 oz/540 mL) diced tomatoes, with juices	1
2 cups	sliced mushrooms	500 mL
1	package (10 oz/300 g) fresh or frozen cheese-filled tortellini	1
1	zucchini, quartered lengthwise and chopped	1
¼ cup	chopped fresh parsley	50 mL
2 tbsp	freshly grated Parmesan cheese	25 mL

1. In a large nonstick skillet, over medium-high heat, cook sausage for 8 to 10 minutes, or until browned, stirring to break up meat. With a slotted spoon, transfer to slow cooker stoneware.
2. Add onion, carrots, stock, Italian seasoning, salt, pepper, tomato sauce, tomatoes and mushrooms to slow cooker.
3. Cover and cook on **Low** for 6 to 10 hours or on **High** for 3 to 4 hours, until vegetables are tender.
4. Meanwhile, cook tortellini according to package directions. Drain. Add tortellini, zucchini and parsley to slow cooker and cook on **High** for 15 to 20 minutes longer, or until heated through and zucchini is tender.
5. Spoon into individual bowls and top with grated Parmesan cheese.

Easy Wieners and Beaners Soup

Serves 4 to 6

This nutrition-packed soup is a sure-fire way to get the kids to eat their vegetables! Try sprinkling a little grated mozzarella cheese on top. Kids love the way it "strings" when they spoon into it.

• • •

Tips

I like to buy veal wieners in the deli department of the supermarket to use in this recipe instead of the pre-packaged hot-dog wieners.

If your family is not fond of vegetable cocktail juice, substitute tomato juice.

Using beans in tomato sauce with added maple syrup adds a little sweetness to the recipe, but you can substitute any canned baked beans. (Baked beans in barbecue sauce will add a spicy punch!)

- Slow cooker size: 3½ to 6 quart

4 cups	tomato vegetable cocktail juice	1 L
2	cans (each 14 oz/398 mL) baked beans in tomato sauce with maple syrup	2
3	carrots, peeled and finely chopped	3
1	small onion, finely chopped	1
1	clove garlic, minced	1
½ cup	fresh or frozen corn kernels (thawed if frozen)	125 mL
1 tsp	Worcestershire sauce	5 mL
½ tsp	dry mustard	2 mL
1	bay leaf	1
4 to 6	wieners or hot dogs, cut into ½-inch (1 cm) pieces	4 to 6
	Salt and freshly ground black pepper	

1. In slow cooker stoneware, combine vegetable juice, beans, carrots, onion, garlic, corn, Worcestershire sauce, dry mustard and bay leaf.
2. Cover and cook on **Low** for 6 to 10 hours or on **High** for 3 to 4 hours, until carrots are tender.
3. Add wieners and cook on **High** for 20 to 30 minutes longer, or until heated through. Discard bay leaf and season soup with salt and pepper.

That's-a-Lotta-Beans Soup

Serves 4 to 6

I can't think of anything better than coming in from the cold and being met by the aroma of this soup simmering in the slow cooker and a loaf of hearty bread baking in the bread machine.

• • •

Tip

If you can't find a can of mixed beans, look for a dried version. Before using, soak the beans: Cover 2 cups (500 mL) dry bean mixture with 8 cups (2 L) water and simmer on stovetop for 1 hour, or until beans are tender. Drain and add to slow cooker as directed.

Make Ahead

This soup can be assembled 12 to 24 hours in advance of cooking (but without adding zucchini and cheese). Prepare ingredients as directed in slow cooker stoneware and refrigerate overnight. The next day, place stoneware in slow cooker and cook as directed.

- Slow cooker size: 3½ to 5 quart

1 lb	mild Italian sausage, casings removed	500 g
2	cans (19 oz/540 mL) mixed beans, with liquid	2
1	can (28 oz/796 mL) diced tomatoes, with juices	1
4	carrots, peeled and diced	4
2 cups	chicken stock	500 mL
1 tsp	dried Italian seasoning	5 mL
2	zucchini, diced	2
	Freshly grated Parmesan cheese	
	Salt and freshly ground black pepper	

1. In a skillet, over medium-high heat, brown sausage, stirring to break up meat. With a slotted spoon, transfer to slow cooker stoneware.
2. Add bean mix (with liquid), tomatoes (with juices), carrots, stock and Italian seasoning to slow cooker.
3. Cover and cook on **Low** for 8 to 10 hours or on **High** for 4 to 6 hours, until vegetables are tender.
4. Add zucchini; cover and cook on **High** for 15 to 20 minutes longer.
5. Spoon into individual bowls and top with grated Parmesan cheese. Season to taste with salt and pepper.

Vegetarian Bean Soup

For a meatless version, omit the sausage. Add 1 tbsp (15 mL) chili powder, 1 tbsp (15 mL) chopped garlic and ½ tsp (2 mL) hot pepper flakes, and increase Italian seasoning to 1 tbsp (15 mL).

Black Bean Cassoulet Soup

Serves 6 to 8

A traditional French cassoulet is chock-full of beans, chicken, sausage, ham and vegetables. This "bistro-style" soup is much easier to make and has a lot of the same great flavor.

• • •

Tips

For a great one-course meal, serve with a tossed salad, lots of crusty French bread and glasses of crisp, cold white wine.

Smoked pork hocks are available in most supermarkets and butcher shops. The hock comes from the pork leg. Hocks make wonderful additions to soups and stews. If you can't find one, use a meaty ham bone instead.

You may want to use the cooking broth and leftover meat from the Slow Cooker Cottage Roll (see recipe, page 295). Substitute 5 cups (1.25 L) cooking liquid for water and 2 cups (500 mL) meat for the smoked pork hock. Do not add the meat as in Step 1, but after the beans have been pureéd.

- Slow cooker size: 3½ to 6 quart

1	onion, diced	1
3	cloves garlic, minced	3
1	smoked pork hock or meaty ham bone (about 2 lbs/1 kg), outer skin removed	1
6 cups	water	1.5 L
1 tsp	ground cumin	5 mL
1 tsp	dried oregano	5 mL
1	bay leaf	1
1 tsp	salt	5 mL
½ tsp	freshly ground black pepper	2 mL
1	can (19 oz/540 mL) black beans, drained and rinsed, or 2 cups (500 mL) home-cooked black beans (page 146)	1
1 lb	hot Italian sausage, browned and cut into 1-inch (2.5 cm) pieces	500 g
1	red bell pepper, diced	1
2 tbsp	chopped fresh parsley (or 1 tbsp/15 mL dried)	25 mL
1 tbsp	dry sherry	15 mL
1 tbsp	packed brown sugar	15 mL
2 tsp	freshly squeezed lemon juice	10 mL
	Sour cream	

1. In slow cooker stoneware, combine onion, garlic, smoked pork hock, water, cumin, oregano, bay leaf, salt, pepper and black beans; stir to mix well.
2. Cover and cook on **Low** for 8 to 10 hours or on **High** for 4 to 6 hours, until meat is tender. Gently remove the pork hock. Shred the meat and set aside. Remove bay leaf and discard. Transfer 1 cup (250 mL) of bean mixture to a food processor or blender and process until smooth. Return to slow cooker with shredded meat.
3. Add cooked sausage, red pepper, parsley, sherry, brown sugar and lemon juice. Cover and cook on **High** for 1 hour longer. Ladle soup into individual bowls and serve garnished with a dollop of sour cream.

Dutch Farmer Bean Soup

Serves 4 to 6

Puréeing some of the soup gives this dish body. Serve it with coleslaw (page 115) with added chopped apples and raisins, accompanied by slices of warm pumpernickel bread.

• • •

Tips

Baby carrots work well in soups. They are already peeled, which eliminates an extra step.

Add the smoked sausages at the end, just to warm through. Since they are already cooked, the skin will toughen if the sausages are left in the soup too long. If you can't find turkey kielbasa, any smoked pork sausage will work.

- Slow cooker size: 3½ to 6 quart

1 cup	baby carrots	250 mL
1	onion, chopped	1
2	cloves garlic, minced	2
4 cups	chicken stock	1 L
1 tsp	dried Italian seasoning	5 mL
2	cans (each 19 oz/540 mL) Great Northern or white kidney beans, drained and rinsed, or 4 cups (1 L) home-cooked white beans (page 146)	2
4	smoked turkey kielbasa sausages, halved lengthwise and cut into ½-inch (1 cm) pieces	4
2 cups	fresh baby spinach	500 mL

1. In slow cooker stoneware, combine carrots, onion, garlic, stock, Italian seasoning and beans.
2. Cover and cook on **Low** for 6 to 10 hours or on **High** for 3 to 4 hours, until vegetables are tender and soup is bubbling.
3. Transfer 2 cups (500 mL) soup to a blender or food processor and process until smooth.
4. Return puréed mixture to slow cooker and add kielbasa and spinach. Cover and cook on **High** for 15 to 20 minutes longer, or until spinach is wilted and kielbasa is heated through.

Dried Italian Seasoning

If you don't have a dried Italian seasoning mix, use a combination of basil, marjoram, thyme and oregano. Instead of 1 tsp (5 mL) Italian seasoning, use ½ tsp (2 mL) dried basil, ¼ tsp (1 mL) dried marjoram, ¼ tsp (1 mL) dried thyme and ¼ tsp (1 mL) dried oregano.

Old World Bean and Beer Soup

Serves 4 to 6

This homey soup is reminiscent of a European-style vegetable soup. Serve lots of extra pretzels to nibble on.

• • •

Tips

For company, serve this soup with a platter of cheeses such as Cheddar, Swiss, Gouda and Jarlsberg. Label the cheeses and arrange them on a platter with grapes and slices of marbled rye and pumpernickel bread.

To let the beer go flat, open it the night before you plan to make the soup and let it sit out overnight.

Make Ahead

This soup can be assembled up to 24 hours before cooking. Combine ingredients in slow cooker stoneware and refrigerate overnight. The next day, place stoneware in slow cooker and continue to cook as directed.

- Slow cooker size: 3½ to 6 quart

1	large onion, finely chopped	1
2	carrots, peeled and chopped	2
2	stalks celery, finely chopped	2
2	cloves garlic, minced	2
4 cups	chicken stock	1 L
1	can (12 oz/341 mL) or bottle dark beer, flat	1
1 tsp	Worcestershire sauce	5 mL
1 tsp	dried thyme	5 mL
½ tsp	dried marjoram	2 mL
½ tsp	hot pepper flakes	2 mL
1 tsp	salt	5 mL
½ tsp	freshly ground black pepper	2 mL
2	cans (each 19 oz/540 mL) white pea (navy) beans, drained and rinsed, or 4 cups (1 L) home-cooked beans (page 146)	2
2 cups	chopped cooked ham	500 mL
¼ cup	chopped fresh parsley	50 mL
2 tbsp	crushed pretzels	25 mL
2 tbsp	chopped green onions	25 mL

1. In slow cooker stoneware, combine onion, carrots, celery, garlic, stock, beer, Worcestershire sauce, thyme, marjoram, hot pepper flakes, salt, black pepper, beans and ham.
2. Cover and cook on **Low** for 6 to 10 hours or on **High** for 3 to 4 hours, until vegetables are tender and soup is bubbling. Stir in parsley.
3. Spoon into individual serving bowls and sprinkle with crushed pretzels and green onions.

Easy Bean and Barley Soup

Serves 6 to 8

This is my idea of a no-fuss family meal — and the kids love it! I like to know that I can reach into the cupboard, pull out some convenient canned products and whip together a healthy soup in no time.

• • •

Variation

For a wonderfully rich, sweet broth, try beans in tomato sauce with maple syrup. Or add 2 tbsp (25 mL) maple syrup to the ingredients.

Make Ahead

This dish can be completely assembled the night before. Follow preparation directions and refrigerate overnight in the slow cooker stoneware. The next day, place stoneware in slow cooker and continue cooking as directed.

- **Slow cooker size: 3½ to 6 quart**

1	can (14 oz/398 mL) beans in tomato sauce	1
2	potatoes, peeled and finely chopped	2
1	stalk celery, finely chopped	1
1	large onion, finely chopped	1
2	leeks (white parts only), trimmed, well rinsed and thinly sliced	2
2	carrots, diced	2
6 cups	beef stock	1.5 L
½ cup	pearl or pot barley, rinsed	125 mL
Pinch	ground nutmeg	Pinch

1. In slow cooker stoneware, combine beans, potatoes, celery, onion, leeks, carrots, stock, barley and nutmeg.
2. Cover and cook on **Low** for 8 to 10 hours or on **High** for 4 to 6 hours, until vegetables are tender and soup is bubbling.

Stews

Chicken Stew with Rosemary Dumplings

Serves 4 to 6

Here's the ultimate comfort food — perfect for the entire family to enjoy while gathered at the kitchen table.

• • •

Tips

This all-in-one meal works especially well in a large slow cooker since it provides plenty of room for the dumplings to cook.

To save some time, make the dumplings with 2 cups (500 mL) prepared biscuit mix combined with ½ tsp (2 mL) crumbled dried rosemary. Add in ¾ cup (175 mL) milk and stir until lumpy. Continue with recipe as directed.

For fluffier dumplings, drop the dough on the chicken pieces rather than into the liquid. This will ensure that the dumplings are steamed and don't become soggy from the liquid. Also, for proper steaming, be sure the stew is piping hot.

• Slow cooker size: 5 to 6 quart

½ cup	all-purpose flour	125 mL
1 tsp	salt	5 mL
½ tsp	freshly ground black pepper	2 mL
1	whole chicken (about 3 lbs/1.5 kg), cut into pieces	1
1 tbsp	vegetable oil	15 mL
4	large carrots, peeled and sliced 1 inch (2.5 cm) thick	4
2	stalks celery, sliced ½ inch (1 cm) thick	2
1	onion, thinly sliced	1
1 tsp	dried rosemary	5 mL
2 cups	chicken stock, divided	500 mL
1 cup	frozen peas	250 mL

Dumplings

1 cup	all-purpose flour	250 mL
2 tsp	baking powder	10 mL
½ tsp	dried rosemary	2 mL
½ tsp	salt	2 mL
½ cup	milk	125 mL
1	egg, lightly beaten	1
	Fresh rosemary sprigs	

1. In a heavy plastic bag, combine flour, salt and pepper. In batches, add chicken pieces to flour mixture and toss to coat.
2. In a large nonstick skillet, heat oil over medium-high heat. Add chicken pieces and cook for 8 to 10 minutes, or until brown on all sides. Set aside.

3. Add carrots, celery, onion and rosemary to slow cooker stoneware. Set chicken pieces over vegetables.
4. Pour ½ cup (125 mL) stock into skillet and cook over medium-high heat, scraping up brown bits from bottom of pan. Pour pan juices into slow cooker along with remaining stock.
5. Cover and cook on **Low** for 8 to 10 hours or on **High** for 4 to 6 hours, until vegetables are tender and stew is bubbling. Add peas and stir gently to combine.
6. *Dumplings:* In a bowl, sift together flour, baking powder, rosemary and salt. In a measuring cup, combine milk and egg. Mix well and add to flour mixture. Stir with a fork to make a lumpy dough (do not overmix — lumps are fine). Drop dumpling mixture over chicken pieces. Cover and cook on **High** for 25 to 30 minutes, or until tester inserted in center of dumpling comes out clean. Serve garnished with fresh rosemary sprigs.

Tip

Cooking times for poultry may be longer for larger slow cookers and/or where there is a relatively high proportion of dark to white meat. For predominantly white-meat dishes, be sure to avoid overcooking.

Moroccan Chicken Stew

Serves 4 to 6

For a simple but satisfying Moroccan-style dinner, serve this stew with warm pita bread, hummus and orange wedges. Or serve the chicken over couscous, which only takes minutes to prepare and will soak up all the delicious sauce. (Prepare the couscous according to package directions.)

• • •

Tip

Turmeric is the ground root of a tropical plant. It has an intense golden yellow color and gingery flavor. If you wish, you can substitute ground ginger. The color won't be as intense, but the flavor will still be good.

- **Slow cooker size: 3½ to 6 quart**

8 to 12	skinless chicken drumsticks	8 to 12
1	can (19 oz/540 mL) chickpeas, drained and rinsed, or 2 cups (500 mL) home-cooked chickpeas (page 146)	1
½ cup	diced tomato	125 mL
1 cup	baby carrots	250 mL
1	can (14 oz/398 mL) pineapple tidbits or chunks, with juices	1
1	large onion, chopped	1
2	cloves garlic, minced	2
2 tbsp	freshly squeezed lemon juice	25 mL
1 tsp	salt	5 mL
1 tsp	dried marjoram	5 mL
1 tsp	paprika	5 mL
½ tsp	ground cumin	2 mL
¼ tsp	ground turmeric	1 mL
Pinch	ground cinnamon	Pinch
1 cup	diced green beans	250 mL
¼ cup	pimento-stuffed green olives	50 mL
¼ cup	chopped fresh mint or cilantro	50 mL

1. Place chicken in slow cooker stoneware. Add chickpeas, tomato and carrots.
2. In a bowl, combine pineapple and juices, onion, garlic, lemon juice, salt, marjoram, paprika, cumin, turmeric and cinnamon. Pour over meat and vegetables.
3. Cover and cook on **Low** for 5 to 7 hours or on **High** for 2½ to 4 hours, until chicken is no longer pink inside.
4. Add green beans. Cover and cook on **High** for 20 to 25 minutes longer, or until beans are tender.
5. Stir in olives and mint.

PBJ Chicken Stew

Serves 4 to 6

Peanut butter, jelly and chicken stew? You bet, and it's delicious! The jelly adds a touch of sweetness and the peanut butter lends a nutty flavor. Of course, you must serve it with slices of white bread to soak up the extra sauce. Accompany with a garden salad and apple pie with ice cream for dessert.

- **Slow cooker size: 3½ to 6 quart**

8	skinless chicken breasts, thighs or drumsticks	8
1	large onion, chopped	1
8 oz	mushrooms, quartered	250 g
2 tbsp	chopped fresh parsley	25 mL
1 cup	chicken stock	250 mL
½ cup	crunchy peanut butter	125 mL
¼ cup	grape jelly or berry jam or jelly	50 mL
1 tbsp	tomato paste	15 mL
½ tsp	salt	2 mL
1	red bell pepper, cut into ½-inch (1 cm) strips	1
2 tbsp	chopped peanuts	25 mL

1. Place chicken pieces in slow cooker stoneware. Sprinkle onion, mushrooms and parsley around and on top of chicken.
2. In a bowl, combine stock, peanut butter, jelly, tomato paste and salt. Pour sauce over chicken and vegetables.
3. Cover and cook on **Low** for 5 to 7 hours or on **High** for 2½ to 4 hours, until chicken is no longer pink inside.
4. Add red pepper. Cover and cook on **High** for 20 to 25 minutes longer, or until pepper is tender.
5. Serve garnished with chopped peanuts.

Brunswick Stew

Serves 6

Dating back to 1828 in Brunswick County, Virginia, this stew was originally made with squirrel and onion, but today chicken is a more popular choice! Serve with coleslaw and warm baking powder biscuits slathered with butter.

Tip

Hot pepper flakes: This fiery flavor booster can be found in the spice section of the supermarket. Leave on the table for a great seasoning alternative to salt and pepper.

- Slow cooker size: 3½ to 6 quart

3	slices bacon	3
2 tbsp	all-purpose flour	25 mL
1 tsp	salt	5 mL
½ tsp	freshly ground black pepper	2 mL
½ tsp	dried marjoram	2 mL
½ tsp	hot pepper flakes	2 mL
2 lbs	boneless skinless chicken thighs, cut into 1-inch (2.5 cm) pieces	1 kg
2 cups	chicken stock, divided	500 mL
2 cups	diced peeled potatoes	500 mL
3	carrots, peeled and cut into 1-inch (2.5 cm) slices	3
2	stalks celery, chopped	2
1	can (19 oz/540 mL) diced tomatoes, with juices	1
2	cloves garlic, minced	2
½ cup	ketchup	125 mL
2 tbsp	packed brown sugar	25 mL
1 tbsp	Worcestershire sauce	15 mL
1 tsp	dry mustard	5 mL
½ tsp	ground ginger	2 mL
2 cups	frozen lima beans, thawed	500 mL
1 cup	fresh or frozen corn kernels (thawed if frozen)	250 mL

1. In a large skillet, over medium-high heat, cook bacon for 5 to 7 minutes, or until crisp. Transfer to a paper towel–lined plate, reserving drippings.
2. In a heavy plastic bag, combine flour, salt, pepper, marjoram and hot pepper flakes. In batches, add chicken to flour mixture and toss to coat.

3. In a skillet, heat reserved bacon drippings over medium-high heat. Cook chicken in batches, stirring occasionally, until browned on all sides. With a slotted spoon, transfer to slow cooker stoneware.
4. Add 1 cup (250 mL) stock to skillet and bring to a boil, stirring to scrape up any browned bits. Transfer stock mixture to slow cooker. Add reserved bacon, remaining stock, potatoes, carrots, celery, tomatoes, garlic, ketchup, brown sugar, Worcestershire sauce, mustard and ginger.
5. Cover and cook on **Low** for 6 to 8 hours or on **High** for 3 to 5 hours, until vegetables are tender and stew is bubbling.
6. Add lima beans and corn. Cover and cook on **High** for 15 to 20 minutes longer, or until beans and corn are heated through.

Quick and Easy Creamy Coleslaw

In a bowl, combine 3 cups (750 mL) finely shredded cabbage, 2 grated carrots and 2 chopped green onions.

In a small bowl or measuring cup, combine ¼ cup (50 mL) mayonnaise, ¼ cup (50 mL) plain yogurt or sour cream, 1 tbsp (15 mL) white vinegar, 1 tsp (5 mL) granulated sugar, ½ tsp (2 mL) celery seed, ½ tsp (2 mL) prepared mustard and ¼ tsp (1 mL) black pepper. Pour over cabbage mixture and toss well. Cover and refrigerate for up to 24 hours. *Serves 4 to 6.*

Tip

While homemade stock is the most flavorful, not everyone has time to make it. The next best choice is canned; use 1 can (10 oz/ 284 mL) broth plus 1 can water. Avoid using bouillon cubes which have less flavor and a lot more salt.

Party-Style Chicken and Sausage Stew

Serves 8

This dish is perfect when you have a houseful of guests and don't want to spend a lot of time in the kitchen. For this quantity, a 6-quart slow cooker is best. If you have a smaller slow cooker (or fewer mouths to feed), simply cut the recipe in half.

• • •

Tip

Cooking times for poultry may be longer for larger slow cookers and/or where there is a relatively high proportion of dark to white meat. For predominantly white-meat dishes, be sure to avoid overcooking.

Make Ahead

This dish can be assembled the night before. Follow preparation directions (but without adding peppers and zucchini) and refrigerate overnight in slow cooker stoneware. The next day, place stoneware in slow cooker and continue cooking as directed.

- Slow cooker size: 5 to 6 quart

1 lb	hot Italian sausage	500 g
1/4 cup	all-purpose flour	50 mL
1/2 tsp	salt	2 mL
1/4 tsp	freshly ground black pepper	1 mL
3 to 4 lbs	chicken legs, separated into thighs and drumsticks, skin removed if desired	1.5 to 2 kg
4	carrots, peeled and chopped	4
2	onions, sliced	2
3	large cloves garlic, halved	3
1	can (28 oz/796 mL) tomatoes, drained and quartered	1
1/2 cup	chicken stock	125 mL
2 tsp	dried Italian seasoning	10 mL
1 tsp	dry mustard	5 mL
1	yellow bell pepper, cut into strips	1
1	red bell pepper, cut into strips	1
2	small zucchini, sliced	2

1. In a large nonstick skillet, over medium-high heat, cook sausages for 6 to 8 minutes, or until browned on all sides. Slice into 1-inch (2.5 cm) pieces and transfer to slow cooker stoneware.
2. In a heavy plastic bag, combine flour, salt and pepper. In batches, add chicken to flour mixture and toss to coat. Transfer chicken to slow cooker. Add carrots, onions, garlic and tomatoes.
3. In a bowl, combine stock, Italian seasoning and dry mustard; stir to mix. Pour into slow cooker.
4. Cover and cook on **Low** for 6 to 8 hours, or until carrots are tender and stew is bubbling.
5. Add yellow pepper, red pepper and zucchini. Cover and cook on **High** for 15 to 20 minutes longer.

Turkey Vegetable Stew with Biscuits

Serves 4 to 6

Vegetables, turkey and biscuits combine here to make a hearty, flavorful stew.

• • •

Tips

While homemade stock is the most flavorful, not everyone has time to make it. The next best choice is canned; use 1 can (10 oz/ 284 mL) broth plus 1 can water. Avoid using bouillon cubes, which have less flavor and a lot more salt.

To debone turkey thighs: Place the thigh, skin side down, on a cutting board. With a sharp knife, cut down to the bone, then along the full length of the bone. To free the ends, slip the knife under the bone, halfway down its length. Cut away from the hand, freeing one end on the bone from the flesh. Turn the thigh around, lift the free end on the bone with one hand and cut the other end free.

• **Slow cooker size: 3½ to 6 quart**

2	boneless skinless turkey thighs or 2 lbs (1 kg) turkey breast, cut into 1-inch (2.5 cm) cubes	2
6	small new potatoes, scrubbed, or 2 regular-size potatoes, cut into 2-inch (5 cm) chunks	6
4	carrots, peeled and chopped	4
3	stalks celery, chopped	3
2	onions, sliced	2
1½ cups	chopped peeled rutabaga	375 mL
¼ cup	all-purpose flour	50 mL
2 cups	chicken stock	500 mL
2 tbsp	tomato paste	25 mL
1 tsp	dried marjoram	5 mL
1 tsp	salt	5 mL
¼ tsp	freshly ground black pepper	1 mL
1	bay leaf	1
2 cups	prepared biscuit mix	500 mL
¾ cup	milk	175 mL

1. Place turkey, potatoes, carrots, celery, onions and rutabaga in slow cooker stoneware. Sprinkle with flour and stir to mix.
2. In a bowl, combine stock, tomato paste, marjoram, salt and pepper; stir into slow cooker. Add bay leaf.
3. Cover and cook on **Low** for 6 to 8 hours or on **High** for 4 to 6 hours, until vegetables are tender and stew is bubbling. Discard bay leaf.
4. In a bowl, combine biscuit mix and milk. Stir with a fork to make a lumpy dough (do not overmix — lumps are fine). Drop spoonfuls of dough over hot stew. Cover and cook on **High** for 20 to 25 minutes longer, or until a tester inserted in center of dumpling comes out clean.

Spicy Cuban Turkey Stew

Serves 4 to 6

This is a highly distinctive stew with Caribbean flavors. Serve it with rice (page 163) for a delicious and substantial meal.

• • •

Tips

Look for turkey parts after a long holiday weekend, when they can be purchased more economically. Freeze them to have on hand for dishes like this one, or for other recipes.

Buy a sweet potato with deep orange flesh for this recipe — they are sweeter and moister than the pale yellow sweet potatoes.

- Slow cooker size: 3½ to 6 quart

1 tbsp	all-purpose flour	15 mL
½ tsp	dried thyme	2 mL
½ tsp	salt	2 mL
¼ tsp	ground allspice	1 mL
¼ tsp	ground ginger	1 mL
¼ tsp	hot pepper flakes	1 mL
Pinch	ground nutmeg	Pinch
2	boneless skinless turkey thighs (about 1¼ lbs/625 g each), cut into 1-inch (2.5 cm) pieces	2
2 tbsp	vegetable oil (approx.)	25 mL
1 cup	chicken stock, divided	250 mL
1	sweet potato, peeled and cut into 1-inch (2.5 cm) cubes	1
1	onion, chopped	1
2	cans (each 19 oz/540 mL) black beans, drained and rinsed, or 4 cups (1 L) home-cooked black beans (page 146)	2
1 cup	orange juice	250 mL
2 tsp	freshly squeezed lime juice	10 mL
1	red bell pepper, coarsely chopped	1
1	green bell pepper, coarsely chopped	1

1. In a heavy plastic bag, combine flour, thyme, salt, allspice, ginger, hot pepper flakes and nutmeg. In batches, add turkey pieces to flour mixture and toss to coat.
2. In a large nonstick skillet, heat half the oil over medium-high heat. Cook turkey in batches, adding more oil as needed, for 5 to 7 minutes, or until browned on all sides. With a slotted spoon, transfer turkey to slow cooker stoneware.

3. Add ½ cup (125 mL) stock to skillet. Bring to a boil, scraping up any browned bits. Transfer to slow cooker. Add sweet potato, onion, black beans, orange juice and remaining stock; mix well to combine.
4. Cover and cook on **Low** for 7 to 9 hours or on **High** for 3 to 5 hours, until vegetables are tender and stew is bubbling.
5. Add lime juice and peppers. Cover and cook on **High** for 15 to 20 minutes longer, or until peppers are tender.

Cooking Poultry in the Slow Cooker

Cooking times for poultry may be longer in large slow cookers and/or where there is a relatively high proportion of dark meat. For predominantly white-meat dishes, be sure to avoid overcooking. Check after the minimum recommended cooking time.

Tip

Refrigerating any leftover stew always improves the flavor (which is why it always tastes better the next day). The fat will rise to the top and solidify; remove it before reheating.

Mom's Old-Fashioned Beef Stew

Serves 6 to 8

This stew is just like one my mother used to make when my sisters and I were little girls and she was the busy mom-on-the-run.

• • •

Tips

Serve with thick slices of crusty bread to soak up every last drop of the rich gravy.

Store any leftovers in the refrigerator for up to 3 days or freeze for up to 3 months. For best consistency, add ½ cup (125 mL) water before reheating.

• • •

Variation

For a slight change of pace, I sometimes make this stew with a can of chunky-style tomatoes with roasted garlic and basil.

- Slow cooker size: 3½ to 5 quart

¼ cup	all-purpose flour	50 mL
1 tsp	salt	5 mL
½ tsp	freshly ground black pepper	2 mL
2 lbs	stewing beef, cut into ½-inch (1 cm) cubes	1 kg
2 tbsp	vegetable oil (approx.)	25 mL
2 cups	beef stock, divided	500 mL
4	carrots, peeled and sliced	4
4	potatoes, peeled and chopped	4
2	stalks celery, chopped	2
1	large onion, diced or 15 to 20 white pearl onions, peeled	1
1	can (19 oz/540 mL) diced tomatoes, with juices	1
1	bay leaf	1
1 tbsp	Worcestershire sauce	15 mL
¼ cup	chopped fresh parsley (or 2 tbsp/25 mL dried)	50 mL
1 cup	frozen peas	250 mL
	Salt and freshly ground black pepper	

1. In a heavy plastic bag, combine flour, salt and pepper. In batches, add beef to flour mixture and toss to coat.
2. In a large nonstick skillet, heat half the oil over medium-high heat. Cook beef in batches, adding more oil as needed, until browned all over. With a slotted spoon, transfer beef to slow cooker stoneware.

3. Add 1 cup (250 mL) stock to skillet and stir to scrape up any brown bits. Transfer stock mixture to slow cooker. Add carrots, potatoes, celery, onion, tomatoes (with juices), remaining stock, bay leaf, Worcestershire sauce and parsley; mix well to combine.
4. Cover and cook on **Low** for 8 to 10 hours or on **High** for 4 to 6 hours, until vegetables are tender and stew is bubbling. Discard bay leaf.
5. Add peas. Cover and cook on **High** for 15 to 20 minutes longer, or until slightly thickened and peas are heated through. Season to taste with salt and pepper.

Make Ahead

This dish can be completely assembled up to 24 hours before cooking (with the exception of beef cubes). Chill browned beef separately before assembling dish. Refrigerate remaining ingredients overnight in slow cooker stoneware. The next day, place stoneware in slow cooker, add browned beef and continue to cook as directed.

Zesty Orange Beef Stew

Serves 4 to 6

This tasty stew gets its name from both the orange zest and the colorful fall vegetables.

Tips

For greater ease of preparation, look for pre-cut squash in the produce department of the supermarket.

Refrigerating any leftover stew always improves the flavor (which is why it always tastes better the next day). The fat will rise to the top and solidify; remove it before reheating.

Make Ahead

This dish can be completely assembled up to 12 hours in advance of cooking. Follow preparation directions and refrigerate overnight in the slow cooker stoneware. The next day, place stoneware in slow cooker and continue cooking as directed.

- Slow cooker size: 3½ to 5 quart

¼ cup	all-purpose flour	50 mL
1 tsp	salt	5 mL
½ tsp	freshly ground black pepper	2 mL
2 lbs	stewing beef, cut into 1-inch (2.5 cm) cubes	1 kg
2 tbsp	vegetable oil (approx.)	25 mL
2 cups	beef stock, divided	500 mL
2	onions, chopped	2
2	large carrots, peeled and chopped	2
2 cups	butternut squash, peeled and cut into 1½-inch (3.5 cm) cubes	500 mL
4	potatoes, peeled and chopped	4
1 cup	red wine	250 mL
2 tbsp	tomato paste	25 mL
¼ cup	chopped fresh parsley (or 2 tbsp/25 mL) dried)	50 mL
1 tsp	grated orange zest	5 mL
1 tsp	dried rosemary	5 mL
	Chopped fresh parsley	

1. In a heavy plastic bag, combine flour, salt and pepper. In batches, add beef to flour mixture and toss to coat.
2. In a large nonstick skillet, heat half the oil over medium-high heat. Cook beef in batches, adding more oil as needed, until browned all over. With a slotted spoon, transfer beef to slow cooker stoneware.
3. Add 1 cup (250 mL) stock to skillet and stir to scrape up any brown bits. Transfer stock mixture to slow cooker. Add onions, carrots, squash and potatoes.
4. In a bowl, combine red wine, remaining stock, tomato paste, parsley, orange zest and rosemary. Pour over vegetables in slow cooker and mix well to combine.
5. Cover and cook on **Low** for 8 to 10 hours or on **High** for 4 to 6 hours, until vegetables are tender and stew is bubbling. Serve garnished with fresh parsley.

Bistro Beef and Beer Stew

Serves 4 to 6

This is a hearty dish full of vegetable chunks and tender beef cubes. The meat slowly bakes in a bold sauce of beer, stock and seasonings until it is fork-tender. Serve it with red wine, a French baguette and light jazz.

• • •

Tips

Select lean stewing beef or trim the excess fat from the meat before using. (Trimming may take a little extra time, but the result will be worth it.)

Use your favorite fresh mushrooms in this stew. Cremini, shiitakes, cèpes and chanterelles can be used in place of all or some of the button mushrooms.

- Slow cooker size: 3½ to 6 quart

¼ cup	all-purpose flour	50 mL
1 tsp	salt	5 mL
½ tsp	dried thyme	2 mL
½ tsp	dried marjoram	2 mL
½ tsp	freshly ground black pepper	2 mL
2 lbs	stewing beef, cut into 1-inch (2.5 cm) cubes	1 kg
2 tbsp	vegetable oil (approx.)	25 mL
1 cup	dark beer, flat (see tip, page 106)	250 mL
1 cup	beef stock	250 mL
2 tbsp	tomato paste	25 mL
1 tbsp	Dijon mustard	15 mL
1 tbsp	red wine vinegar	15 mL
2 tsp	Worcestershire sauce	10 mL
1	large onion, chopped	1
4	cloves garlic, minced	4
2 cups	baby carrots	500 mL
8 oz	button mushrooms	250 g
½ cup	sour cream	125 mL

1. In a heavy plastic bag, combine flour, salt, thyme, marjoram and pepper. Add beef to flour mixture in batches and toss to coat.
2. In a large nonstick skillet, heat half the oil over medium-high heat. Cook beef in batches, adding more oil as needed, until browned all over. With a slotted spoon, transfer beef to slow cooker stoneware.
3. Add beer and stock to skillet and bring to a boil, stirring to scrape up any brown bits. Transfer to slow cooker. Add tomato paste, mustard, vinegar, Worcestershire sauce, onion, garlic, carrots and mushrooms; mix well to combine.
4. Cover and cook on **Low** for 8 to 10 hours or on **High** for 4 to 6 hours, until vegetables are tender and stew is bubbling. Stir in sour cream just before serving.

Mahogany Beef Stew

Serves 6

Grab a cushion and a blanket. This rich and hearty beef stew is perfect for a cozy fireside supper. Serve with horseradish mashed potatoes (page 255).

• • •

Tip

Hoisin sauce is used extensively in Chinese cuisine, both in cooking and as a condiment. Made from soybeans, garlic and chilies, the thick red-brown sauce has a sweet, spicy flavor.

- Slow cooker size: 3½ to 6 quart

2 tbsp	all-purpose flour	25 mL
1 tsp	dried thyme	5 mL
½ tsp	dry mustard	2 mL
½ tsp	ground ginger	2 mL
2 lbs	stewing beef, cut into 1-inch (2.5 cm) cubes	1 kg
2 tbsp	vegetable oil (approx.)	25 mL
1 cup	dry red wine	250 mL
1	can (19 oz/540 mL) Italian-style stewed tomatoes, with juices (see box, page 97)	1
⅓ cup	hoisin sauce	75 mL
3	carrots, peeled and chopped	3
2	parsnips, peeled and chopped	2
1	large onion, chopped	1
2	cloves garlic, minced	2
2	bay leaves	2
	Salt and freshly ground black pepper	
2 tbsp	chopped fresh parsley	25 mL

1. In a heavy plastic bag, combine flour, thyme, mustard and ginger. In batches, add beef to flour mixture and toss to coat.
2. In a large nonstick skillet, heat half the oil over medium-high heat. Cook beef in batches, adding more oil as needed, until browned all over. With a slotted spoon, transfer beef to slow cooker stoneware.
3. Add wine to skillet and bring to a boil, scraping up brown bits stuck to pan. Transfer to slow cooker. Add tomatoes, hoisin sauce, carrots, parsnips, onion, garlic and bay leaves; stir to combine.
4. Cover and cook on **Low** for 8 to 10 hours or on **High** for 4 to 6 hours, until meat and vegetables are tender and stew is bubbling. Discard bay leaves. Season with salt and pepper. Serve garnished with fresh parsley.

Sauerbraten Beef Stew

Serves 6

Sauerbraten is a German specialty made by marinating beef roast in a sweet-tangy marinade for 2 to 3 days. The roast is then browned and simmered in the marinade until it is tender. This slow-cooked version is ready in a fraction of the time it takes to prepare the traditional recipe.

• • •

Tips

For a traditional German meal, serve this sauerbraten with spätzle, tiny dumplings that often accompany saucy German main dishes.

To make the gingersnap crumbs, process cookies in a food processor or blender or place cookies in a resealable plastic bag. Squeeze all air out of bag and seal. Crush cookies with a rolling pin until crumbs are formed.

- Slow cooker size: 3½ to 6 quart

2 tbsp	vegetable oil (approx.)	25 mL
2 lbs	stewing beef, cut into 1-inch (2.5 cm) cubes	1 kg
1 cup	beef stock, divided	250 mL
2	onions, chopped	2
4	large carrots, peeled and cut into 1-inch (2.5 cm) chunks	4
½ cup	cider vinegar	125 mL
¼ cup	packed brown sugar	50 mL
2	bay leaves	2
¼ tsp	salt	1 mL
¼ tsp	freshly ground black pepper	1 mL
Pinch	ground allspice	Pinch
Pinch	ground cloves	Pinch
½ cup	gingersnap cookie crumbs	125 mL
1 cup	frozen green beans, thawed and chopped (optional)	250 mL
¼ cup	raisins (optional)	50 mL
2 tbsp	chopped fresh parsley	25 mL

1. In a large nonstick skillet, heat half the oil over medium-high heat. Cook beef in batches, adding more oil as needed, until browned all over. With a slotted spoon, transfer beef to slow cooker stoneware.
2. Add ½ cup (125 mL) stock to skillet and bring to a boil, scraping up any brown bits in bottom of pan. Transfer to slow cooker. Stir in remaining stock, onions, carrots, vinegar, brown sugar, bay leaves, salt, pepper, allspice and cloves.
3. Cover and cook on **Low** for 8 to 10 hours or on **High** for 4 to 6 hours, until meat and carrots are tender and stew is bubbling. Discard bay leaves.
4. Add cookie crumbs, green beans and raisins, if using. Cover and cook on **High** for 20 minutes longer, or until beans are tender. Sprinkle with parsley.

Burgundy Beef and Wild Mushroom Stew

Serves 4 to 6

If you love the combination of beef and mushrooms, this stew is sure to be one of your favorites.

• • •

Tips

There are many types of dried mushrooms, including varieties such as shiitake and chanterelles. When they are properly rehydrated, their flavor and texture are as good as fresh. And if the soaking liquid is incorporated into the recipe, it adds even more flavor. Besides hot water, you can try using red wine or beef stock to soak the mushrooms for this stew.

For an extra-peppery flavor, try adding the optional freshly cracked black peppercorns to the flour used for dredging the beef.

- Slow cooker size: 3½ to 6 quart

1	package (5 oz/142 g) dried mushrooms, such as shiitake or chanterelles	1
1 cup	boiling water	250 mL
¼ cup	all-purpose flour	50 mL
2 tsp	freshly cracked black pepper (optional)	10 mL
½ tsp	dried basil	2 mL
½ tsp	dried oregano	2 mL
½ tsp	salt	2 mL
2 lbs	stewing beef, cut into 1-inch (2.5 cm) cubes	500 g
2 tbsp	vegetable oil (approx.)	25 mL
1 cup	beef stock	250 mL
2	carrots, peeled and cut lengthwise in half, then crosswise into thirds	2
1	onion, chopped (or 15 to 20 pearl onions, peeled)	1
2	cloves garlic, minced	2
8 oz	button mushrooms, quartered	250 g
½ cup	red wine	125 mL
2 tbsp	tomato paste	25 mL
1 tbsp	balsamic vinegar	15 mL
1	bay leaf	1

1. In a 2-cup (500 mL) measuring cup, combine dried mushrooms and boiling water. Let stand for 20 to 30 minutes.

2. In a heavy plastic bag, combine flour, pepper (if using), basil, oregano and salt. In batches, add beef to flour mixture and toss to coat.
3. In a large nonstick skillet, heat half the oil over medium-high heat. Cook beef in batches, adding more oil as needed, until browned all over. With a slotted spoon, transfer beef to slow cooker stoneware.
4. Add stock to skillet; stir to scrape up brown bits and transfer to slow cooker. Add carrots, onion, garlic, button mushrooms, wine, tomato paste, vinegar and bay leaf.
5. With a slotted spoon, remove rehydrated mushrooms from soaking liquid; coarsely chop and add to slow cooker along with soaking liquid; stir well to combine beef-vegetable mixture.
6. Cover and cook on **Low** for 8 to 10 hours or on **High** for 4 to 6 hours, until vegetables are tender and stew is bubbling. Discard bay leaf.

Tip

Select lean stewing beef or trim the excess fat from the meat before using. (Trimming may take a little extra time, but the result will be worth it.)

Mediterranean Veal Stew

Serves 4 to 6

Impress your dinner guests with this delicately flavored veal stew.

• • •

Tips

For an authentic Mediterranean flavor, serve with a Greek salad (chopped tomatoes, cucumbers and black olives, tossed with a lemon-oregano vinaigrette).

Green peppers can become bitter if they are cooked too long. Adding them at the end of cooking allows them to soften slightly while preserving their sweet flavor.

- Slow cooker size: 3½ to 6 quart

¼ cup	all-purpose flour	50 mL
2 tsp	dried oregano	10 mL
½ tsp	dried thyme	2 mL
1 tsp	salt	5 mL
¼ tsp	freshly ground black pepper	1 mL
2 lbs	veal shoulder or leg, well-trimmed and cut into 1-inch (2.5 cm) cubes	1 kg
2 tbsp	vegetable oil (approx.)	25 mL
1 cup	chicken stock	250 mL
2	cloves garlic, minced	2
1	onion, chopped	1
1	can (7½ oz/221 mL) tomato sauce	1
2 tbsp	red wine vinegar	25 mL
¼ cup	oil-packed sun-dried tomatoes, drained and chopped	50 mL
1	green bell pepper, coarsely chopped	1
½ cup	crumbled feta cheese	125 mL
2 tbsp	chopped fresh parsley	25 mL

1. In a heavy plastic bag, combine flour, oregano, thyme, salt and pepper. In batches, add veal to flour mixture and toss to coat.
2. In a large nonstick skillet, heat half the oil over medium-high heat. Cook veal in batches, adding more oil as needed, until browned all over. With a slotted spoon, transfer veal to slow cooker stoneware.
3. Add stock to skillet and stir to scrape up any brown bits. Transfer stock mixture to slow cooker. Add garlic, onion, tomato sauce, vinegar and sun-dried tomatoes.

4. Cover and cook on **Low** for 8 to 10 hours or on **High** for 4 to 6 hours, until meat is tender and stew is bubbling.
5. Stir in green pepper. Cover and cook on **High** for 15 to 20 minutes longer, or until heated through.
6. Spoon stew into individual serving bowls and top each with crumbled feta cheese and parsley.

Veal

Veal is sold in milk-fed or grain-fed varieties. Milk-fed veal has a soft creamy pink color and is considered superior. Grain-fed veal is redder but is still delicately flavored. For convenience, look for pre-cut cubes of stewing veal. If you can't get veal, use stewing beef instead.

Make Ahead

This dish can be completely assembled up to 24 hours before cooking (with the exception of veal cubes). Chill browned veal separately before assembling dish. Refrigerate remaining ingredients overnight in slow cooker stoneware. The next day, place stoneware in slow cooker, add browned veal and continue to cook as directed.

Hearty Veal Stew with Red Wine and Sweet Peppers

Serves 6

In this Italian-inspired stew, chunks of veal cook in a rich tomato sauce seasoned with garlic and sage. Capers lend a tangy contrast to the sweet bell peppers. Serve over egg noodles with a bottle of red wine.

- Slow cooker size: 3½ to 6 quart

¼ cup	all-purpose flour	50 mL
1 tsp	salt	5 mL
½ tsp	freshly ground black pepper	2 mL
2 lbs	veal stewing meat, cut into 1-inch (2.5 cm) cubes	1 kg
2 tbsp	vegetable oil (approx.)	25 mL
2 tbsp	butter (approx.)	25 mL
3	cloves garlic, peeled and crushed	3
¾ cup	dry red wine	175 mL
1	can (19 oz/540 mL) Italian-style stewed tomatoes, with juices	1
1 tsp	dried sage	5 mL
2	red bell peppers, cut into ½-inch (1 cm) pieces	2
2 tbsp	drained capers	25 mL

1. In a heavy plastic bag, combine flour, salt and pepper. In batches, add veal to flour mixture and toss to coat.
2. In a large nonstick skillet, heat 1 tbsp (15 mL) oil and 1 tbsp (15 mL) butter over medium-high heat. Add garlic. Cook, stirring, for 1 minute. With a slotted spoon, transfer to slow cooker stoneware.
3. Add veal to skillet in batches and cook, adding more oil and butter as needed, until browned all over. With a slotted spoon, transfer veal to slow cooker.
3. Add wine to skillet and bring to a boil, scraping up any browned bits from bottom of pan. Transfer to slow cooker. Add tomatoes and sage; stir to combine.
4. Cover and cook on **Low** for 8 to 10 hours or on **High** for 4 to 6 hours, until meat is tender.
5. Add peppers and capers. Cover and cook on **High** for 15 to 20 minutes longer, or until heated through.

Creamy Veal and Mushroom Ragoût

Serves 4 to 6

This wonderfully creamy, rich stew can be served to company, as well as family. Make sure you serve it over hot cooked egg noodles.

• • •

Tip

For convenience, look for pre-cut veal stewing cubes in the meat department of the supermarket. Or ask your butcher to cut the veal into cubes for you.

Make Ahead

This dish can be completely assembled up to 12 hours in advance of cooking. Follow preparation directions and refrigerate overnight in the slow cooker stoneware. The next day, place stoneware in slow cooker and continue cooking as directed.

- Slow cooker size: 3½ to 5 quart

¼ cup	all-purpose flour	50 mL
1 tsp	salt	5 mL
½ tsp	freshly ground black pepper	2 mL
½ tsp	dried thyme	2 mL
1	boneless veal shoulder or leg (about 3 lbs/1.5 kg), well trimmed and cubed	1
2 tbsp	vegetable oil (approx.)	25 mL
8 oz	small button mushrooms or large white mushrooms, quartered	250 g
2	onions, chopped	2
2	cloves garlic, minced	2
1 cup	beef stock	250 mL
¼ cup	dry sherry	50 mL
2 tbsp	tomato paste	25 mL
¼ cup	whipping (35%) cream	50 mL
2 cups	frozen green peas	500 mL
	Salt and freshly ground black pepper	
	Hot cooked egg noodles	

1. In a heavy plastic bag, combine flour, salt, pepper and thyme. In batches, add veal to flour mixture and toss to coat. In a large skillet, heat half the oil over medium-high heat. Cook veal in batches, adding more oil as needed, until browned all over. With a slotted spoon, transfer veal to slow cooker stoneware. Add mushrooms, onions and garlic.
2. In a 2-cup (500 mL) glass measure, combine stock, sherry and tomato paste; mix well. Pour into slow cooker and stir to combine. Cover and cook on **Low** for 8 to 10 hours or on **High** for 4 to 6 hours, until meat is tender and sauce is bubbling.
3. Add cream and peas. Cover and cook on **High** for 15 to 20 minutes longer, or until heated through. Season to taste with salt and pepper. Serve over hot noodles.

Ham and Lentil Ragoût

Serves 8

Lentils are a staple in Indian and Middle Eastern cooking. They come in three varieties — brown, red and green. I prefer green lentils for this dish, since they hold their shape well during the long slow-cooking process.

Tip

Serve with crusty Italian buns and cold beer on the side.

Variation

For a livelier version of this dish, try using a spicy smoked sausage in place of the ham.

Make Ahead

This dish can be completely assembled up to 12 hours in advance of cooking. Prepare the ingredients in the slow cooker up to the cooking stage (without adding the parsley) and refrigerate in the stoneware. The next day, place stoneware in slow cooker and continue cooking as directed.

- Slow cooker size: 5 to 6 quart

3 cups	chopped cooked ham	750 mL
2	carrots, peeled and finely chopped	2
2	stalks celery, finely chopped	2
1	onion, finely chopped	1
2 cups	dried green lentils	500 mL
2 cups	chicken stock	500 mL
4 cups	water	1 L
2 tsp	paprika	10 mL
1 tsp	dried thyme	5 mL
1/4 cup	chopped fresh parsley	50 mL

1. In slow cooker stoneware, combine ham, carrots, celery, onion, lentils, stock, water, paprika and thyme; mix well.
2. Cover and cook on **Low** for 6 to 8 hours or on **High** for 3 to 4 hours, until vegetables and lentils are tender. Stir in parsley and serve.

Spicy White Bean and Sausage Ragoût

Serves 4

This dish packs plenty of heat. But if you're not a big fan of spicy food, use mild Italian sausage — it has lots of flavor, but without the zap. Serve with a crisp Caesar salad and a hearty red wine.

• • •

Tips

Use Fia's Favorite Pasta Sauce (see recipe, page 182) in place of store-bought pasta sauce.

Green peppers can become bitter if they are cooked too long. Adding them at the end of cooking allows them to soften slightly while preserving their sweet flavor.

- Slow cooker size: 5 to 6 quart

1 lb	hot Italian sausages	500 g
2 cups	store-bought chunky-style pasta sauce	500 mL
1 cup	beef stock	250 mL
2	stalks celery, chopped	2
4	cloves garlic, minced	4
1 tsp	dried Italian seasoning	5 mL
2	cans (each 19 oz/540 mL) white kidney beans, drained and rinsed or 4 cups (1 L) home-cooked beans (page 146)	2
1	green bell pepper, coarsely chopped	1

1. In a skillet, over medium-high heat, cook sausages for 10 minutes, or until browned on all sides. Cut into 1-inch (2.5 cm) slices. Using a slotted spoon, transfer sausages to slow cooker stoneware. Add pasta sauce, stock, celery, garlic, Italian seasoning and kidney beans; stir to combine.
2. Cover and cook on **Low** for 6 to 7 hours or on **High** for 3 to 4 hours, until stew is hot and bubbling.
3. Stir in green pepper. Cover and cook on **High** for 20 minutes longer.

Italian Meatball and Bean Ragoût

Serves 4 to 6

This thick, hearty stew is loaded with moist, tender meatballs, vegetables and beans. Serve it with toasted garlic bread.

• • •

Tips

Italian sausage is highly seasoned and adds a wallop of great flavor. For less heat, stick to the mild variety.

Look for flavored tomato paste such as roasted garlic or Italian-style. It will add a little more gusto to this dish.

- Slow cooker size: 3½ to 6 quart

Italian Meatballs

½ lb	hot or mild Italian sausages, casings removed	250 g
½ lb	lean ground pork	250 g
½ cup	dry bread crumbs	125 mL
1	small onion, finely chopped	1
3 tbsp	milk	45 mL
1	egg, lightly beaten	1
2 tbsp	freshly grated Parmesan cheese	25 mL
2 tbsp	chopped fresh parsley	25 mL
¼ tsp	Worcestershire sauce	1 mL
¼ tsp	salt	1 mL
Pinch	freshly ground black pepper	Pinch

Ragoût

1 cup	beef stock	250 mL
1	can (19 oz/540 mL) Italian-style stewed tomatoes, with juices (see box, page 97)	1
2 tbsp	tomato paste	25 mL
1	carrot, peeled and chopped	1
1	stalk celery, chopped	1
1	can (19 oz/540 mL) white kidney or navy beans, drained and rinsed, or 2 cups (500 mL) home-cooked beans (page 146)	1
½ tsp	dried oregano	2 mL
½ tsp	salt	2 mL
¼ tsp	freshly ground black pepper	1 mL
2 tbsp	freshly grated Parmesan cheese	25 mL

1. *Italian meatballs:* In a bowl, combine sausage meat, ground pork, bread crumbs, onion, milk, egg, Parmesan, parsley, Worcestershire sauce, salt and pepper. Mix well and shape into 1-inch (2.5 cm) balls.
2. Arrange meatballs in a single layer on a foil-lined baking sheet and bake in a preheated 400°F (200°C) oven for 10 to 12 minutes, or until no longer pink inside. Drain off any accumulated juices and transfer to slow cooker stoneware.
3. *Ragoût:* In a bowl, combine stock, tomatoes, tomato paste, carrot, celery, beans, oregano, salt, pepper; mix well and pour over meatballs.
4. Cover and cook on **Low** for 4 to 5 hours, or until sauce is bubbling, meatballs are hot and vegetables are tender.
5. Spoon into bowls and sprinkle with Parmesan.

Toasted Garlic Bread

Cut a loaf of French bread into 1-inch (2.5 cm) slices.

In a bowl, combine ¼ cup (50 mL) softened butter and 3 minced cloves garlic or 1 tsp (5 mL) garlic powder. Spread garlic butter on bread slices.

Place bread on broiler rack, butter side up, and broil 5 to 6 inches (12 to 15 cm) from heat for 2 to 3 minutes, or until lightly golden brown.

For cheesy garlic bread, sprinkle with ¾ cup (175 mL) grated mozzarella cheese and broil for 3 minutes, or until cheese is melted. *Serves 8 to 10.*

Make Ahead

Ragoût can be assembled up to 24 hours before cooking. Refrigerate overnight in slow cooker stoneware. The next morning, add meatballs to ragoût and place stoneware in slow cooker. Continue to cook as directed. Meatballs can also be cooked up to a month in advance and frozen. Defrost at room temperature for about 30 minutes before adding to ragoût.

Cider Pork Stew

Serves 6

The tang of the vinegar and sweetness of the onion blend well in this easy-to-assemble dinner. Serve with garlic mashed potatoes (page 303) or steamed rice (page 163).

• • •

Variation

Orange Fennel Pork Stew: Replace thyme with 2 tsp (10 mL) crushed fennel seeds. Replace apple cider with 1 cup (250 mL) orange juice concentrate. Add 2 tbsp (25 mL) grated gingerroot to slow cooker with peppers. Omit bay leaves and garnish with orange slices instead of apple.

- Slow cooker size: 3½ to 6 quart

2	onions, sliced	2
4	cloves garlic, minced	4
⅓ cup	all-purpose flour	75 mL
1 tbsp	dried thyme	15 mL
1 tsp	salt	5 mL
½ tsp	freshly ground black pepper	2 mL
4 lbs	boneless pork shoulder butt roast, trimmed of excess fat, cut into 1-inch (2.5 cm) cubes	2 kg
¼ cup	vegetable oil (approx.)	50 mL
1 cup	apple cider	250 mL
¼ cup	cider vinegar	50 mL
2	bay leaves	2
2	red bell peppers, coarsely chopped	2
1	red apple, unpeeled, thinly sliced	1
1 tbsp	chopped fresh parsley	15 mL

1. Layer onions and garlic in slow cooker stoneware.
2. In a heavy plastic bag, combine flour, thyme, salt and pepper. In batches, add pork to flour mixture and toss to coat.
3. In a large nonstick skillet, heat half the oil over medium-high heat. Cook pork in batches, adding oil as needed, until browned all over. With a slotted spoon, transfer pork to slow cooker stoneware.
4. Add apple cider and vinegar to skillet and bring to a boil, scraping up any brown bits on bottom of pan. Pour over pork in slow cooker. Add bay leaves.
5. Cover and cook on **Low** for 8 to 10 hours or on **High** for 3 to 4 hours, until pork is tender. Discard bay leaves.
6. Stir in peppers. Cover and cook on **High** for 1 hour longer. Skim fat from sauce. Taste and adjust seasonings if necessary. Serve topped with apple slices and parsley.

Hungarian Pork Goulash

Serves 4 to 6

Don't be alarmed by the amount of paprika in this recipe. The large quantity adds a rich color to the sauce, but not a lot of spiciness. Omit the optional sauerkraut if you wish, but it gives this dish an authentic European character.

Tips

If you only have hot paprika, reduce the amount by half.

Try replacing canned sauerkraut with the fresh variety. It can generally be found in the fresh meat or deli department of the grocery store.

Make Ahead

Stew can be assembled 12 hours in advance. Prepare the ingredients in the slow cooker up to the cooking stage (without sour cream) and refrigerate in stoneware insert overnight. The next day, place stoneware in slow cooker and continue cooking as directed.

- Slow cooker size: 5 to 6 quart

1 tbsp	vegetable oil	15 mL
2 lbs	boneless pork shoulder roast, cut into 1½-inch (3.5 cm) cubes	1 kg
2	onions, sliced	2
2	cloves garlic, minced	2
¼ cup	mild paprika	50 mL
½ tsp	salt	2 mL
½ tsp	freshly ground black pepper	2 mL
1	can or jar (19 oz/540 mL) sauerkraut, drained and rinsed (optional)	1
1	can (19 oz/540 mL) diced tomatoes, with juices	1
1 cup	beef stock	250 mL
1 cup	light sour cream	250 mL
	Hot cooked egg noodles	
	Sour cream (optional)	

1. In a large nonstick skillet, heat oil over medium-high heat. Add pork cubes, onions and garlic; cook for 4 to 5 minutes, or until pork is browned all over. Sprinkle with paprika, salt and pepper; cook for 1 minute longer. With a slotted spoon, transfer pork and seasonings to slow cooker stoneware. Add sauerkraut (if using), tomatoes (with juices) and stock.
2. Cover and cook on **Low** for 8 to 10 hours or on **High** for 4 to 6 hours, until meat is tender.
3. Reduce heat to **Low**. Stir in sour cream and cook for 5 minutes longer. Serve over hot noodles. If desired, garnish with additional sour cream.

Pork and Parsnip Stew with Apricots

Serves 4 to 6

After many years of developing recipes for the pork industry, I'm convinced that fruit is just about the perfect accompaniment to any pork dish. Here, dried apricots, prunes and orange juice sweeten this savory stew.

• • •

Tips

When browning the meat in hot oil, avoid cooking too many cubes in the skillet at one time. The meat will steam rather than brown. Turn the meat frequently and remove with a slotted spoon as quickly as possible.

Adding a splash of balsamic vinegar to soups and stews helps to tenderize the meat and give it a sweet zing of flavor.

- Slow cooker size: 3½ to 5 quart

¼ cup	all-purpose flour	50 mL
½ tsp	salt	2 mL
¼ tsp	freshly ground black pepper	2 mL
2 lbs	boneless pork shoulder butt roast, cut into 1-inch (2.5 cm) cubes	1 kg
2 tbsp	vegetable oil (approx.)	25 mL
2	onions, finely chopped	2
2	large parsnips, peeled and cut into 1-inch (2.5 cm) slices	2
2	carrots, peeled and cut into 1-inch (2.5 cm) slices	2
1½ cups	chicken stock	375 mL
1 cup	orange juice	250 mL
2 tbsp	balsamic vinegar	25 mL
½ tsp	ground allspice	2 mL
	Salt and freshly ground black pepper	
½ cup	dried apricots	125 mL
½ cup	pitted prunes	125 mL

1. In a heavy plastic bag, combine flour, salt and pepper. In batches, add pork to flour mixture and toss to coat.
2. In a large nonstick skillet, heat half the oil over medium-high heat. Cook pork in batches, adding more oil as needed, until browned all over. With a slotted spoon, transfer pork to slow cooker stoneware. Add onions, parsnips, carrots, stock, orange juice, vinegar, allspice, salt and pepper; stir to combine.

3. Cover and cook on **Low** for 8 to 10 hours or on **High** for 4 to 6 hours, until vegetables are tender and stew is bubbling.
4. Gently stir in apricots and prunes. Cover and cook on **High** for 15 to 20 minutes longer, or until heated through. Season to taste with salt and pepper.

Parsnips

Parsnips are a wonderful winter vegetable that resemble white carrots. (At least that's the description I give my vegetable-wary children when they ask, "What's that?") Parsnips have a slightly sweet flavor and make a delicious addition to many soups and stews.

Make Ahead

Stew can be assembled 12 hours in advance. Prepare the ingredients in the slow cooker up to the cooking stage (without adding apricots and prunes) and refrigerate in stoneware insert overnight. The next day, place stoneware in slow cooker and continue cooking as directed.

Hawaiian Pork Stew

Serves 4 to 6

Serve this with a tropical fruit plate and fragrant rice (page 163). Use bright orange sweet potatoes in this recipe. They are sweeter, moister and more colorful than the pale yellow sweet potatoes.

• • •

Tip

Green peppers can become bitter if they are cooked too long. Adding them at the end of cooking allows them to soften slightly while preserving their sweet flavor.

- Slow cooker size: 3½ to 6 quart

3 tbsp	all-purpose flour	45 mL
1 tsp	salt	5 mL
1 tsp	freshly ground black pepper	5 mL
½ tsp	ground cinnamon	2 mL
¼ tsp	dried oregano	1 mL
¼ tsp	ground cloves	1 mL
2 lbs	boneless pork shoulder butt roast, cut into 1-inch (2.5 cm) cubes	1 kg
2 tbsp	vegetable oil (approx.)	25 mL
1 cup	chicken stock	250 mL
1	onion, chopped	1
2	cloves garlic, minced	2
1	can (19 oz/540 mL) diced tomatoes, with juices	1
1	large sweet potato, peeled and cubed	1
1 tbsp	packed brown sugar	15 mL
1 cup	fresh or canned pineapple chunks	250 mL
¼ cup	sliced pimento-stuffed green olives	50 mL
½	green bell pepper, chopped	½
¼ cup	chopped fresh parsley	50 mL

1. In a heavy plastic bag, combine flour, salt, pepper, cinnamon, oregano and cloves. In batches, add pork to flour mixture and toss to coat.
2. In a large nonstick skillet, heat half the oil over medium-high heat. Cook pork in batches, adding more oil as needed, until browned all over. With a slotted spoon, transfer pork to slow cooker stoneware.

3. Add stock to skillet and bring to a boil, stirring to scrape up any browned bits from bottom of pan. Transfer to slow cooker. Add onion, garlic, tomatoes, sweet potato and brown sugar; stir to combine.
4. Cover and cook on **Low** for 8 to 10 hours or on **High** for 4 to 6 hours, until meat and potatoes are tender and stew is bubbling.
5. Stir in pineapple chunks, olives, green pepper and parsley. Cover and cook on **High** for 15 to 20 minutes longer, or until heated through.

Tip

Refrigerating any leftover stew always improves the flavor (which is why it always tastes better the next day). The fat will rise to the top and solidify; remove it before reheating.

Garlic

Chopped garlic in the jar is a convenient alternative to fresh garlic. It's easy to use and will keep in the refrigerator for up to 6 months.

Easy Jambalaya

Serves 6 to 8

This one-pot wonder originates from the deep South — New Orleans, in fact — and traditionally features a mix of chicken, sausage and shrimp. This scaled-down version uses only ham and shrimp, but still packs a piquant punch. All you need is a crisp garden salad to top it off.

• • •

Tips

You can replace the ham with any spicy sausage, such as andouille, chorizo or hot Italian.

Make Ahead

Jambalaya can be assembled 12 hours in advance. Prepare the ingredients in the slow cooker up to the cooking stage (but without adding the shrimp and green pepper) and refrigerate in stoneware insert overnight. The next day, place stoneware in slow cooker and continue cooking as directed.

• **Slow cooker size: 3½ to 4 quart**

1	large onion, finely chopped	1
2	stalks celery, finely chopped	2
3	cloves garlic, minced	3
1	can (19 oz/540 mL) diced, tomatoes, with juices	1
1	can (14 oz/398 mL) tomato sauce	1
2 cups	chopped ham	500 mL
2 tbsp	dried parsley	25 mL
1 tsp	dried thyme	5 mL
½ tsp	salt	2 mL
½ tsp	hot pepper flakes	2 mL
¼ tsp	freshly ground black pepper	1 mL
12 oz	medium shrimp, uncooked, peeled and deveined	375 g
1	green bell pepper, coarsely chopped	1
	Hot cooked rice	

1. In slow cooker stoneware, combine onion, celery, garlic, tomatoes (with juices), tomato sauce, ham, parsley, thyme, salt, hot pepper flakes and black pepper.
2. Cover and cook on **Low** for 6 to 8 hours or on **High** for 3 to 4 hours, until vegetables are tender.
3. Add shrimp and green pepper. Cover and cook on **Low** for 15 to 20 minutes longer, or until shrimp are pink and firm. Serve over hot rice.

South African Lamb Stew

Serves 6 to 8

My friend Gill Ireland hails from South Africa, where lamb is very much a staple. She passed this delicately flavored stew along to me and I have adapted it to the slow cooker.

• • •

Tips

Enjoy the stew with a hearty South African red wine and a thick, crusty loaf of bread.

The best cuts for lamb stew come from the shoulder or shank. Avoid using loin — it can be very expensive and overcooks quickly.

Make Ahead

Stew can be assembled 12 hours in advance. Prepare the ingredients in the slow cooker up to the cooking stage (without adding green peas, lemon zest and parsley) and refrigerate in stoneware insert overnight. The next day, place stoneware in slow cooker and continue cooking as directed.

- Slow cooker size: 3½ to 5 quart

¼ cup	all-purpose flour	50 mL
½ tsp	salt	2 mL
¼ tsp	freshly ground black pepper	1 mL
1 lb	boneless lamb shoulder roast, trimmed and cut into 1-inch (2.5 cm) cubes	500 g
2 tbsp	vegetable oil (approx.)	25 mL
1	large onion, chopped	1
3	carrots, peeled and chopped	3
3	large potatoes, peeled and chopped	3
1½ cups	chopped peeled rutabaga	375 mL
1	can (19 oz/540 mL) diced tomatoes, with juices	1
2 cups	beef stock	500 mL
1 tbsp	soy sauce	15 mL
1 tsp	granulated sugar	5 mL
1 cup	frozen peas	250 mL
1 tbsp	grated lemon zest	15 mL
1 tbsp	chopped fresh parsley	15 mL

1. In a heavy plastic bag, combine flour, salt and pepper. In batches, add lamb to flour mixture and toss to coat.
2. In a large nonstick skillet, heat half the oil over medium-high heat. Cook lamb in batches, adding more oil as needed, until browned all over. With a slotted spoon, transfer to slow cooker stoneware. Add onion, carrots, potatoes, rutabaga, tomatoes (with juices), stock, soy sauce and sugar; stir to combine.
4. Cover and cook on **Low** for 8 to 10 hours or on **High** for 4 to 6 hours, until vegetables are tender and stew is bubbling.
5. Gently stir in peas. Cover and cook on **High** for 15 to 20 minutes longer.
6. Spoon into serving bowls and sprinkle with lemon zest and parsley.

Chilies and Beans

Dried Beans

Cooking dried beans from scratch takes a little extra time, but it's very economical and, in many people's opinion, gives a better-tasting result than using canned beans. When using dried beans, remember that the beans will more than double in size after cooking. One pound (500g) dried beans yields approximately 4 to 5 cups (1 to 1.25 L) cooked beans. Also bear in mind that beans must be completely cooked before combining with sugar or acidic foods such as molasses or tomatoes. (Sugar and acid tend to prevent beans from softening.)

Preparing Dried Beans

Transforming the hard, dried legume into a tender, edible bean requires four steps: cleaning, soaking, rinsing and cooking. Soaking the beans helps to replace the water that has been lost in the drying process. It also speeds up the cooking time. Cooking times for beans (see chart below) depend on the type of slow cooker used, as well as the variety, age and quality of the beans, altitude and whether hard or soft water is used in cooking. The best way to test for doneness is to taste them. Cooked beans are free of any raw, starchy taste, are fork-tender, and easy to squash between your fingers.

Begin by picking the beans over to remove any that are broken or cracked, then place them in a colander or sieve and rinse well under cold running water. In a pot of boiling water (enough to cover beans), simmer on the stovetop for 10 minutes; drain and rinse well. Transfer beans to a slow cooker and cover with 6 cups (1.5 L) fresh water per pound (500 g) beans. Cover and cook on Low for about 12 hours. Discard water unless otherwise stated. Beans are now recipe-ready. (Hint: Let the beans do the initial cooking in the slow cooker while you are sleeping and they will be recipe-ready in the morning.)

Storing Cooked Beans

Cooked beans store well in the refrigerator in resealable plastic bags or covered containers for up to 5 days. Cooked beans can also be kept in the freezer for up to 6 months. For convenient, easy meals, it's a good idea to pack them in measured amounts, such as 1 cup (250 mL) or 2 cups (500 mL) — amounts usually called for in recipes.

Canned Beans

For convenience, the same variety of canned beans may be substituted for cooked, dried beans in any of the recipes in this book. One 19-oz (540 mL) can of any bean variety can be substituted for 2 cups of cooked beans. Canned beans are already cooked and are recipe-ready. Before adding to any recipe, rinse well under cold running water to remove brine. Canned beans should be stored in a cool, dry place and, for best flavor and texture, should be used within a year of purchase.

Bean Type	Suggested Cooking Time
Red Kidney Beans	10 to 12 hours on **Low**
Light Red Kidney Beans	10 to 12 hours on **Low**
White Kidney Beans	10 to 12 hours on **Low**
White Pea or Navy Beans	10 to 12 hours on **Low**
Black Beans	8 to 10 hours on **Low**
Romano/Cranberry Beans	8 to 10 hours on **Low**
Chickpeas/Garbanzo Beans	10 to 12 hours on **Low**

Hearty Vegetarian Chili

Serves 6

This dish is a spicy blend of squash, carrots, black beans and more — you'll never miss the meat!

Tips

You can substitute 2 large sweet potatoes (peeled and chopped) for the squash.

Canned green chilies are found in the Mexican food section of the supermarket. They are sold whole or chopped.

Make Ahead

This chili can be assembled 12 hours in advance of cooking. Follow preparation directions and refrigerate overnight in slow cooker stoneware. The next day, place stoneware in slow cooker and continue cooking as directed.

- **Slow cooker size: 3½ to 5 quart**

1	medium-sized butternut squash, peeled and cut into ¾-inch (2 cm) cubes	1
2	carrots, diced	2
1	onion, finely chopped	1
1	can (28 oz/796 mL) diced tomatoes, with juices	1
2	cans (each 19 oz/540 mL) black beans, drained and rinsed, or 4 cups (1 L) home-cooked beans (page 146)	2
1	can (4½ oz/127 mL) chopped green chilies, with liquid	1
1 cup	vegetable or chicken stock	250 mL
3 tbsp	chili powder	45 mL
½ tsp	salt	2 mL
¼ cup	chopped fresh cilantro	50 mL
	Sour cream	
	Fresh cilantro, chopped	

1. In slow cooker stoneware, combine squash, carrots, onion, tomatoes (with juices), black beans, chilies (with liquid), stock, chili powder and salt; stir to mix well.
2. Cover and cook on **Low** for 6 to 8 hours or on **High** for 3 to 4 hours, until hot and bubbling.
3. Add cilantro; cover and cook on **High** for 15 to 20 minutes longer.
4. Spoon into serving bowls and top with a dollop of sour cream and additional chopped fresh cilantro.

Vegetable Chili with Sour Cream Topping

Serves 6

This vegetarian chili contains lots of fresh vegetables simmered in a rich sauce. The cocoa gives it an authentic Mexican flavor. Serve with cornmeal muffins or breadsticks.

• • •

Tips

Use a food processor to make quick work of chopping the vegetables.

The tomato purée gives the chili a smooth consistency.

Make Ahead

This chili can be completely assembled up to 24 hours before cooking. Refrigerate overnight in the slow cooker stoneware. The next day, place stoneware in slow cooker and continue to cook as directed. Prepare the sour cream topping and refrigerate until serving.

- Slow cooker size: 3½ to 6 quart

1	zucchini, quartered lengthwise and sliced	1
1	stalk celery, chopped	1
1	carrot, peeled and chopped	1
1	onion, finely chopped	1
2	cloves garlic, minced	2
2	cans (each 14 oz/398 mL) kidney beans, drained and rinsed, or 3 cups (750 mL) home-cooked beans (page 146)	2
1	can (19 oz/540 mL) diced tomatoes, with juices	1
1	can (14 oz/398 mL) tomato purée or crushed tomatoes	1
½ cup	vegetable stock	125 mL
1 tbsp	chili powder	15 mL
1 tbsp	unsweetened cocoa powder	15 mL
½ tsp	dried oregano	2 mL
½ tsp	ground cumin	2 mL
Dash	hot pepper sauce	Dash
½ tsp	salt	2 mL
¼ tsp	freshly ground black pepper	1 mL
½ cup	sour cream	125 mL
½ cup	shredded Cheddar cheese	125 mL
4	green onions, chopped	4

1. In slow cooker stoneware, combine zucchini, celery, carrot, onion, garlic, kidney beans, tomatoes, tomato purée, stock, chili powder, cocoa, oregano, cumin, hot pepper sauce, salt and pepper.
2. Cover and cook on **Low** for 6 to 8 hours or on **High** for 3 to 4 hours, until hot and bubbling.
3. In a small bowl, combine sour cream, Cheddar and green onions. Spoon chili into individual serving bowls and add topping.

Stratford's Sweet Chili

Serves 6 to 8

My childhood friend Joy Stratford has been a vegetarian for many years. Not only is she a busy mom and great soccer player, she is also a fantastic cook! This is one of her favorite recipes.

• • •

Tips

If you find this chili too sweet, reduce the honey by 2 tbsp (25 mL).

Substitute 1 cup (250 mL) frozen corn for canned corn.

Beans are an excellent source of fiber and protein, and give this chili a hearty, filling consistency that satisfies even a die-hard meat eater. Don't be afraid to add an additional can of beans to this recipe. Several varieties of shapes and colors add interest and texture.

- Slow cooker size: 5 to 6 quart

1	can (19 oz/540 mL) chickpeas, drained and rinsed, or 2 cups (500 mL) home-cooked chickpeas (page 146)	1
1	can (19 oz/540 mL) red kidney beans or black beans, drained and rinsed, or 2 cups (500 mL) home-cooked beans (page 146)	1
1	can (28 oz/796 mL) diced tomatoes with herbs and spices	1
1	can (10 oz/284 mL) corn kernels, drained	1
2	carrots, peeled and diced	2
2	large cloves garlic, minced	2
1	red onion, finely chopped	1
1 cup	ketchup	250 mL
1/4 cup	liquid honey	50 mL
3 tbsp	chili powder	45 mL
1/2 tsp	cayenne pepper	2 mL
1	green bell pepper, diced	1
1	red bell pepper, diced	1
1	yellow bell pepper, diced	1
	Sour cream	
	Cheddar cheese, shredded	

1. In slow cooker stoneware, combine chickpeas, kidney beans, tomatoes, corn, carrots, garlic and red onion.
2. In a bowl, combine ketchup, honey, chili powder and cayenne; mix well and pour into slow cooker. Stir mixture to combine.
3. Cover and cook on **Low** for 8 to 10 hours or on **High** for 4 to 6 hours, until hot and bubbling.
4. Add green pepper, red pepper and yellow pepper. Cover and cook on **High** for 20 to 25 minutes longer.
5. Serve in bowls with a dollop of sour cream and shredded Cheddar cheese.

Anthony's Awesome Chili Con Carne

Serves 6 to 8

My friend Anthony Scian gave me his "secret" recipe for this very flavorful chili. It's cocoa powder — something Mexican cooks have used for centuries to make their mole sauces.

• • •

Tips

For those who like their chili a little spicier, add more cayenne pepper.

Small quantities of leftover chili should never go to waste. Try spooning this chili over hot baked potatoes. Garnish with grated Cheddar cheese.

Make Ahead

This chili can be assembled 12 hours in advance of cooking (but without adding the green pepper). Follow preparation directions and refrigerate overnight in slow cooker stoneware. The next day, place stoneware in slow cooker and continue cooking as directed.

- Slow cooker size: 5 to 6 quart

2 lbs	lean ground beef	1 kg
2	large cloves garlic, minced	2
2	stalks celery, finely chopped	2
2	large onions, finely chopped	2
2 tbsp	chili powder	25 mL
½ tsp	dried oregano	2 mL
¼ tsp	cayenne pepper	1 mL
1	can (28 oz/796 mL) diced tomatoes, with juices	1
1	can (19 oz/540 mL) red kidney beans, drained and rinsed, or 2 cups (500 mL) home-cooked beans (page 146)	1
2 tbsp	unsweetened cocoa powder	25 mL
1 tbsp	packed brown sugar	15 mL
3 or 4	whole cloves	3 or 4
1 tsp	white vinegar	5 mL
½ tsp	freshly ground black pepper	2 mL
1	green bell pepper, finely chopped	1
	Salt and freshly ground black pepper	

1. In a large nonstick skillet, over medium heat, cook ground beef, garlic, celery and onions, breaking up beef with back of a spoon, until vegetables are tender and beef is no longer pink. Add chili powder, oregano and cayenne; cook for 1 minute longer. With a slotted spoon, transfer mixture to slow cooker stoneware.
2. Add tomatoes (with juices), kidney beans, cocoa, brown sugar, cloves, vinegar and pepper to slow cooker; stir to combine.
3. Cover and cook on **Low** for 6 to 8 hours or on **High** for 3 to 4 hours, until hot and bubbling.
4. Add green pepper and stir to combine. Cover and cook on **High** for 20 to 25 minutes longer. Season to taste with salt and pepper.

Football Sunday Chili

Serves 4 to 6

Everyone needs a good chili for football season, whether it's a tailgate party or in the comfort of your own home. This is also a perfect potluck tote! It's a mildly hot chili with a slightly sweet flavor.

• • •

Tips

If you have a large (6-quart) slow cooker, this recipe can easily be doubled. I love to serve this with hot garlic bread or buttered toast.

When handling hot peppers, make sure you keep your hands away from your eyes. Better yet, wear rubber gloves and wash hands and utensils afterwards.

Make Ahead

This chili can be assembled 12 hours in advance of cooking (but without adding the green pepper). Follow preparation directions and refrigerate overnight in slow cooker stoneware. The next day, place stoneware in slow cooker and continue cooking as directed.

- Slow cooker size: 3½ to 6 quart

2 lbs	lean ground beef	1 kg
2	large onions, chopped	2
2	hot red chili peppers, finely chopped	2
2 tbsp	chili powder	25 mL
1 tsp	ground ginger	5 mL
1 tsp	ground cinnamon	5 mL
½ tsp	ground allspice	2 mL
½ tsp	ground nutmeg	2 mL
1	can (28 oz/796 mL) diced tomatoes, with juices	1
1	can (10 oz/284 mL) condensed tomato soup	1
2	cans (19 oz/540 mL) red kidney beans, drained and rinsed, or 2 cups (500 mL) home-cooked beans (page 146)	2
½ cup	cider vinegar	125 mL
¼ cup	packed brown sugar	50 mL
2	green bell peppers, finely chopped	2

1. In a large nonstick skillet, over medium-high heat, cook ground beef, onions and hot peppers, breaking up beef with back of a spoon, until beef is no longer pink. Add chili powder, ginger, cinnamon, allspice and nutmeg; cook for 1 minute longer. With a slotted spoon, transfer seasoned meat to slow cooker stoneware.
2. Add tomatoes (with juices), tomato soup, kidney beans, vinegar and brown sugar to slow cooker; stir to combine.
3. Cover and cook on **Low** for 8 to 10 hours or on **High** for 4 to 6 hours, until hot and bubbling.
4. Add green pepper and stir to combine. Cover and cook on **High** for 20 to 25 minutes longer.

Pepperoni Pizza Chili

Serves 6 to 8

All the kids' favorite ingredients rolled into a pot of chili! Serve with Italian bread and a Caesar salad.

• • •

Tips

You can substitute equal amounts of lean ground turkey or chicken for the ground beef. You can also use a blend of pre-shredded pizza cheese in place of the mozzarella.

If your kids love Italian food but prefer it plain, omit the mushrooms and red pepper and serve them as toppings for the adults.

Make Ahead

This dish can be completely assembled up to 24 hours before cooking. Chill cooked meat and vegetables separately. Then assemble dish and refrigerate overnight in slow cooker stoneware. The next day, place stoneware in slow cooker and continue to cook as directed.

- **Slow cooker size: 3½ to 6 quart**

1 lb	lean ground beef	500 g
2	cloves garlic, minced	2
1	can (19 oz/540 mL) pinto or Romano beans, drained and rinsed, or 2 cups (500 mL) home-cooked beans (page 146)	1
1	can (7½ oz/213 mL) pizza sauce	1
1	can (19 oz/540 mL) Italian-style stewed tomatoes, with juices (see box, page 97)	1
1	can (7½ oz/213 mL) tomato sauce	1
4 oz	pepperoni, sliced	125 g
1 cup	sliced mushrooms	250 mL
1	red bell pepper, finely chopped	1
1 tsp	dried Italian seasoning (see box, page 105)	5 mL
½ tsp	salt	2 mL
½ cup	shredded mozzarella cheese	125 mL

1. In a large nonstick skillet, over medium-high heat, cook beef and garlic, breaking up beef with back of a spoon, until beef is no longer pink. With a slotted spoon, transfer meat to slow cooker stoneware.
2. Add beans, pizza sauce, tomatoes (with juices), tomato sauce, pepperoni, mushrooms, red pepper, Italian seasoning and salt to slow cooker; stir to combine.
3. Cover and cook on **Low** for 8 to 10 hours or on **High** for 4 to 5 hours, until hot and bubbling.
4. Spoon chili into individual serving bowls and top with mozzarella cheese.

Rock'n and Roast'n Chili

Serves 6 to 8

Red alert! For those who like a little kick to their meal, this meaty beef chili will knock the socks off anyone who can take it. A loaf of crusty bread is a must, along with a few cold beers.

• • •

Tips

If you can't find Italian-style stewed tomatoes, use regular stewed tomatoes and add ½ tsp (2 mL) dried Italian seasoning or a combination of dried basil, marjoram, oregano and thyme.

Mild green chilies are found in the Mexican foods section of the supermarket. They are sold whole or chopped.

- **Slow cooker size: 3½ to 6 quart**

2 tbsp	vegetable oil (approx.)	25 mL
2 lbs	stewing beef, cut into 1-inch (2.5 cm) cubes	1 kg
2 tbsp	chili powder	25 mL
Pinch	ground cumin	Pinch
½ cup	chopped drained pickled hot banana peppers (stems and seeds removed)	125 mL
1	onion, chopped	1
3	cloves garlic, minced	3
1	fresh jalapeño or banana pepper, seeded and chopped	1
1	can (19 oz/540 mL) Italian-style stewed tomatoes, with juices	1
1	can (5½ oz/156 mL) tomato paste	1
1	can (19 oz/540 mL) red kidney beans, drained and rinsed, or 2 cups (500 mL) home-cooked beans (page 146)	1
1	can (4½ oz/127 mL) chopped mild green chilies, including liquid	1
1 tsp	hot pepper sauce (approx.)	5 mL
1 tsp	salt	5 mL

1. In a large nonstick skillet, heat half the oil over medium-high heat. Cook beef in batches, adding more oil as needed, until browned all over. Return all beef to skillet.
2. Add chili powder and cumin to skillet and cook, stirring, for 1 minute. With a slotted spoon, transfer meat to slow cooker stoneware.
3. Add pickled peppers, onion, garlic, jalapeño, tomatoes (with juices), tomato paste, beans, green chilies, hot pepper sauce and salt to slow cooker, stir to combine.
4. Cover and cook on **Low** for 8 to 10 hours or on **High** for 4 to 6 hours, until meat is tender. Taste and add more hot pepper sauce if desired.

Shredded Barbecued Beef Chili

Serves 10 to 12

This recipe is meant to feed a crowd of hungry people, providing at least 10 hearty servings. It's the perfect dish to prepare for a football or skating party. For extra heat, add more cayenne.

• • •

Tips

Slow cooking helps to tenderize less expensive cuts of meat. Pot roast benefits from a longer cooking time on **Low**, but if you're short of time, count on 4 hours of simmering on **High** to produce fork-tender meat.

Any beans can be used in place of Great Northern or white kidney beans. Try pinto, red kidney or black beans.

- Slow cooker size: 5 to 6 quart

2 tbsp	chili powder	25 mL
1 tbsp	garlic powder	15 mL
2 tsp	celery seed	10 mL
1 tsp	freshly ground black pepper	5 mL
1/4 tsp	cayenne pepper	1 mL
1	boneless beef pot roast, cross rib, rump or brisket (about 3 to 4 lbs/1.5 to 2 kg)	1
1	small onion, chopped	1
2 cups	tomato-based chili sauce	500 mL
1 cup	ketchup	250 mL
1/2 cup	barbecue sauce	125 mL
1/3 cup	packed brown sugar	75 mL
1/4 cup	cider vinegar	50 mL
1/4 cup	Worcestershire sauce	50 mL
1 tsp	dry mustard	5 mL
2	cans (each 19 oz/540 mL) Great Northern or white kidney beans, drained and rinsed, or 4 cups (1 L) home-cooked beans (page 146)	2

1. In a small bowl, combine chili powder, garlic powder, celery seed, black pepper and cayenne.
2. Cut roast into 4 smaller portions and rub seasoning mixture on all sides of chunks. Place in slow cooker stoneware.
3. In a bowl, combine onion, chili sauce, ketchup, barbecue sauce, brown sugar, vinegar, Worcestershire sauce and dry mustard. Pour over meat.

4. Cover and cook on **Low** for 8 to 10 hours or on **High** for 4 to 5 hours, until meat is fork-tender.
5. With a slotted spoon, transfer meat chunks to a large bowl. Using two forks, shred meat.
6. Skim fat from sauce. Return shredded meat to slow cooker and add beans. Cover and cook on **Low** for 1 hour longer, or until heated through.

Make Ahead

This dish can be made a day ahead. In fact, letting it sit for 24 hours enhances the flavors. Cook meat, shred and cool completely before returning meat to slow cooker. Refrigerate overnight. The next day, add beans and cook on High for 1 to 2 hours, or until hot and bubbling.

Chunky Beef Chili

Serves 4 to 6

Instead of making chili with ground beef, try this chunky chili, which uses stewing beef. You can substitute kidney beans or black beans for the chickpeas.

Tip

A good chili depends on the quality of chili powder used. Most chili powders are a blend of ground chilies, cumin, oregano, garlic and salt. Don't confuse chili powder with cayenne pepper or dried crushed red chilies. These are much hotter.

Make Ahead

This dish can be completely assembled up to 24 hours before cooking (with the exception of beef). Chill browned beef separately before assembling dish. Refrigerate remaining ingredients overnight in slow cooker stoneware. The next day, place stoneware in slow cooker, add beef mixture and continue to cook as directed.

- Slow cooker size: 3½ to 6 quart

2 tbsp	vegetable oil (approx.)	25 mL
2 lbs	stewing beef, cut into ½-inch (1 cm) cubes	1 kg
2 tbsp	chili powder	25 mL
1 tsp	ground cumin	5 mL
1 tsp	dried oregano	5 mL
¾ tsp	salt	4 mL
2	onions, chopped	2
2	carrots, chopped	2
2	stalks celery, chopped	2
1	can (19 oz/540 mL) diced tomatoes, with juices	1
1	can (19 oz/540 mL) chickpeas, drained and rinsed, or 2 cups (500 mL) home-cooked chickpeas (page 146)	1
1 cup	beef stock	250 mL
½	can (5½ oz/156 mL) tomato paste	½
1	red bell pepper, chopped	1

1. In a large nonstick skillet, heat half the oil over medium-high heat. Cook beef in batches, adding more oil as needed, until browned all over. Return all beef to skillet.
2. Add chili powder, cumin, oregano and salt to skillet and cook for 1 minute longer. With a slotted spoon, transfer meat to slow cooker stoneware.
3. Add onions, carrots, celery, tomatoes (with juices), chickpeas, stock and tomato paste to slow cooker; stir to combine.
4. Cover and cook on **Low** for 8 to 10 hours or on **High** for 4 to 6 hours, until meat is tender.
5. Add red pepper; stir to combine. Cover and cook on **High** for 20 to 25 minutes longer.

Adobe Pork and Bean Chili

Serves 6 to 8

Here's a Southwest version of pork and beans. Everyone in the family will enjoy this dish, since half the fun is putting on all the toppings. Serve with bowls of sour cream, crushed tortilla chips and grated Cheddar cheese.

• • •

Tips

If you can't find Italian-style stewed tomatoes, use regular stewed tomatoes and add $\frac{1}{2}$ tsp (2 mL) dried Italian seasoning or a combination of dried basil, marjoram, oregano and thyme.

- Slow cooker size: 3$\frac{1}{2}$ to 6 quart

2 tbsp	vegetable oil (approx.)	25 mL
3 lbs	boneless pork shoulder butt roast, trimmed of excess fat, cut into 1-inch (2.5 cm) cubes	1.5 kg
1	onion, chopped	1
2	cloves garlic, minced	2
2 tbsp	chili powder	25 mL
$\frac{1}{2}$ tsp	cayenne pepper	2 mL
$\frac{1}{2}$ tsp	freshly ground black pepper	2 mL
1 cup	beef stock	250 mL
1	can (19 oz/540 mL) black beans, drained and rinsed, or 2 cups (500 mL) home-cooked beans (page 146)	1
1	can (19 oz/540 mL) Italian-style stewed tomatoes, with juices	1
1	can (7$\frac{1}{2}$ oz/213 mL) tomato sauce	1
1 cup	fresh or frozen corn kernels (thawed if frozen)	250 mL

1. In a large nonstick skillet, heat half the oil over medium-high heat. Cook pork in batches, adding more oil as needed, until browned all over. With a slotted spoon, transfer pork to slow cooker stoneware.
2. Add onion to skillet and cook, stirring, for 3 to 4 minutes, or until softened. Add garlic, chili powder, cayenne and black pepper to skillet and cook, stirring, for 1 minute. Add stock to skillet. Bring to a boil, stirring to scrape up all bits, and pour into slow cooker.
3. Add black beans, tomatoes and tomato sauce to slow cooker; stir to combine.
4. Cover and cook on **Low** for 8 to 10 hours or on **High** for 4 to 5 hours, until pork is tender.
5. Stir in corn; cover and cook on **High** for 20 to 25 minutes longer, or until corn is hot.

Party Pleas'n Chili

Serves 8 to 10

This dish goes down beautifully with a bottle of full-bodied red wine.

• • •

Tips

The best cut of beef to buy for this chili is an economical round steak or stewing beef. Don't use an expensive cut like flank steak; it will just fall apart from the long slow-cooking process.

Hot pepper flakes: This fiery flavor booster can be found in the spice section of the supermarket. Leave on the table for a great seasoning alternative to salt and pepper.

- Slow cooker size: 5 to 6 quart

1 tbsp	vegetable oil (approx.)	15 mL
1 lb	round steak, cut into 1-inch (2.5 cm) cubes	500 g
1 lb	hot Italian sausage, casings removed	500 g
2	large onions, finely chopped	2
1	can (28 oz/796 mL) diced tomatoes, with juices	1
1	can (19 oz/540 mL) red kidney beans, drained and rinsed, or 2 cups (500 mL) home-cooked beans (page 146)	1
1	can (19 oz/540 mL) black beans, drained and rinsed, or 2 cups (500 mL) home-cooked beans (page 146)	1
1	can (5½ oz/156 mL) tomato paste	1
½ cup	red wine	125 mL
4	cloves garlic, minced	4
2 tbsp	chili powder	25 mL
1 tbsp	dried oregano	15 mL
1 tbsp	Dijon mustard	15 mL
1 tsp	freshly ground black pepper	5 mL
½ tsp	hot pepper flakes (optional)	2 mL
½ tsp	salt	2 mL
1	red bell pepper, finely chopped	1
1	green bell pepper, finely chopped	1
	Chopped red onions	
	Shredded Monterey Jack cheese	
	Tortilla chips	

1. In a large nonstick skillet, heat oil over medium-high heat. Add steak cubes and cook until browned on all sides. With a slotted spoon, transfer to slow cooker stoneware, reserving juices.

2. Return pan with juices to heat. Cook sausage and onions, breaking up meat with a spoon and adding more oil if necessary, until meat is no longer pink inside. Drain and transfer to slow cooker.
3. Add tomatoes (with juices), kidney beans, black beans, tomato paste, red wine, garlic, chili powder, oregano, Dijon mustard, pepper, hot pepper flakes (if using) and salt to slow cooker; stir to combine.
4. Cover and cook on **Low** for 8 to 10 hours or on **High** for 4 to 6 hours, until hot and bubbling.
5. Add red pepper and green pepper; stir to combine. Cover and cook on **High** for 20 to 25 minutes longer.
6. Serve with chopped red onions, shredded Monterey Jack cheese and tortilla chips.

Make ahead

This dish can be completely assembled up to 24 hours before cooking (with the exception of steak cubes and sausage). Chill meat mixture separately before assembling dish. Refrigerate remaining ingredients overnight in slow cooker stoneware. The next day, place stoneware in slow cooker, add cooked meat mixture and continue to cook as directed.

Saucy Blonde Chili

Serves 4 to 6

Made with lean ground pork, chicken or turkey, this saucy dish is lighter in color than the average chili.

Variation

Make a second meal out of Molasses Baked Beans (see recipe, page 168) by using them in this recipe instead of canned beans. The results will be completely different, but taste great! If desired, serve over hot cooked rice or noodles.

Make Ahead

This chili can be assembled 12 hours in advance of cooking. Follow preparation directions and refrigerate overnight in slow cooker stoneware. The next day, place stoneware in slow cooker and continue cooking as directed.

- Slow cooker size: 3½ to 5 quart

1 tbsp	vegetable oil	15 mL
1½ lbs	lean ground pork, chicken or turkey	750 g
1	onion, finely chopped	1
2	cloves garlic, minced	2
1 tbsp	chili powder	15 mL
½ tsp	ground cumin	2 mL
2	cans (each 14 oz/398 mL) beans in tomato sauce	2
1 cup	chicken stock	250 mL
1	can (4½ oz/127 mL) chopped green chilies, with liquid	1
	Salt and freshly ground black pepper	

1. In a nonstick skillet, heat oil over medium-high heat. Cook pork, onion and garlic, breaking up pork with back of a spoon, until meat is no longer pink and onion is translucent. Add chili powder and cumin; cook for 1 minute longer. With a slotted spoon, transfer mixture to slow cooker stoneware.
2. Add beans, stock and chilies (with liquid) to slow cooker; stir to combine.
3. Cover and cook on **Low** for 6 to 8 hours or on **High** for 3 to 4 hours, until hot and bubbling. Season to taste with salt and pepper.

Zesty Orange Beef Stew (page 122)

Bistro Beef and Beer Stew (page 123)

Stratford's Sweet Chili (page 149)

Vegetable Chili with Sour Cream Topping (page 148)

Creamy Spinach Ricotta Noodles (page 183)

Vegetable Pastitsio (page 184)

Simple Salmon Pie with Creamy Dill Sauce (page 176)

Winter Chicken and Corn Chili

Serves 4 to 6

For convenience, roasted red peppers are available in jars or can be found fresh in the deli section of some supermarkets. To make your own, preheat broiler and cut red peppers in half, removing pith and seeds. Place cut side down on a baking sheet. Broil until all skin turns black. Place in paper bag and close up. Allow peppers to sweat for approximately 30 minutes. Peel off skins and chop as needed.

Make Ahead

Peppers can be broiled or grilled, peeled, then frozen for later use. They will keep up to 3 months in the freezer.

- Slow cooker size: 3½ to 5 quart

1 tbsp	vegetable oil	15 mL
2 lbs	ground chicken	1 kg
3 or 4	green onions, finely chopped	3 or 4
2 tsp	chili powder	10 mL
½ tsp	dried oregano	2 mL
Pinch	cayenne pepper	Pinch
2	roasted red bell peppers, diced	2
2 tbsp	pickled jalapeño peppers, finely chopped	25 mL
3	cloves garlic, minced	3
1	bay leaf	1
1	can (19 oz/540 mL) navy beans or white kidney beans, drained and rinsed, or 2 cups (500 mL) home-cooked beans (page 146)	1
1½ cups	frozen corn kernels	375 mL
1½ cups	chicken stock	375 mL
½ cup	chopped fresh cilantro	125 mL
2 tbsp	freshly squeezed lime juice	25 mL
1 tbsp	granulated sugar	15 mL
½ tsp	salt	2 mL
	Sour cream	

1. In a nonstick skillet, heat oil over medium-high heat. Cook chicken and green onions, breaking up meat with back of a spoon, until chicken is no longer pink. Add chili powder, oregano and cayenne; cook for 1 minute longer. With a slotted spoon, transfer mixture to slow cooker stoneware.
2. Add roasted peppers, jalapeño peppers, garlic, bay leaf, beans, corn and stock to slow cooker; stir to combine.
3. Cover and cook on **Low** for 6 to 8 hours or on **High** for 3 to 4 hours. Discard bay leaf.
4. Stir in cilantro, lime juice, sugar and salt. Cover and cook on **High** for 10 minutes longer.
5. Ladle into bowls and garnish with a dollop of sour cream.

Shredded White Chicken Chili

Serves 6 to 8

This creamy, stew-like chili is different from the typical red tomato-based versions. Nevertheless, the flavors are bold, making it a delicious alternative. Serve it with steamed rice (see box, opposite) or bread.

• • •

Tips

To save time, you can use lean ground chicken in place of the chicken thighs. Reduce the oil to 1 tbsp (15 mL), brown the meat in the oil with the spices, then add to the slow cooker along with the stock, beans and chilies. You will not have to shred the meat.

Chopped garlic in the jar is a convenient alternative to fresh garlic. It's easy to use and will keep in the refrigerator for up to 6 months.

- Slow cooker size: 3½ to 6 quart

3 tbsp	vegetable oil, divided	45 mL
2 lbs	boneless skinless chicken thighs	1 kg
1	onion, finely chopped	1
2	cloves garlic, minced	2
1 tsp	ground cumin	5 mL
1 tsp	dried oregano	5 mL
½ tsp	freshly ground black pepper	2 mL
¼ tsp	cayenne pepper	1 mL
1	can (10 oz/284 mL) condensed chicken broth, undiluted	1
2	cans (each 19 oz/540 mL) white kidney beans, drained and rinsed, 4 cups (1 L) home-cooked beans (page 146)	2
2	cans (each 4½ oz/127 mL) chopped mild green chilies, including liquid	2
1 tsp	salt	5 mL
1 cup	sour cream	250 mL
½ cup	whipping (35%) cream	125 mL
1 cup	shredded Monterey Jack cheese	250 mL

1. In a large nonstick skillet, heat 2 tbsp (25 mL) oil over medium-high heat. Add chicken and cook for 5 to 7 minutes per side, or until browned. Place chicken in slow cooker stoneware.
2. Add remaining oil to skillet and heat. Add onion, garlic, cumin, oregano, black pepper and cayenne. Cook, stirring, for 3 minutes, or until onion is softened. Transfer to slow cooker.

3. Pour chicken broth into skillet and bring to a boil, scraping up any browned bits. Pour over chicken and seasonings in slow cooker.
4. Cover and cook on **Low** for 5 to 7 hours or on **High** for 3 to 4 hours, until hot and bubbling and chicken is no longer pink inside.
5. Remove chicken from slow cooker and shred with a fork. Return shredded chicken to slow cooker. Stir in beans, chilies, salt, sour cream and whipping cream. Cover and cook on **High** for 15 to 20 minutes longer, or until heated through.
7. Spoon into serving bowls and sprinkle with shredded cheese.

Tip

Mild green chilies are found in the Mexican foods section of the supermarket. They are sold whole or chopped.

Steamed Rice

This no-fail method works with many types of rice, including basmati or any white or brown rice.

In a saucepan with a tight-fitting lid, bring 2½ cups (625 mL) water and ¼ tsp (1 mL) salt to a boil over medium-high heat. Stir in 1¼ cups (300 mL) rice. Cover and reduce heat to low. Simmer white rice for 20 minutes and brown rice for 45 minutes, or until rice is tender and liquid has been absorbed. Fluff with a fork.

Leftover rice will keep in the refrigerator for 2 days or in the freezer for 1 month. *Serves 4.*

Chicken and Black Bean Chili in Tortilla Bowls

Serves 6

This chili cooks in less time than other meat chilies because it uses lean chicken breast. You can substitute cooked ground chicken if you prefer. Since canned beans and salsa tend to be salty, you may not need additional salt.

• • •

Tips

You can vary the spiciness of this chili by the selection of salsa. Hot salsa gives a burst of heat while mild salsa will appeal to those with timid taste buds.

Soft flour tortilla shells come in a variety of flavors and colors. Don't be afraid to experiment!

- Slow cooker size: 3½ to 6 quart

Chili

1 tbsp	vegetable oil	15 mL
2 lbs	boneless skinless chicken breast, cut into ½-inch (1 cm) cubes	1 kg
1	onion, finely chopped	1
2	cloves garlic, minced	2
1	can (19 oz/540 mL) diced tomatoes, with juices	1
1	can (12 oz/341 mL) corn kernels or 1½ cups (375 mL) frozen corn	1
1	can (19 oz/540 mL) black beans, drained and rinsed, or 2 cups (500 mL) home-cooked beans (page 146)	1
2 cups	mild or hot salsa	500 mL
1 tbsp	chili powder	15 L
½ tsp	salt	2 mL

Tortilla Bowls

6	large flour tortilla shells	6
	Lettuce leaves, washed	
1	tomato, diced	1
2	jalapeño peppers, chopped	2

1. *Chili:* In a large nonstick skillet, heat oil over medium heat. Add chicken and cook, stirring frequently, until chicken is no longer pink. With a slotted spoon, transfer to slow cooker stoneware.

2. Add onion, garlic, tomatoes (with juices), corn, black beans, salsa, chili powder and salt to slow cooker; stir to combine.
3. Cover and cook on **Low** for 4 to 6 hours or on **High** for 2 to 3 hours, until hot and bubbling.
4. *Tortilla bowls:* Mold a piece of foil around the inside of a 6-cup (1.5 L) mixing bowl. Gently press one tortilla into foil bowl. Remove foil and tortilla together and place on a large baking sheet. (Tortilla will have folds.) Repeat with more foil and tortillas to make 2 more tortilla bowls. Bake in a 350°F (180°C) oven for 15 to 20 minutes, or until tortillas are crisp and golden. Place tortillas on a wire rack to cool. Repeat bowl-making procedure, using same foil, to make another 3 tortilla bowls, for a total of 6 bowls.
5. To assemble, place one tortilla bowl on each plate. Line each bowl with lettuce leaves. Spoon in chili and garnish with tomato and jalapeño peppers.

Make ahead

This dish can be completely assembled up to 24 hours before cooking (with the exception of chicken). Chill cooked chicken separately before assembling dish. Refrigerate remaining ingredients overnight in slow cooker stoneware. The next day, place stoneware in slow cooker, add cooked chicken and continue to cook as directed.

Spicy Turkey Chili

Serves 4 to 6

My children love chili served with tortilla chips. Look for yellow or blue ones — either way, everyone will enjoy scooping and eating.

Tip

Ground turkey is a tasty low-fat alternative to ground beef. It has a very mild flavor, so it needs a lot of additional seasoning. Adjust the quantity of hot pepper flakes to suit your taste.

Variation

For a vegetarian version, omit the turkey and add 1 can (19 oz/540 mL) red kidney beans in addition to the navy beans.

Make Ahead

This chili can be assembled 12 hours in advance of cooking. Follow preparation directions and refrigerate overnight in slow cooker stoneware. The next day, place stoneware in slow cooker and continue cooking as directed.

- Slow cooker size: 3½ to 6 quart

1 tbsp	vegetable oil	15 mL
2 lbs	ground turkey	1 kg
1	onion, finely chopped	1
1 tsp	hot pepper flakes	5 mL
1 tsp	ground coriander	5 mL
1 tsp	ground cumin	5 mL
½ tsp	salt	2 mL
¼ tsp	freshly ground black pepper	1 mL
2	cans (19 oz/540 mL) navy or white pea beans, drained and rinsed, or 2 cups (500 mL) home-cooked beans (page 146)	2
2 cups	chicken stock	500 mL
1	can (12 oz/341 mL) corn kernels or 1½ cups (375 mL) frozen corn	1
1	can (4½ oz/127 mL) chopped mild green chilies, drained	1
1 cup	chopped fresh cilantro	250 mL

1. In a nonstick skillet, heat oil over medium heat. Cook ground turkey, onion, hot pepper flakes, coriander and cumin, breaking up meat with back of a spoon, until no longer pink. With a slotted spoon, transfer seasoned turkey to slow cooker.
2. Add salt, pepper, 1 can of beans, stock, corn and chilies to slow cooker.
3. In a bowl, with a potato masher, or in a food processor, mash or purée remaining can of beans. Add to slow cooker and stir to combine.
4. Cover and cook on **Low** for 6 to 10 hours or on **High** for 3 to 4 hours, until hot and bubbling.
5. Add cilantro; cover and cook on **High** for 15 to 20 minutes longer.

Best-Ever Baked Beans

Serves 12 to 15

I like to take this dish to our annual skating party and sleigh ride. When there are a lot of people, it's the perfect pot to pack.

• • •

Tip

Serve these beans with garlic bread and a green salad.

Make Ahead

This dish can be assembled in the slow cooker the day before. Refrigerate until ready to cook.

• Slow cooker size: 3½ to 5 quart

8 oz	bacon	250 g
1 lb	lean ground beef	500 g
2	onions, sliced and separated into rings	2
4 cups	Molasses Baked Beans (see recipe, page 168) or 2 cans (each 14 oz/398 mL) beans in tomato sauce	1 L
1	can (19 oz/540 mL) red kidney beans, drained and rinsed, or 2 cups (500 mL) home-cooked beans (page 146)	1
1	can (19 oz/540 mL) chickpeas, drained and rinsed, or 2 cups (500 mL) home-cooked chickpeas (page 146)	1
2 cups	ketchup	500 mL
¼ cup	granulated sugar	50 mL
¼ cup	packed brown sugar	50 mL
3 tbsp	white vinegar	45 mL
1 tbsp	Dijon mustard	15 mL

1. In a large nonstick skillet, over medium-high heat, cook bacon for 5 minutes, or until slightly cooked but not crisp. Remove from skillet and place on paper towel–lined plate. Let cool and coarsely chop. Drain excess fat from skillet.
2. Add ground beef and onions to skillet; cook, breaking up meat with back of a spoon, until meat is no longer pink and onions are translucent. With a slotted spoon, transfer meat mixture to slow cooker stoneware.
3. Add baked beans, kidney beans, chickpeas, ketchup, granulated sugar, brown sugar, vinegar, mustard and bacon; stir to combine.
4. Cover and cook on **Low** for 7 to 9 hours or on **High** for 3 to 4 hours, until hot and bubbling.

Molasses Baked Beans

Serves 4 to 6

Nothing is as heartwarming as a pot of these comfy baked beans. The marriage of ketchup, molasses and sugar is what makes them so flavorful. Not only are they extremely tasty, they are also very nutritious and a good source of protein and fiber.

• • •

Tip

White pea beans, also known as navy beans or *alubias chicas*, are the type of cooked bean you will find in "pork and beans" or, as will be called for in many recipes, "beans in tomato sauce." The term "navy bean" was adopted during the Second World War, when this dish was regularly fed to the troops. It is important to soak the beans first to replace the water lost in drying.

• • •

Variation

Salsa Beans: Substitute bottled salsa for ketchup and add 1 tsp (5 mL) ground cumin and 1 tsp (5 mL) dried oregano. Increase black pepper to 1 tsp (5 mL).

- **Slow cooker size: 3½ to 6 quart**

4 cups	water	1 L
1 lb	dry white pea or navy beans	500 g
6 cups	cold water	1.5 L
1	onion, chopped	1
1	can (5½ oz/156 mL) tomato paste	1
¾ cup	ketchup	175 mL
¾ cup	molasses	175 mL
2	cloves garlic, minced	2
⅓ cup	packed brown sugar	75 mL
2 tsp	dry mustard	10 mL
½ tsp	salt	2 mL
¼ tsp	freshly ground black pepper	1 mL

1. In a large pot, over medium-high heat, bring water to a boil. Add beans and simmer for 10 minutes. Drain and rinse.
2. Transfer beans to slow cooker stoneware and add about 6 cups (1.5 L) cold water, or enough to completely cover beans. Cover and cook on **Low** for 10 to 12 hours, or until fork-tender. Drain, reserving 2 cups (500 mL) cooking liquid.
3. In a bowl, combine onion, tomato paste, ketchup, molasses, garlic, brown sugar, mustard, salt and pepper; stir to mix well. Add to slow cooker with beans and reserved liquid.
4. Cover and cook on **Low** for 4 to 6 hours or on **High** for 2 to 3 hours, until hot and bubbling.

Cowpoke Baked Beans

Serves 8 to 10

Cowpokes (just another word for cowboys) called dried beans prairie strawberries, because the varieties they used tended to be reddish-brown in color (i.e., red kidney and pinto). These beans make a great vegetarian main course, but you can also add chopped cooked bacon, or serve them alongside ribs (pages 291, 292, 293 and 294) and coleslaw (page 115).

Make Ahead

This dish can be completely assembled up to 24 hours before cooking. Refrigerate overnight in the slow cooker stoneware. The next day, place stoneware in slow cooker and continue to cook as directed.

- Slow cooker size: 3½ to 6 quart

2 tbsp	vegetable oil	25 mL
2	onions, chopped	2
4	stalks celery, finely chopped	4
3	cloves garlic, minced	3
2	cans (each 19 oz/540 mL) pinto or Romano beans, drained and rinsed, or 4 cups (1 L) home-cooked beans (page 146)	2
1	can (19 oz/540 mL) red kidney beans, drained and rinsed, or 2 cups (500 mL) home-cooked beans (page 146)	1
1½ cups	salsa	375 mL
1 cup	barbecue sauce	250 mL
½ cup	fancy molasses	125 mL
¼ cup	Dijon mustard	50 mL
1	bottle (12 oz/341 mL) beer	1
¼ cup	chopped fresh parsley	50 mL
	Salt and freshly ground black pepper	

1. In a large nonstick skillet, heat oil over medium-high heat. Cook onions, celery and garlic, stirring occasionally, for 3 minutes, or until vegetables are softened. With a slotted spoon, transfer onion mixture to slow cooker stoneware.
2. Add pinto and kidney beans, salsa, barbecue sauce, molasses, mustard, beer and parsley to slow cooker; stir to combine.
3. Cover and cook on **Low** for 6 to 10 hours or on **High** for 3 to 4 hours, until hot and bubbling. Season with salt and pepper.

Cuban-Style Black Beans

Serves 6 to 8

Black beans (turtle beans) are a Cuban staple. Top this chili with shredded Monterey Jack cheese, chopped tomato and, for an extra kick, a dollop of chipotle-flavored sour cream (combine 1 cup/250 mL sour cream and 1 tsp/5 mL minced chipotles in adobo sauce).

Make Ahead
This dish can be assembled up to 24 hours before cooking. Refrigerate overnight in slow cooker stoneware. The next day, place stoneware in slow cooker and continue to cook as directed.

- Slow cooker size: 3½ to 6 quart

1	large onion, finely chopped	1
4	cloves garlic, minced	4
3	cans (each 19 oz/540 mL) black beans, drained and rinsed, or 6 cups (1.5 L) home-cooked beans (page 146)	3
1 cup	vegetable stock	250 mL
2 tbsp	granulated sugar	25 mL
2 tbsp	freshly squeezed lime juice	25 mL
¼ tsp	salt	1 mL
¼ tsp	freshly ground black pepper	1 mL
¼ tsp	dried oregano	1 mL
1	bay leaf	1
1	red bell pepper, finely chopped	1
2 tbsp	finely chopped cilantro	25 mL

1. In slow cooker stoneware, combine onion, garlic, beans, stock, sugar, lime juice, salt, pepper, oregano and bay leaf.
2. Cover and cook on **Low** for 6 to 10 hours or on **High** for 3 to 4 hours, until hot and bubbling.
3. Discard bay leaf. Transfer 1 cup (250 mL) hot bean mixture to a bowl and mash slightly with a potato masher. Return to slow cooker.
4. Stir in red pepper and cilantro. Cover and cook on **High** for 15 to 20 minutes longer, or until heated through.

Chipotle Peppers

Chipotle peppers are smoked jalapeños, and are considerably hotter than fresh or canned jalapeños. They are available dried or canned in adobo sauce. Freeze any leftover chipotles in the sauce in ice cube trays and then transfer the small portions to a plastic freezer bag.

Farmer-Style Cannellini Beans

Serves 4 to 6

This simple combination of white kidney beans (cannellini) seasoned tomatoes and vegetables makes a perfect meatless main course. It also makes a wonderful accompaniment to poultry or meat, and is terrific served cold as a salad. For a non-vegetarian version, garnish with crumbled cooked bacon.

• • •

Tip

Kale is a dark green, leafy vegetable that is a great source of fiber and many essential nutrients. Remove the stems and any tough veins from the leaves before using.

Make Ahead

This dish can be assembled up to 24 hours before cooking. Refrigerate overnight in slow cooker stoneware. The next day, place stoneware in slow cooker and continue to cook as directed.

- Slow cooker size: 3½ to 6 quart

1	can (19 oz/540 mL) white kidney beans, drained and rinsed, or 2 cups (500 mL) home-cooked beans (page 146)	1
1	can (19 oz/540 mL) stewed tomatoes, with juices	1
½ cup	vegetable stock	125 mL
1	stalk celery, finely chopped	1
1	onion, finely chopped	1
2	cloves garlic, minced	2
2	bay leaves	2
2 tbsp	olive oil	25 mL
½ tsp	dried sage	2 mL
½ tsp	dried rosemary, crumbled	2 mL
2 tbsp	dry red wine	25 mL
1 cup	chopped kale	250 mL

1. In slow cooker stoneware, combine beans, tomatoes, stock, celery, onion, garlic, bay leaves, olive oil, sage and rosemary.
2. Cover and cook on **Low** for 6 to 10 hours or on **High** for 3 to 4 hours, until hot and bubbling.
3. Stir in wine and kale. Cover and let stand for 5 minutes to wilt kale leaves. Discard bay leaves.

Seafood and Vegetarian Main Courses

Perfectly Poached Salmon

Serves 4 to 6

On one of my girls-only outings, I attended a cooking class luncheon. Our instructor, Roger (pronounced the French way), served us a lovely moist poached salmon, and I have adapted the dish to the slow cooker. Serve the salmon hot or cold as part of a buffet, and garnish with slices of lemon and sprigs of parsley and dill.

- Slow cooker size: 5 to 6 quart

Poaching Liquid

6 cups	water	1.5 L
1 cup	dry white wine	250 mL
2	stalks celery, sliced	2
2	sprigs parsley	2
1	onion, peeled and cut into wedges	1
1	carrot, peeled and sliced	1
1 tsp	dried thyme	5 mL
½ tsp	salt	2 mL
½ tsp	whole black peppercorns	2 mL
1	bay leaf	1

Salmon

1	salmon fillet (about 3 to 4 lbs/1.5 to 2 kg)	1

Cucumber Dill Sauce

1 cup	mayonnaise	250 mL
1 cup	sour cream	250 mL
½ cup	finely chopped cucumber	125 mL
1 tsp	chopped fresh dill	5 mL
½ tsp	salt	2 mL
¼ tsp	freshly ground black pepper	1 mL

1. *Poaching liquid:* In a saucepan, combine water, wine, celery, parsley, onion, carrot, thyme, salt, peppercorns and bay leaf. Bring to a boil, reduce heat and simmer for 30 minutes. Strain through a sieve and discard solids. Reserve liquid.

2. *Salmon:* Preheat slow cooker on **High** for 15 minutes. Line slow cooker stoneware with a double thickness of cheesecloth or fold a 2-foot (60 cm) piece of foil in half lengthwise and lay on bottom of slow cooker. Place salmon on top of cheesecloth or foil and pour hot poaching liquid over salmon. Cover and cook on **High** for 1 hour.
3. With oven mitts, remove stoneware from slow cooker and let salmon cool in poaching liquid for 20 minutes. (If serving cold, stoneware can be stored in refrigerator to allow salmon to chill in liquid.)
4. Lift salmon out of stoneware using cheesecloth or foil handles and gently place on a platter.
5. *Cucumber dill sauce:* In a bowl, combine mayonnaise, sour cream, cucumber, dill, salt and pepper; mix well. Serve salmon with sauce.

Make Ahead

Poaching liquid can be made up to 24 hours in advance. Refrigerate until ready to use and reheat on the stove before placing in slow cooker.

Simple Salmon Pie with Creamy Dill Sauce

Serves 4 to 6

My mother, Evelyn Pye, spent countless hours with my sisters and me at the dance studio. When we got home, one of her specialties (and one of our favorites) was salmon loaf. This slow-cooker version is easy to make and can quickly be put together. And of course, you must serve it with steaming green peas — the only way, according to Ev!

• • •

Tips

For an economical pie, use 1 can (7½ oz/213 g) sockeye salmon and 1 can (7½ oz/213 g) of the less expensive pink salmon.

For a larger pie, double all ingredients, using 4 cans salmon.

This pie makes a wonderful complete meal when served with boiled new potatoes and green peas.

- Slow cooker size: 3½ to 6 quart

2	cans (each 7½ oz/213 g) red sockeye salmon, drained, skin removed	2
¼ cup	finely crushed saltine crackers	50 mL
1	small onion, finely chopped	1
1	egg, lightly beaten	1
2 tbsp	milk or light (5%) cream	25 mL
1 tbsp	freshly squeezed lemon juice	15 mL
1 tbsp	chopped fresh parsley (or 1 tsp/5 mL dried)	15 mL
1 tbsp	chopped fresh dill (or 1 tsp/5 mL dried)	15 mL
½ tsp	freshly ground black pepper	2 mL

Creamy Dill Sauce

1 tbsp	butter or margarine	15 mL
1 tbsp	all-purpose flour	15 mL
½ tsp	salt	2 mL
¼ tsp	freshly ground black pepper	1 mL
1 cup	milk	250 mL
2 tbsp	chopped fresh dill (or 2 tsp/10 mL dried)	25 mL

1. Cut a 2-foot (60 cm) length of foil in half lengthwise. Fold each strip in half lengthwise, forming two long strips. Crisscross the strips in the bottom of the slow cooker, bringing the ends of the foil strips up and clear of the stoneware rim.

2. In a bowl, combine salmon, crackers, onion, egg, milk, lemon juice, parsley, dill and pepper. Using a fork or wooden spoon, gently mix until evenly combined. Press evenly into foil-lined slow cooker stoneware, tucking foil ends under lid. (For a large oval-style slow cooker, salmon mixture can be shaped into a loaf and set on foil handles.)
3. Cover and cook on **Low** for 4 to 6 hours or on **High** for 2 to 2½ hours. Turn off heat and let stand for 5 minutes. Remove lid, gently run a knife around outside edge of pie and grasp ends of foil strips to lift out pie. Set on plate and place lifter between loaf and foil; lift loaf from foil, remove foil and set loaf on serving plate.
4. *Creamy dill sauce:* In a saucepan, melt butter over medium heat. Add flour, salt and pepper; cook, stirring, for 1 minute. Gradually whisk in milk; cook, stirring constantly, for 5 minutes, or until boiling and thickened. Stir in dill. Serve over salmon.

Make Ahead

This dish can be completely assembled up to 12 hours in advance of cooking. Follow preparation directions and refrigerate overnight in the slow cooker stoneware. The next day, place stoneware in slow cooker and continue cooking as directed.

Cheesy Salmon Chowder

Serves 4 to 6

My family are big fish eaters, and salmon is their favorite. This hearty chowder is one they ask for again and again. It can be made using fresh, canned or smoked salmon. If you are using canned salmon, be sure to remove the dark skin and large bones first.

• • •

Tip

You can replace the evaporated milk with 1½ cups (375 mL) cream if you wish.

- **Slow cooker size: 3½ to 6 quart**

1	large onion, chopped	1
3	potatoes, peeled and cut into ½-inch (1 cm) cubes	3
1	large carrot, peeled and finely chopped	1
1	stalk celery, finely chopped	1
1	clove garlic, minced	1
¼ cup	long-grain parboiled (converted) white rice	50 mL
3 cups	chicken or vegetable stock	750 mL
¾ tsp	salt	4 mL
½ tsp	dried thyme	2 mL
¼ tsp	freshly ground black pepper	1 mL
1 cup	flaked cooked salmon	250 mL
1	can (13 oz/385 mL) evaporated milk	1
1 cup	shredded Cheddar cheese	250 mL

1. In slow cooker stoneware, combine onion, potatoes, carrot, celery, garlic, rice, stock, salt, thyme and pepper.
2. Cover and cook on **Low** for 8 to 10 hours, or until vegetables and rice are tender.
3. Stir in salmon, milk and cheese. Cover and cook on **High** for 15 minutes longer, or until salmon is heated through.

Tuscan Pepper and Bean Soup

Serves 4 to 6

This tasty vegetarian soup is filling and flavorful, and it is even better reheated the next day. Serve it with bruschetta and fresh fruit.

• • •

Tip

Leeks must be cleaned carefully, since they contain a lot of sand. Remove most of the green part and cut the white part into halves lengthwise. Rinse thoroughly under cold running water and drain in a colander.

- Slow cooker size: 3½ to 6 quart

1	leek (white and light green part only), well rinsed and sliced	1
1	potato, peeled and diced	1
2	cloves garlic, minced	2
4	roasted red peppers (see box, page 310), finely chopped	4
4 cups	vegetable or chicken stock	1 L
¼ tsp	dried thyme	1 mL
¼ tsp	dried rosemary	1 mL
½ tsp	salt	2 mL
¼ tsp	freshly ground black pepper	1 mL
1	can (19 oz/540 mL) white kidney beans, drained and rinsed, or 2 cups (500 mL) home-cooked beans (page 146)	1
1 cup	cooked bow tie, rotini or other small pasta (optional)	250 mL

1. In slow cooker stoneware, combine leek, potato, garlic, red peppers, stock, thyme, rosemary, salt, pepper and beans.
2. Cover and cook on **Low** for 6 to 10 hours or on **High** for 3 to 4 hours, until hot and bubbling.
3. Add cooked pasta, if using. Cover and cook on **High** for 15 to 20 minutes longer, or until heated through.

Spicy Vegetable-Lentil Soup

Serves 4 to 6

Don't worry about any overwhelming spiciness here. This surprisingly sweet tasting soup will warm you to your toes.

Tips

Red lentils are available in cans, but the dried variety cook up so fast that they're the better (and cheaper) choice. It is important to pick over lentils to remove any sticks or broken pieces, then rinse and drain before using. If the holes in your strainer are too large, line it with a paper towel before rinsing.

Make Ahead

This soup can be assembled 12 to 24 hours in advance. Follow preparation directions and refrigerate overnight in slow cooker stoneware. The next day, place stoneware in slow cooker and cook as directed.

- **Slow cooker size: 3½ to 6 quart**

4	carrots, diced	4
2	stalks celery, diced	2
1	large onion, diced	1
1	Granny Smith apple, peeled and diced	1
1 tbsp	grated gingerroot	15 mL
1	large clove garlic, minced	1
1 tbsp	curry powder	15 mL
¾ tsp	ground cumin or cumin seeds	4 mL
4 cups	vegetable or chicken stock	1 L
½ cup	dried red lentils, rinsed (see tip, at left)	125 mL
	Plain low-fat yogurt	
	Toasted whole wheat pitas	

1. In slow cooker stoneware, combine carrots, celery, onion, apple, ginger, garlic, curry, cumin, stock and lentils; stir to mix well.
2. Cover and cook on **Low** for 8 to 10 hours or on **High** for 4 to 6 hours, until thick and bubbling.
3. Transfer mixture in batches to a blender or food processor and process until smooth. Return to slow cooker and process to keep warm.
4. Ladle soup into individual bowls and top each with a dollop of yogurt. Serve with whole wheat pitas.

Pizza Fondue

Serves 4 to 6

This is a wonderful appetizer dip, but it also makes a great weekend family meal, as well as a perfect potluck dish. Prepare all the ingredients in the slow cooker and cook as directed in Step 1. Unplug the slow cooker and wrap in a towel or newspapers to insulate, then place in a container that will stay flat in the car. Attach rubber bands around the handles and lid to secure while traveling. Once you arrive, plug in slow cooker and set on Low to stay warm.

• • •

Tip

You can also serve this with breadsticks, pretzels and veggies such as cauliflower and broccoli.

- **Slow cooker size: 3½ to 6 quart**

1	processed cheese loaf (about 1 lb/ 500 g), cut into ½-inch (1 cm) cubes	1
2 cups	shredded mozzarella cheese	500 mL
1	can (19 oz/540 mL) Italian-style stewed tomatoes, with juices (see box, page 97)	1
1	loaf Italian bread, cut into 1-inch (2.5 cm) cubes	1

1. Place cheese cubes, mozzarella and tomatoes in lightly greased slow cooker stoneware. Cover and cook on **High** for 45 to 60 minutes, or until cheeses melt.
2. Stir to combine and scrape down sides of slow cooker with a rubber spatula to prevent scorching. Reduce heat to **Low**. (Fondue will stay warm for up to 4 hours.)
3. Serve with bread cubes for dipping.

Fia's Favorite Pasta Sauce

Makes about 12 cups (3 L)

My friend Fia grew up in an Italian household in Toronto. She has fond schoolday memories of coming home, where a pot of pasta sauce was always simmering on the stove. She passed her secret sauce along to me and I've adapted it for the slow cooker. Now my children always ask for Fiasauce.

• • •

Tip

Freeze sauce in 2-cup (500 mL) batches and thaw for quick use in other recipes. Try it with Vegetable Pastitsio (see recipe, page 184), Cheesy Tortellini Bake (see recipe, page 187) or Spicy White Bean and Sausage Ragoût (see recipe, page 133).

Make Ahead

This sauce can be completely assembled 12 to 24 hours in advance. Place all ingredients in slow cooker stoneware and refrigerate overnight. The next day, place stoneware in slow cooker and cook as directed.

- Slow cooker size: 3½ to 6 quart

4	cans (each 28 oz/796 mL) Italian-style stewed tomatoes, coarsely chopped, with juices (see box, page 97)	4
1 cup	red wine	250 mL
½ cup	olive oil	125 mL
¼ cup	freshly chopped parsley (or 2 tbsp/25 mL dried)	50 mL
4	cloves garlic, minced	4
2 tsp	salt	10 mL
1 tsp	hot pepper flakes	5 mL
1 tsp	dried oregano	5 mL
8	fresh basil leaves (or 1 tsp/5 mL dried)	8
1 tsp	freshly ground black pepper	5 mL
	Hot cooked pasta	
	Freshly grated Parmesan cheese	

1. In slow cooker stoneware, combine tomatoes (with juices), wine, olive oil, parsley, garlic, salt, hot pepper flakes, oregano, basil and pepper.
2. Cover and cook on **Low** for 8 to 10 hours or on **High** for 4 to 6 hours, until sauce is hot and bubbling.
3. Serve over hot cooked pasta and sprinkle with Parmesan cheese.

Creamy Spinach Ricotta Noodles

Serves 6 to 8

Serve up comfort food to your family with this quick-to-assemble meatless dish.

• • •

Tip

In Italian, ricotta means "recooked," a reference to it being made with leftover whey from milk previously heated for mozzarella and provolone cheese. Ricotta is a fresh white cheese used in both savory and sweet dishes.

• **Slow cooker size: 3½ to 6 quart**

2 cups	dried fusilli or other medium pasta	500 mL
2 tbsp	butter	25 mL
1	onion, finely chopped	1
⅓ cup	all-purpose flour	75 mL
2½ cups	milk	625 mL
2 tsp	Dijon mustard	10 mL
1 tsp	salt	5 mL
½ tsp	freshly ground black pepper	2 mL
2 cups	ricotta cheese	500 mL
½ cup	shredded Asiago or Parmesan cheese	125 mL
1	package (10 oz/300 g) frozen chopped spinach, thawed and squeezed dry	1
2	roasted red peppers (see box, page 310), chopped	2
2 tbsp	dry bread crumbs (see box, page 197)	25 mL
2 tbsp	freshly grated Parmesan cheese	25 mL

1. In a large pot of boiling salted water, cook pasta according to package directions. Drain and set aside.
2. In a large saucepan, melt butter over medium heat. Add onion and cook for 5 minutes, stirring occasionally, until softened. Add flour and cook, stirring, for 1 minute. Whisk in milk and cook, stirring constantly, for 8 to 10 minutes, or until thickened. Stir in mustard, salt and pepper. Stir in cooked noodles, ricotta, Asiago, spinach and red peppers.
3. Transfer mixture to lightly greased slow cooker stoneware and sprinkle with bread crumbs and Parmesan.
4. Cover and cook on **Low** for 6 to 8 hours or on **High** for 3 to 4 hours, until hot and bubbly.

Vegetable Pastitsio

Serves 6 to 8

A savory vegetable mixture is layered over spinach and creamy pasta in this delicious variation of lasagna.

• • •

Tips

Evaporated milk holds up extremely well in slow cookers and will not curdle. Don't confuse this milk with the sweetened condensed milk used in desserts and candies.

You can use 1 cup (250 mL) Fia's Favorite Pasta Sauce (see recipe, page 182) in place of canned tomato sauce.

To grease slow cooker stoneware, use a vegetable nonstick spray. Or use cake pan grease, which is available in specialty cake-decorating or bulk-food stores.

- Slow cooker size: 5 to 6 quart

Pasta Custard Layer

3 cups	dried penne or any small pasta	750 mL
1/4 cup	butter or margarine	50 mL
1/4 cup	all-purpose flour	50 mL
1	can (13 oz/385 mL) evaporated milk	1
1/2 tsp	ground nutmeg	2 mL
1/2 tsp	salt	2 mL
1/4 tsp	freshly ground black pepper	1 mL
2	eggs, lightly beaten	2
1 cup	small-curd cottage cheese	250 mL
1 cup	shredded mozzarella cheese	250 mL

Vegetable Layer

1 tbsp	vegetable oil	15 mL
1	onion, finely chopped	1
2	cloves garlic, minced	2
1	small zucchini, finely chopped (about 1 cup/250 mL)	1
1	carrot, peeled and grated	1
1 cup	frozen corn kernels	250 mL
1	can (7 1/2 oz/213 mL) tomato sauce	1
1/2 tsp	dried oregano	2 mL
1/4 tsp	ground cinnamon	1 mL
1/4 tsp	freshly ground black pepper	1 mL
1	package (10 oz/300 g) frozen chopped spinach, thawed	1
1/4 cup	freshly grated Parmesan cheese	50 mL

1. *Pasta custard layer:* In a pot of boiling salted water, cook pasta according to package directions. Drain and rinse well with cold water. Set aside.

2. In a heavy saucepan, heat butter over medium heat. Add flour and cook, stirring constantly to prevent browning, for 2 minutes. Gradually add milk, whisking constantly, until smooth. Cook for 5 minutes, or until thickened. Stir in nutmeg, salt and pepper.
3. In a large bowl, combine eggs with about ½ cup (125 mL) sauce, mixing well. Add remaining sauce, cottage cheese, mozzarella cheese and reserved pasta. Set aside.
4. *Vegetable layer:* In a large skillet, heat oil over medium heat. Add onion, garlic, zucchini and carrot; cook for 5 minutes, or until vegetables are softened. Add corn, tomato sauce, oregano, cinnamon and pepper. Bring to a boil, reduce heat and simmer for 5 minutes.
5. Spoon pasta mixture into lightly greased slow cooker stoneware. Spread spinach over pasta and spoon vegetable mixture over spinach. Sprinkle with Parmesan cheese.
6. Cover and cook on **Low** for 6 to 9 hours or on **High** for 3 to 4 hours, until mixture is bubbling. Let stand for 10 minutes before serving.

Make Ahead

This dish takes quite a bit of preparation time, but fortunately it can be completely assembled up to 24 hours in advance. Follow preparation directions and refrigerate overnight in the slow cooker stoneware. The next day, place stoneware in slow cooker and continue cooking as directed. It's perfect for a buffet supper or potluck reunion.

Slow-Cooked Macaroni and Cheese

Serves 8 to 10

Everyone likes good old mac 'n' cheese. While there are many versions, this is one of my quick-and-easy favorites for the slow cooker. The recipe is made even easier with the use of condensed Cheddar cheese soup, which holds up well during the long slow-cooking process.

• • •

Tip

Use a rolling pin, blender or food processor to crush the melba toast crackers. They will give the casserole a tasty crunch.

• • •

Variation

Add 1 cup (250 mL) chopped cooked ham and 1 chopped roasted red pepper (see box, page 310) to macaroni with egg mixture.

- Slow cooker size: 5 to 6 quart

3 cups	dried elbow macaroni or other small pasta	750 mL
¼ cup	butter, melted	50 mL
2	eggs, lightly beaten	2
1	can (13 oz/385 mL) evaporated milk	1
2	cans (each 10 oz/284 mL) condensed Cheddar cheese soup, undiluted	2
1 tsp	dry mustard	5 mL
3 cups	shredded Cheddar cheese, divided	750 mL
Pinch	paprika	Pinch
6	melba toast crackers, crushed (optional)	6

1. In a large pot of boiling salted water, cook pasta according to package directions. Drain and place in lightly greased slow cooker stoneware. Pour melted butter over macaroni and toss to coat.
2. In a bowl, whisk together eggs, evaporated milk, cheese soup, mustard and 2 cups (500 mL) shredded Cheddar. Add to macaroni and stir together.
3. Cover and cook on **Low** for 3 to 4 hours, or until bubbling and edges are lightly browned.
4. In a small bowl, combine remaining Cheddar, paprika and crushed crackers, if using. Sprinkle mixture over macaroni. Cover and cook on **Low** for 15 to 20 minutes longer, or until cheese has melted.

Cheesy Tortellini Bake

Serves 6 to 8

This recipe is perfect family fare or as a potluck take-along.

• • •

Tips

For a great meal, serve with bruschetta (see recipe, at right), a tossed green salad, and cappuccino ice cream.

Roasted red pepper sauce is widely available in many grocery stores. Look for it in the refrigerated deli department near the fresh pasta. If you can't find any, substitute 3 cups (750 mL) of your favorite canned or bottled pasta sauce or Fia's Favorite Pasta Sauce (see recipe, page 182) for the roasted red pepper sauce and tomato sauce.

Make Ahead

Assemble and refrigerate overnight in slow cooker stoneware. The next day, place stoneware in liner and cook as directed.

- Slow cooker size: 3½ to 5 quart

2 lbs	cheese-filled tortellini	1 kg
1	container (about 14½ oz/415 g) roasted red pepper sauce	1
1	can (7½ oz/213 mL) tomato sauce	1
1	can (19 oz/540 mL) diced Italian-style stewed tomatoes, with juices (see box, page 97)	1
2 cups	shredded Cheddar cheese	500 mL
2 tbsp	freshly grated Parmesan cheese	25 mL
	Chopped fresh parsley	

1. In a large pot of boiling salted water, cook pasta according to package directions. Drain and set aside.
2. In a bowl, combine red pepper sauce and tomato sauce; mix well.
3. Spoon one-third of the red pepper sauce mixture in bottom of lightly greased slow cooker stoneware. Layer with half the cooked noodles, all the tomatoes (with juices), one-third of the red pepper sauce mixture and half the Cheddar cheese. Cover with remaining noodles, remaining one-third red pepper sauce mixture and remaining Cheddar cheese. Sprinkle with grated Parmesan cheese and chopped parsley.
4. Cover and cook on **Low** for 4 to 6 hours or on **High** for 2 to 3 hours, until bubbling.

Bruschetta

In a bowl, combine 4 finely chopped tomatoes, 2 minced cloves garlic, ¼ cup (50 mL) chopped fresh basil, 2 tbsp (25 mL) olive oil, ½ tsp (2 mL) salt and ¼ tsp (1 mL) black pepper. Spoon mixture onto 12 toasted or grilled baguette slices and sprinkle with ¼ cup (50 mL) freshly grated Parmesan cheese. Broil or grill for 1 minute, or until cheese melts. *Makes 12 pieces.*

Kids' Favorite Tuna Noodle Casserole

Serves 4 to 6

Who can resist this all-time favorite family classic? Here, the traditional (and salty) cream soup has been replaced with a light cream-cheese sauce. When my children tested this one, they asked for seconds. That means it's a keeper.

• • •

Tips

Serve this casserole with a crisp green salad.

Evaporated milk holds up extremely well in slow cooking and will not curdle. In this dish, you can use the low-fat 2% partly skimmed type. Don't confuse this milk with "condensed milk" — the sweet sugary one used in desserts and candy.

• Slow cooker size: 3½ to 5 quart

1 tbsp	butter or margarine	15 mL
8 oz	mushrooms, sliced or finely chopped	250 g
1	onion, finely chopped	1
2 tbsp	all-purpose flour	25 mL
1 cup	chicken stock	250 mL
1	can (13 oz/385 mL) evaporated milk	1
4 oz	light cream cheese, cut into ½-inch (1 cm) cubes	125 g
1	can (6½ oz/184 g) solid white tuna, drained and flaked	1
1 cup	frozen peas	250 mL
	Salt and freshly ground black pepper	
8 oz	penne or rotini pasta, uncooked	250 g

Topping

½ cup	crushed corn flakes cereal	125 mL
1 tbsp	melted butter	15 mL
1 cup	shredded Cheddar cheese	250 mL

1. In a large nonstick skillet, heat butter over medium heat. Add mushrooms and onion; cook for 5 minutes, or until mushrooms have released their juices and onion is softened.
2. Add flour, stirring to blend. Pour in stock and evaporated milk. Bring mixture to a boil, stirring constantly until slightly thickened. Stir in cream cheese until melted. Add tuna and peas, stirring to combine. Remove from heat. Season to taste with salt and pepper.

3. Meanwhile, cook pasta in a pot of boiling salted water according to package directions, or until tender but firm. Drain and toss with tuna mixture. Transfer mixture to lightly greased slow cooker stoneware.
4. *Topping:* In a bowl, toss together cereal and melted butter. Add Cheddar cheese, stirring to combine. Sprinkle over noodles in slow cooker.
5. Cover and cook on **Low** for 4 to 6 hours or on **High** for $1\frac{1}{2}$ to 2 hours, until bubbling and heated through.

Make Ahead

This dish can be completely assembled (but without adding topping mixture) up to 12 hours in advance of cooking. Follow preparation directions and refrigerate overnight in slow cooker stoneware.

Mexican Rice and Beans

Serves 4 to 6

This is a wonderful meatless meal the entire family can enjoy. Serve it with a tossed green salad.

Make Ahead

This dish can be assembled and partially prepared up to 24 hours before cooking. Prepare to the end of Step 4 and refrigerate overnight in slow cooker stoneware. The next day, place stoneware in the slow cooker and continue to cook as directed. Cook the rice and prepare the green pepper, cilantro and cheese the night before for an easy dinner preparation when you get home at the end of the day.

- Slow cooker size: 3½ to 6 quart

1 tbsp	vegetable oil	15 mL
1	onion, finely chopped	1
2	cloves garlic, minced	2
1 tbsp	chili powder	15 mL
1 tsp	ground cumin	5 mL
¼ tsp	cayenne pepper	1 mL
¼ tsp	freshly ground black pepper	1 mL
1	can (19 oz/540 mL) diced tomatoes, with juices	1
1	can (19 oz/540 mL) red kidney beans, drained and rinsed, or 2 cups (500 mL) home-cooked beans (page 146)	1
1 cup	fresh or frozen corn kernels (thawed if frozen)	250 mL
2	roasted red peppers (page 310), finely chopped	2
2 cups	cooked rice (about ⅔ cup/150 mL uncooked)	500 mL
½	green bell pepper, chopped	½
1 tbsp	chopped fresh cilantro	15 mL
1 cup	shredded Cheddar cheese	250 mL

1. In a large nonstick skillet, heat oil over medium-high heat. Add onion and garlic and cook, stirring occasionally, for 5 minutes, or until softened and translucent. Stir in chili powder, cumin, cayenne and pepper and cook, stirring, for 1 minute.
2. Add tomatoes and bring to a boil. Cook, stirring, for 3 minutes, scraping up any bits from bottom of pan. Transfer vegetable mixture to slow cooker stoneware. Stir in kidney beans, corn and roasted red peppers.
3. Cover and cook on **Low** for 6 to 10 hours or on **High** for 3 to 4 hours, until bubbling.
4. Stir in rice, green pepper and cilantro. Sprinkle top with cheese. Cover and cook on **High** for 15 to 20 minutes longer, or until heated through and cheese has melted.

Tailgating Four-Bean Hot Dish

Serves 8 to 10

Infamous for brutally cold late-fall temperatures, Green Bay, Wisconsin, is also famous for its football field and tailgate parties. Although fans huddle around grills in boots and parkas, it's still all about the food. A spinoff from traditional baked beans, this hot and hearty combination also goes well with grilled bratwurst or pork chops.

• • •

Tips

Although you can use canned beans in this recipe, home-cooked dried beans are not only economical, they tend to be better tasting.

For a non-vegetarian version, omit the oil and cook 3 slices chopped bacon with the onion.

- Slow cooker size: 3½ to 6 quart

1 tbsp	vegetable oil	15 mL
1	large onion, finely chopped	1
1	can (19 oz/540 mL) white kidney beans, drained and rinsed, or 2 cups (500 mL) home-cooked beans (page 146)	1
1	can (19 oz/540 mL) red kidney beans, drained and rinsed, or 2 cups (500 mL) home-cooked beans	1
1	can (19 oz/540 mL) chickpeas, drained and rinsed, or 2 cups (500 mL) home-cooked chickpeas	1
1	can (7½ oz/213 mL) tomato sauce	1
½ cup	ketchup	125 mL
2 tbsp	packed brown sugar	25 mL
2 tsp	prepared mustard	10 mL
2 cups	frozen green beans, thawed	500 mL

1. In a large nonstick skillet, heat oil over medium-high heat. Add onion and cook, stirring occasionally, for 5 minutes, or until tender. Transfer onion to slow cooker stoneware.
2. Add white and red kidney beans, chickpeas, tomato sauce, ketchup, brown sugar and mustard to slow cooker; stir to combine.
3. Cover and cook on **Low** for 6 to 10 hours or on **High** for 3 to 4 hours, until hot and bubbling.
4. Add green beans. Cover and cook on **High** for 20 to 30 minutes longer, or until green beans are heated through.

Black Bean Moussaka

Serves 6 to 8

In this vegetarian version of Greek-style lasagna, noodles and meat are replaced with hearty eggplant and black beans. It's a wonderful make-ahead for a buffet supper at the chalet.

• • •

Tips

Tired of opening a whole can of tomato paste when all you need is a small amount? Look for the squeeze tubes of tomato paste sold in most supermarkets.

If not salted first, eggplant develops a bitter flavor in the slow cooker. Sprinkle cut eggplant with salt. Place in a colander, cover with a plate and weight down with heavy cans. Allow eggplant to drain for 1 hour, then rinse under cold water to remove salt and pat dry with paper towels.

- Slow cooker size: 3½ to 5 quart

1	large eggplant, peeled and cut into 2-inch (5 cm) cubes	1
	Salt	
2 tbsp	olive oil	25 mL
1	large onion, finely chopped	1
1	can (19 oz/540 mL) diced tomatoes, with juices	1
¼ cup	red wine	50 mL
2 tbsp	tomato paste	25 mL
1 tsp	dried oregano	5 mL
¼ tsp	ground cinnamon	1 mL
2	cans (each 19 oz/540 mL) black beans, drained and rinsed, or 4 cups (1 L) home-cooked beans (page 146)	1

Topping

1	can (13 oz/385 mL) evaporated milk	1
2	eggs	2
2 tbsp	butter or margarine	25 mL
2 tbsp	all-purpose flour	25 mL
½ tsp	salt	2 mL
¼ tsp	freshly ground black pepper	1 mL
¼ tsp	ground nutmeg	1 mL
½ cup	shredded mozzarella cheese	125 mL

1. Place chopped eggplant in a colander and sprinkle with salt; cover with a plate. Let stand for 1 hour or until the eggplant releases its juices. Rinse well under cold running water to remove salt, then drain. Squeeze out any excess moisture and pat dry with paper towels.

2. In a large skillet, heat half the oil over medium-high heat. Add eggplant and sauté for 10 minutes, or until lightly browned. Remove to a plate and set aside.
3. Return skillet to heat and add remaining 1 tbsp (15 mL) oil. Add onion and sauté for 5 minutes, or until tender. Add tomatoes (with juices), red wine, tomato paste, oregano and cinnamon. Bring mixture to a boil, reduce heat and simmer for 5 minutes. Stir in black beans and set aside.
4. *Topping:* In a 2-cup (500 mL) measure, combine milk and eggs. Mix well and set aside. In a saucepan, heat butter over medium-low heat. Add flour, stirring to combine. Increase heat to medium and gradually whisk in egg mixture, whisking constantly, until slightly thickened. Add salt, pepper and nutmeg.
5. To assemble, place half the sautéed eggplant in lightly greased slow cooker stoneware. Spoon tomato-bean mixture over eggplant. Add remaining eggplant and cover with topping. Sprinkle with mozzarella cheese.
6. Cover and cook on **Low** for 8 to 10 hours or on **High** for 4 to 6 hours, until bubbling. Let stand for 5 minutes before serving.

Make Ahead

This chili can be assembled 12 hours in advance of cooking. Follow preparation directions and refrigerate overnight in slow cooker stoneware. The next day, place stoneware in slow cooker and continue cooking as directed.

Lentil Curry with Squash and Cashews

Serves 6

For the vegetarian in the family or for adding to your array of meatless entrées, try this Middle Eastern–inspired dish.

• • •

Tips

A bowlful of this curry makes a hearty meal. Serve with warm pita bread.

While cooked green lentils are available in cans, the dried variety are fast and easy to cook. It is important to pick over lentils to remove any sticks or broken pieces, then rinse and drain before using.

- Slow cooker size: 3½ to 5 quart

2 tsp	vegetable oil	10 mL
1	onion, chopped	1
2	cloves garlic, minced	2
2 tbsp	all-purpose flour	25 mL
1 tbsp	curry powder	15 mL
1 tbsp	grated gingerroot (or 1 tsp/5 mL ground ginger)	15 mL
1 tsp	ground cumin	5 mL
1 tsp	fennel seeds	5 mL
1 tsp	salt	5 mL
2 cups	vegetable or chicken stock	500 mL
1 cup	water or apple juice	250 mL
1 cup	dried green lentils, picked over and rinsed	250 mL
2 cups	peeled chopped butternut squash	500 mL
1	large potato, chopped into 1-inch (2.5 cm) cubes	1
6 cups	fresh spinach, washed and trimmed	1.5 L
½ cup	cashews (salted or unsalted)	125 mL

1. In a skillet, heat oil over medium heat. Add onion and garlic and cook for 5 minutes, or until softened and translucent. Stir in flour, curry, ginger, cumin, fennel seeds and salt; mix well.
2. Stir in stock and water; bring to a boil, scraping up bits from bottom of skillet. Transfer mixture to slow cooker stoneware.
3. Add lentils, squash and potato to slow cooker; stir to combine.

4. Cover and cook on **Low** for 7 to 9 hours or on **High** for 3 to 4 hours, until hot and bubbling.
5. Add spinach leaves; stir to combine. Cover and cook on **High** for 15 minutes longer, or until leaves have wilted. Spoon into individual bowls and sprinkle with cashews.

Fresh Gingerroot

There is no need to peel gingerroot before grating. Use a standard kitchen grater with fine holes. Wrap any unused ginger in plastic wrap and freeze. Frozen gingerroot can be grated without defrosting.

Variation

For a meaty version, add chopped leftover chicken at the same time that you add the spinach.

Remarkable Ratatouille

Serves 6 to 8

Here's my version of the classic Mediterranean vegetarian dish. It can be eaten as a main course with a crisp green salad or as a side dish with salmon or chicken. Any way you serve it, this ratatouille is excellent!

• • •

Tips

Eggplant can become bitter in the slow cooker if it is not salted first. Small eggplants do not need salting as much as large, since their water content is not as high.

If you don't have a dried Italian seasoning mix, use a combination of basil, marjoram, thyme and oregano.

- Slow cooker size: 3½ to 5 quart

3	small eggplants, cut into 1-inch (2.5 cm) cubes	3
1 tsp	salt	5 mL
3 tbsp	olive oil	45 mL
1 tbsp	butter or margarine	15 mL
1	large onion, thinly sliced and separated into rings	1
8 oz	mushrooms, sliced	250 g
1	can (28 oz/796 mL) Italian-style stewed tomatoes, with juices, chopped (see box, page 97)	1
2 tbsp	freshly grated Parmesan cheese	25 mL
¼ cup	fine dry bread crumbs	50 mL
1 tsp	dried Italian seasoning (see tip, at left)	5 mL
1 cup	shredded mozzarella cheese	250 mL

1. In a large colander, toss eggplants with salt. Let stand for 1 hour or until cubes release their juices. Rinse well under cold running water to remove salt, then drain. Squeeze out any excess moisture and pat dry with paper towels. Set aside.
2. In a large nonstick skillet, heat 1 tbsp (15 mL) oil and the butter over medium heat. Add onion and mushrooms; sauté for 10 minutes, or until softened. Remove with a slotted spoon to a plate and set aside.
3. Return skillet to heat and add remaining 2 tbsp (25 mL) olive oil. In batches, sauté drained eggplant cubes over medium heat for 10 minutes, or until lightly browned.

4. Layer half the eggplant cubes in slow cooker stoneware. Top with onion mixture and half the tomatoes (with juices). Sprinkle with Parmesan cheese, then add remaining eggplant cubes and chopped tomatoes.
5. In a bowl, combine bread crumbs, Italian seasoning and mozzarella cheese; mix well and spoon over tomatoes and eggplant.
6. Cover and cook on **Low** for 8 to 10 hours or on **High** for 4 to 6 hours, until hot and bubbling.

Homemade Bread Crumbs

To make your own dry bread crumbs, spread bread slices on a flat surface and let stand overnight, until completely dry and brittle. Break bread into pieces and place in a food processor or blender. Process until bread is in fine crumbs.

Make Ahead

This dish can be completely assembled up to 12 hours in advance of cooking. Follow preparation directions and refrigerate overnight in the slow cooker stoneware. The next day, place stoneware in slow cooker and continue cooking as directed.

Moroccan Vegetable Hotpot

Serves 4 to 6

This hearty Moroccan-inspired stew combines squash and chickpeas, lightly scented with fragrant cinnamon. It is best served over hot, fluffy couscous.

• • •

Tip

For a meaty version, stir in 2 cups (500 mL) chopped cooked chicken when adding parsley. Cook for 15 to 20 minutes longer or until heated through.

Make Ahead

This dish can be completely assembled the night before. Follow preparation directions and refrigerate overnight in the slow cooker stoneware. The next day, place stoneware in slow cooker and continue cooking as directed.

- Slow cooker size: 3½ to 5 quart

2	carrots, sliced	2
1	butternut squash, peeled and cut into 1-inch (2.5 cm) cubes	1
1	onion, chopped	1
1	can (19 oz/540 mL) chickpeas, drained and rinsed	1
1	can (19 oz/540 mL) diced tomatoes, with juices	1
1 cup	vegetable or chicken stock	250 mL
½ cup	chopped pitted prunes	125 mL
1 tsp	ground cinnamon	5 mL
½ tsp	hot pepper flakes	2 mL
2 tbsp	chopped fresh parsley or cilantro	25 mL
	Salt and freshly ground black pepper	
	Hot couscous	

1. In slow cooker stoneware, combine carrots, squash, onion, chickpeas, tomatoes (with juices), stock, prunes, cinnamon and hot pepper flakes; stir to mix well.
2. Cover and cook on Low for 6 to 8 hours or on High for 3 to 4 hours, until all vegetables are tender.
3. Stir parsley into stew and season to taste with salt and black pepper. Serve over hot cooked couscous.

Couscous

Couscous is another name for semolina, the milled center of durum wheat. It is traditionally served with North African dishes — particularly those from Morocco, Algeria and Tunisia — and it takes less time to prepare than rice.

Corn and Green Chili Tamale Casserole

Serves 4 to 6

I'm always looking for interesting ways to make an easy weeknight meal. Sometimes a few prepared ingredients can be whipped up into a tasty casserole like this one. It's a big hit with my family.

Tips

Mexican cuisine includes many raw and cooked salsas based on tomatoes or tomatillos with chilies. Salsa verde is green in color and is found in the Mexican food aisle. If you have difficulty finding it, substitute regular salsa.

Cut the burritos when they are only slightly thawed so the filling doesn't ooze out.

- Slow cooker size: 3½ to 6 quart

6	prepared bean and cheese burritos, slightly thawed	6
2 cups	fresh or frozen corn kernels (thawed if frozen)	500 mL
1	can (4½ oz/127 mL) chopped mild green chilies, including liquid	1
3	green onions, chopped	3
¼ cup	chopped fresh cilantro, divided	50 mL
1 cup	whipping (35%) cream or sour cream	250 mL
1	can (7 oz/200 mL) salsa verde	1
1 tsp	chili powder	5 mL
½ tsp	ground cumin	2 mL
¼ tsp	salt	1 mL
¼ tsp	freshly ground black pepper	1 mL
1½ cups	shredded Monterey Jack cheese	375 mL
1	avocado, peeled and cut into wedges (optional)	1

1. Cut each burrito into 4 slices and place in a single layer in bottom of slow cooker stoneware. (If you are using a smaller slow cooker, you will have to make two layers of burritos.) Sprinkle burritos with corn, chilies, green onions and 2 tbsp (25 mL) cilantro.
2. In a bowl, whisk together cream, salsa verde, chili powder, cumin, salt and pepper. Pour over burritos and vegetables.
3. Cover and cook on **Low** for 4 to 6 hours or on **High** for 2 to 3 hours, until heated through and bubbling.
4. Sprinkle casserole with cheese. Cover and cook on **High** for 20 to 30 minutes longer, or until cheese melts. Garnish with remaining cilantro and avocado, if using.

Barbecued Veggie Joes

Serves 8

This is a yummy vegetarian twist on a family favorite. For a Middle Eastern flair, stuff these lentils into pita breads lined with lettuce leaves. The lettuce helps to keep the lentils from soaking the bread.

• • •

Tip

Lentils are an inexpensive source of protein, as well as being high in fiber, complex carbohydrates and B vitamins. It's best to use green or brown lentils in the slow cooker, not the smaller red or yellow lentils, which break down during cooking.

- Slow cooker size: 3½ to 6 quart

1 cup	dried lentils, rinsed and sorted	250 mL
2 cups	water	500 mL
1½ cups	finely chopped celery	375 mL
1½ cups	finely chopped carrots	375 mL
1	large onion, finely chopped	1
¾ cup	ketchup	175 mL
2 tbsp	packed brown sugar	25 mL
2 tbsp	Worcestershire sauce	25 mL
2 tbsp	cider vinegar	25 mL
8	kaiser buns, halved and lightly toasted	8
8	slices Cheddar cheese (optional)	8

1. In a saucepan, combine lentils and water. Bring to a boil and reduce heat. Cover and simmer for 10 minutes. Transfer lentils and water to slow cooker stoneware.
2. Add celery, carrots, onion, ketchup, brown sugar and Worcestershire sauce to slow cooker; stir to combine.
3. Cover and cook on **Low** for 10 to 12 hours or on **High** for 4 to 6 hours, until lentils are tender. Just before serving, stir in vinegar.
4. Spoon ½ cup (125 mL) filling onto bottoms of toasted kaisers. Top with Cheddar, if using, and top halves of buns.

Veggie-Stuffed Baked Potatoes

Serves 6

No one will believe you made these in the slow cooker. They make a satisfying vegetarian main course, or you can serve them as a side dish with grilled chicken or steak.

• • •

Tips

If you are pressed for time, omit the mashing step and just serve the baked potatoes with a variety of toppings, including sour cream, ranch dip, bacon bits, crumbled blue cheese and salsa. Or serve with hot baked beans or leftover spaghetti sauce and grated mozzarella cheese.

Tossing the potatoes with oil before cooking helps keep the skins soft. Salt and pepper the skins, too, for those who like to eat the whole potato, skins and all!

- Slow cooker size: 3½ to 6 quart

6	large baking potatoes, unpeeled (about 3 lbs/1.5 kg total)	6
2 tbsp	vegetable oil	25 mL
1½ tsp	salt, divided	7 mL
¾ tsp	freshly ground black pepper, divided	4 mL
2 tbsp	butter	25 mL
½ cup	milk	125 mL
½ cup	sour cream	125 mL
1 tsp	Dijon mustard	5 mL
½ tsp	salt	2 mL
1 cup	small broccoli florets	250 mL
1	carrot, peeled and shredded or finely chopped	1
½ cup	chopped red bell pepper	125 mL
½ cup	shredded Cheddar cheese	125 mL

1. Pierce potatoes all over with a fork. Rub potato skins with oil and sprinkle with 1 tsp (5 mL) salt and ½ tsp (2 mL) pepper. Wrap potatoes individually in foil and place in slow cooker stoneware.
2. Cover and cook on **Low** for 6 to 10 hours, or until potatoes are tender.
3. Remove potatoes from slow cooker and unwrap. Slice ¼ inch (5 mm) off each potato. Scoop potato flesh into a bowl, leaving skins intact.
4. Add butter, milk, sour cream, mustard and remaining salt and pepper to potato flesh and mash until smooth and blended. Stir in broccoli, carrot, red pepper and cheese. Spoon mashed potato mixture back into skins.
5. Place potatoes on a baking sheet and bake in a preheated 400°F (200°C) oven for 15 to 20 minutes, or until tops are golden.

Poultry

Coq au Vin

Serves 4 to 6

This is another great choice for entertaining. Coq au vin *means "chicken in wine," but I have also added brandy for an extra kick. If you prefer, substitute dry white wine for the red.*

• • •

Tip

Cooking times for poultry may be longer for larger slow cookers and/or where there is a relatively high proportion of dark to white meat. For predominantly white-meat dishes, be sure to avoid overcooking.

Make Ahead

This dish is best prepared a day ahead. After cooking, cool slightly and place stoneware in refrigerator overnight. The chicken will improve as the flavors meld. The next day, remove any accumulated fat from the surface. Transfer to an ovenproof casserole. Place in pre-heated 350°F (180°C) oven for 20 to 30 minutes, or until warmed through.

- **Slow cooker size: 3½ to 6 quart**

1	whole chicken, cut into parts (about 9 pieces)	1
¼ cup	all-purpose flour	50 mL
8	slices bacon, chopped	8
2	onions, sliced	2
8 oz	small button mushrooms, cleaned	250 g
16	small new potatoes, scrubbed	16
4	cloves garlic, minced	4
¼ cup	chopped fresh parsley (or 2 tbsp/25 mL dried)	50 mL
½ tsp	dried thyme	2 mL
1	bay leaf	1
½ tsp	salt	2 mL
¼ tsp	freshly ground black pepper	1 mL
2 tbsp	brandy	25 mL
1 cup	red wine	250 mL
1 cup	chicken stock	250 mL

1. In a bowl, dredge chicken pieces in flour. Transfer to slow cooker stoneware.
2. In a skillet, over medium heat, cook bacon until crisp. Drain on paper towels. Transfer bacon to slow cooker. Add onions, mushrooms, potatoes, garlic, parsley, thyme, bay leaf, salt, pepper, brandy, wine and stock.
3. Cover and cook on **Low** for 6 to 8 hours, until juices run clear when chicken is pierced with a fork. Discard bay leaf.

Baked Chicken with Mustard Barbecue Sauce

Serves 6

A century ago, spicy English mustards were too pungent for the North American palate. In the early 1900s, bright yellow prepared mustard was invented and we now slather it on everything from sandwiches to pretzels. It also adds a tangy zip to this barbecue sauce. Serve the chicken with creamy coleslaw (page 115) and steamed corn.

- **Slow cooker size: 3½ to 6 quart**

12	skinless chicken drumsticks	12
1	can (19 oz/540 mL) tomatoes, drained	1
¼ cup	packed brown sugar	50 mL
3 tbsp	cider vinegar	45 mL
2 tbsp	prepared mustard	25 mL
1½ tsp	Worcestershire sauce	7 mL
1 tsp	salt	5 mL
½ tsp	freshly ground black pepper	2 mL

1. Place chicken in slow cooker stoneware.
2. In a blender or food processor, purée tomatoes, brown sugar, vinegar, mustard, Worcestershire sauce, salt and pepper until smooth. Pour sauce over chicken.
3. Cover and cook on **Low** for 5 to 7 hours or on **High** for 2½ to 4 hours, until juices run clear when chicken is pierced with a fork.
4. For a thicker sauce, transfer chicken to a serving platter and keep warm. Transfer sauce to a saucepan and bring to a boil. Boil gently until reduced by half or sauce reaches desired consistency. Pour sauce over chicken.

Chicken with Orange Gremolata

Serves 4 to 6

This is a chicken version of an Italian dish that is traditionally made with veal shanks. Pass any extra gremolata — a flavorful mix of parsley, garlic and orange zest (be sure to grate the zest before juicing the orange)

• • •

Tips

To extract the most juice from oranges, use fruit that has been sitting at room temperature. Roll firmly on a flat surface using the palm of your hand. Or microwave a whole orange on High for 30 seconds, and then roll. Juice can be frozen in ice cube trays, then stored in recloseable plastic bags for later use. Peel can also be wrapped and frozen for later use.

To zest an orange, use the fine edge of a cheese grater, ensuring you don't grate the white pith underneath. Or use a zester to remove the zest, then finely chop. Zesters are inexpensive and widely available at specialty kitchen shops.

- **Slow cooker size: 5 to 6 quart**

1	roasting chicken (3 to 6 lbs/1.5 to 3 kg)	1
1 tbsp	vegetable oil	15 mL
1	onion, finely chopped	1
1	stalk celery, finely chopped	1
2	cloves garlic, minced	2
2	carrots, peeled and sliced	2
1	red bell pepper, coarsely chopped	1
1 tsp	dried rosemary, crumbled	5 mL
½ tsp	dried thyme	2 mL
1	can (19 oz/540 mL) stewed tomatoes, with juices	1
	Juice of 1 orange	
2 tbsp	dry white wine or chicken stock	25 mL

Gremolata

⅓ cup	chopped fresh parsley	75 mL
1 tsp	grated orange zest	5 mL
1	clove garlic, minced	1

1. Rinse chicken inside and out and pat dry. Trim off excess fat. Truss chicken loosely.
2. In a large nonstick skillet, heat oil over medium-high heat. Brown chicken on all sides, beginning with breast side down (this should take about 20 minutes in total). Use two wooden spoons to turn bird so you don't puncture skin. Place chicken in slow cooker stoneware, breast side up.
3. Drain off all but 1 tbsp (15 mL) fat from skillet and reduce heat to medium. Add onion, celery, garlic, carrots, red pepper, rosemary and thyme. Cook, stirring, for about 5 minutes, or until vegetables are soft.

4. Add tomatoes, with juices, orange juice and wine to skillet. Bring to a boil, reduce heat and simmer for 5 minutes, or until thickened. Pour over chicken.
5. Cover and cook on **Low** for 7 to 9 hours or on **High** for 3½ to 4 hours, until a meat thermometer inserted in thigh reads 170°F (77°C).
6. Transfer chicken to a plate and cover loosely with foil. Let sit for 10 minutes before carving. Skim fat from sauce.
7. *Gremolita:* In a bowl, combine parsley, orange zest and garlic.
8. Serve chicken with vegetable sauce and sprinkle gremolata over each serving.

Tips

Removing lid of slow cooker releases heat, which will lengthen the cooking time. Do not remove lid until minimum cooking time.

For an authentic Italian meal, serve this with risotto and a good Italian red wine.

Drunken Roast Chicken

Serves 6 to 8

While roasting is something we typically associate with the oven, you can also "roast" in a slow cooker — with very tasty results. In this recipe, the garlic creates a wonderful aroma and imparts a subtle flavor to the chicken.

• • •

Tips

For a complete Sunday night dinner or easy weeknight meal, add chopped carrots and potatoes to the bottom of the slow cooker at the beginning of Step 3, then place chicken on top of vegetables and proceed with recipe as directed.

If you have thyme growing in your herb garden, substitute a few fresh sprigs for the dried thyme called for in this recipe.

If whole chicken is too large to fit in your slow cooker, cut it into pieces with a sharp knife.

- Slow cooker size: 5 to 6 quart

1	roasting chicken (about 3½ to 4 lbs/1.75 to 2 kg)	1
4 to 6	cloves garlic, halved	4 to 6
1	onion, quartered	1
1	stalk celery, with leaves, cut into 3 pieces	1
1 tsp	dried thyme	5 mL
½ tsp	paprika	2 mL
½ cup	chicken stock	125 mL
½ cup	dry white wine	125 mL
1 tbsp	Worcestershire sauce	15 mL

Gravy

1 tbsp	butter	15 mL
1 tbsp	all-purpose flour	15 mL
	Salt and freshly ground black pepper	

1. Rinse chicken inside and out and pat dry with paper towels. With your fingers, gently loosen skin from chicken breast to form a pocket. Insert garlic halves under the skin. Place onion and celery in the cavity.
2. With kitchen twine, tie chicken legs together and secure wings to body, leaving an extra length of twine at each end. You will use the ends to lift the chicken from slow cooker.
3. Place chicken in slow cooker stoneware, breast side up. Sprinkle with thyme and paprika. Pour in stock, wine and Worcestershire sauce.
4. Cover and cook on **Low** for 8 to 10 hours, or until a meat thermometer inserted in thigh reads 170°F (77°C).
5. Gently remove chicken from slow cooker and transfer to a platter. Cover with foil to keep warm. If desired, brown chicken under preheated broiler for 5 to 7 minutes.

6. *Gravy:* Pour 1 cup (250 mL) juices from slow cooker into a glass measure; skim any fat from surface. In a saucepan, melt butter over medium-high heat. Add flour and cook, stirring, for 1 minute. Add measured juices and bring mixture to a boil; cook, stirring, until sauce is smooth and thickened. Season to taste with salt and pepper. Serve gravy over chicken.

Stock

"Stock" refers to the strained liquid that results from cooking poultry, meat or vegetables and seasonings in water. Other terms for this include "broth" and "bouillon." The best stock is homemade, but if time won't allow, use canned stock (dilute as directed) or refrigerated stocks sold in tetra paks. Try to avoid using bouillon powder or cubes since these tend to be quite salty and don't give the same rich taste. If you do use powdered stock or cubes, add salt to taste at the end of the cooking.

Tip

Cooking times for poultry may be longer for larger slow cookers and/or where there is a relatively high proportion of dark to white meat. For predominantly white-meat dishes, be sure to avoid overcooking.

Chicken-in-a-Pot

Serves 4 to 6

Kids love this simple poached chicken and so will you. It's tasty, simple and the ingredients take just minutes to prepare.

• • •

Tips

Serve chicken and sauce on a bed of rice.

If whole chicken is too large to fit into your slow cooker, cut it into pieces with a sharp knife.

• • •

Variation

For a more sophisticated version, replace Parsley Sauce with *Creamed Curry Sauce*: In a saucepan, melt butter with 1 tsp (5 mL) curry powder. Blend in flour and cook 1 minute, stirring constantly. Gradually whisk in 1½ cups (375 mL) strained cooking liquid (from Step 3) and ½ cup (125 mL) whipping (35%) cream, stirring for 3 minutes, or until sauce boils and thickens. Season to taste with salt and pepper.

● **Slow cooker size: 5 to 6 quart**

1	roasting chicken (3 to 6 lbs/1.5 to 3 kg)	1
2 cups	chicken stock	500 mL
3	leeks (white and light green part only), cut crosswise into 4-inch (10 cm) pieces	3
1	stalk celery (with leaves), cut in half	1
1	carrot, peeled and cut in half	1
1 tsp	salt	5 mL
6	whole black peppercorns	6
3 or 4	sprigs fresh parsley (or 1 tbsp/15 mL dried)	3 or 4
2	sprigs whole fresh thyme (or ½ tsp/2 mL dried)	2
2	whole cloves	2
1	small bay leaf	1

Parsley Sauce

¼ cup	butter or margarine	50 mL
¼ cup	all-purpose flour	50 mL
2 cups	strained cooking liquid (from chicken) or chicken stock	500 mL
¼ cup	chopped fresh parsley (or 2 tbsp/25 mL dried)	50 mL
	Salt and freshly ground black pepper	

1. Rinse chicken inside and out and pat dry. (Discard bag of giblets but reserve chicken neck, if desired.) Place in slow cooker stoneware, breast side up. Add stock, leeks, celery, carrot, salt, peppercorns, parsley, thyme, cloves and bay leaf. Pour in enough water to almost completely cover chicken, leaving 1 inch (2.5 cm) headspace at top of slow cooker.
2. Cover and cook on **Low** for 8 to 10 hours, or until a meat thermometer inserted in thigh reads 170°F (77°C).

3. Carefully lift chicken from liquid and transfer to a plate; allow to rest for 15 to 20 minutes. Strain vegetables and cooking liquid, discarding vegetables and reserving liquid. Skim any fat from surface of liquid.
4. *Parsley sauce:* In a saucepan over medium heat, melt butter. Blend in flour and cook for 1 minute, stirring constantly. Gradually whisk in strained cooking liquid, stirring for about 5 minutes, or until sauce boils and thickens. Remove from heat and stir in parsley. Season to taste with salt and pepper. Serve sauce over chicken.

Leeks

Leeks have a wonderful mellow flavor when they are cooked gently before being added to sauces or other dishes. They must be cleaned carefully before using, since they tend to contain a lot of sand. Remove the roots and dark-green tops. Cut the leek in half lengthwise. Rinse thoroughly under cold running water and drain in a colander.

Tip

Cooking times for poultry may be longer for larger slow cookers and/or where there is a relatively high proportion of dark to white meat. For predominantly white-meat dishes, be sure to avoid overcooking.

Chicken in Honey-Mustard Sauce

Serves 4

For a larger crowd, you can double the chicken in this recipe and — of course — the sauce for drizzling over it.

• • •

Tips

If your liquid honey has crystallized or you use solid creamed honey, place the jar (or as much as you need in a small bowl) in a saucepan of hot water, heating gently until melted. Or heat in microwave until melted.

When measuring honey, rub measuring cup with a little vegetable oil, then measure honey. It will easily pour out, with no sticky mess!

Cooking times for poultry may be longer for larger slow cookers and/or where there is a relatively high proportion of dark to white meat. For predominantly white-meat dishes, be sure to avoid overcooking.

- **Slow cooker size: 3½ to 6 quart**

¼ cup	butter or margarine	50 mL
½ cup	liquid honey	125 mL
¼ cup	Dijon mustard	50 mL
1 tbsp	curry powder	15 mL
1 tsp	salt	5 mL
8	chicken pieces (legs and breasts), skin removed, if desired	8

1. In a small saucepan over medium heat (or in a small glass bowl in the microwave), melt butter. Add honey, mustard, curry powder and salt; stir until dissolved.
2. Place chicken in slow cooker stoneware. Pour honey-mustard sauce over top.
3. Cover and cook on **Low** for 6 to 8 hours, until juices run clear when chicken is pierced with a fork. Skim off any fat from sauce and serve drizzled over chicken.

Vegetable-Stuffed Chicken with Mushroom Sauce

Serves 4

Using inexpensive chicken thighs makes this dish an economical family meal. But don't let the recipe fool you — it's perfect for entertaining as well. Serve over cooked noodles or steamed rice (page 163).

Tips

The French term *julienne* refers to food cut in matchstick-sized pieces. To julienne carrots, first cut in half widthwise, then cut into thin strips.

Purchase chicken thighs in economical family packs. Divide into meal-sized portions, wrap in plastic wrap and freeze in freezer bags.

- Slow cooker size: 3½ to 6 quart

8	boneless skinless chicken thighs	8
1 tsp	salt	5 mL
½ tsp	freshly ground black pepper	2 mL
1	small carrot, peeled and cut in julienne strips	1
½	red bell pepper, cut into 16 strips	½
2	green onions, cut in thin strips	2
2 cups	sliced mushrooms	500 mL
1	onion, finely chopped	1
½ tsp	dried thyme	2 mL
½ tsp	dried sage	2 mL
3 tbsp	all-purpose flour	45 mL
1	can (13 oz/385 mL) evaporated milk	1
1 tbsp	chopped fresh parsley	15 mL

1. Place chicken thighs, smooth side down, on work surface. Sprinkle with salt and pepper. Lay 2 or 3 carrot strips, 2 pepper strips and a few green onion strips along one end of thigh. Roll up and secure each with a toothpick.
2. Lay chicken bundles in bottom of slow cooker stoneware. Sprinkle mushrooms, onion, thyme and sage on top of chicken.
3. In a small saucepan, whisk flour into milk. Cook on medium heat, stirring constantly, for 5 to 7 minutes, or until thickened. Pour over chicken and vegetables in slow cooker.
4. Cover and cook on **Low** for 6 to 8 hours, or until juices run clear when chicken is pierced with a fork.
5. With a slotted spoon, transfer chicken bundles to serving plate. Whisk sauce in slow cooker until smooth and pour over chicken. Sprinkle with chopped parsley.

Lemony Herbed Drumsticks

Serves 4 to 6

Kids love this dish made with apple juice. Substitute white wine for a more adult version.

• • •

Tips

Be sure to crumble the rosemary between your fingers before adding it to the marinade. This helps to release the full aromatic flavor of the herb.

Cooking times for poultry may be longer for larger slow cookers and/or where there is a relatively high proportion of dark to white meat. For predominantly white-meat dishes, be sure to avoid overcooking.

- Slow cooker size: 3½ to 5 quart

3 to 4 lbs	chicken drumsticks	1.5 to 2 kg
¼ cup	freshly squeezed lemon juice	50 mL
1 cup	apple juice or dry white wine	250 mL
1 tbsp	olive oil	15 mL
1	onion, finely chopped	1
2	cloves garlic, minced	2
1 tsp	dried rosemary, crumbled	5 mL
½ tsp	salt	2 mL
¼ tsp	freshly ground black pepper	1 mL

1. In a large bowl or plastic bag, place chicken, lemon juice, apple juice, olive oil, onion, garlic, rosemary, salt and pepper. Cover or seal bag and marinate for 4 to 6 hours or overnight in refrigerator.
2. Transfer chicken and marinade to slow cooker stoneware.
3. Cover and cook on **Low** for 6 to 8 hours, or until chicken is lightly browned and juices run clear when chicken is pierced with a fork.

Apple Chicken

Serves 4 to 6

This is a wonderful dish to serve when the weather turns cooler and the nights are longer. Use apples that keep their shape and texture during cooking, such as Ida Red, Mutsu (Crispin) or Northern Spy.

• • •

Tip

A quick way to mix cornstarch with a liquid is to use a jar. Screw the lid on tightly and shake the jar until the mixture is smooth. (This is faster than trying to stir or whisk until all the cornstarch is dissolved.)

- Slow cooker size: 3½ to 6 quart

12	skinless chicken drumsticks or thighs	12
1 tsp	dried thyme	5 mL
½ tsp	salt	2 mL
½ tsp	freshly ground black pepper	2 mL
2	apples, unpeeled, thickly sliced	2
1	onion, sliced	1
½ cup	apple cider or apple juice	125 mL
1½ tsp	cider vinegar	7 mL
1 tbsp	cornstarch	15 mL

1. Place chicken in slow cooker stoneware. Sprinkle with thyme, salt and pepper. Add apples and onion. Pour apple cider over chicken.
2. Cover and cook on **Low** for 5 to 7 hours or on **High** for 2½ to 4 hours, until juices run clear when chicken is pierced with a fork. Transfer chicken to a serving plate and keep warm.
3. In a small bowl or jar, combine vinegar and cornstarch (see tip, at left). Whisk into slow cooker. Cover and cook on **High** for 15 to 20 minutes longer, or until thickened. Spoon over chicken.

Plum-Good Chicken

Serves 4

Don't think that plums are only good for pies. They're also great with chicken.

• • •

Tips

There are many varieties of vinegar to choose from. Here we use rice wine vinegar — a light, low-acid, slightly sweet variety from Japan, which goes particularly well in Asian dishes. White wine vinegar (and herb vinegars, such as tarragon) also add a delightful flavor to chicken.

• • •

Variation

Peachy-Good Chicken: Prepare recipe as directed but substitute canned sliced or halved peaches for the plums.

Very-Cherry Chicken: 1 can (14 oz/398 mL) black cherries can be substituted for the plums.

- Slow cooker size: 3½ to 5 quart

¼ cup	all-purpose flour	50 mL
½ tsp	paprika	2 mL
½ tsp	salt	2 mL
¼ tsp	freshly ground black pepper	1 mL
Pinch	cayenne	Pinch
8	chicken pieces (breasts or thighs), skin removed, if desired	8
1	can (14 oz/398 mL) purple plums	1
1 tsp	ground ginger	5 mL
2 tbsp	soy sauce	25 mL
2 tbsp	rice vinegar or white wine vinegar	25 mL
1 tbsp	packed brown sugar	15 mL
2 tbsp	cornstarch	25 mL
2 tbsp	water	25 mL
½ tsp	ground cinnamon	2 mL

1. In a shallow dish or plastic bag, combine flour, paprika, salt, black pepper and cayenne. Toss chicken in flour mixture to coat on all sides. Place in slow cooker stoneware.
2. Drain plums (reserving juice) and chop, discarding pits. Add to slow cooker.
3. In a bowl, combine reserved plum juice, ginger, soy sauce, vinegar and brown sugar, mixing well. Pour over chicken and plums in slow cooker.
4. Cover and cook on **Low** for 6 to 8 hours, until juices run clear when chicken is pierced with a fork.
5. In a small bowl, combine cornstarch, water and cinnamon, stirring until smooth. Add to slow cooker; cover and cook on **High** for 20 to 25 minutes longer, or until sauce has thickened.

Caramelized Onion Chicken

Serves 4 to 6

In this dish, a sweet, tangy sauce forms as the chicken cooks. Serve with boiled or baked potatoes or, for a change, try serving with potato dumplings, German spätzle or Italian gnocchi. You'll find them in the fresh pasta/deli aisle or frozen food section of the supermarket. Toss the cooked dumplings with melted butter and add a sprinkle of chopped fresh parsley or dill for a touch of color and flavor.

• • •

Tip

Cooking times for poultry may be longer for larger slow cookers and/or where there is a relatively high proportion of dark to white meat. For predominantly white-meat dishes, be sure to avoid overcooking.

- Slow cooker size: 3½ to 6 quart

12	skinless chicken thighs or drumsticks	12
½ tsp	salt	2 mL
¼ tsp	freshly ground black pepper	1 mL
1 tbsp	butter	15 mL
1	sweet onion, sliced	1
½ cup	raspberry jam, preferably seedless	125 mL
1 tbsp	red wine vinegar	15 mL
1 tbsp	soy sauce	15 mL
2 tsp	grated gingerroot (or 1 tsp/5 mL ground ginger)	10 mL
½ tsp	dried rosemary, crumbled	2 mL

1. Place chicken thighs in slow cooker stoneware and sprinkle with salt and pepper.
2. In a medium skillet, melt butter on medium-high heat. Add onion and cook, stirring, for 2 minutes. Reduce heat to medium and cook for 10 to 12 minutes longer, stirring often, until onions are tender and golden brown. Spread over top of chicken.
3. In a bowl, combine jam, vinegar, soy sauce, ginger and rosemary. Pour over chicken and onions.
4. Cover and cook on **Low** for 5 to 7 hours or on **High** for 2½ to 4 hours, until juices run clear when chicken is pierced with a fork.

Sweet Onions

Sweet onions such as Vidalia, Maui, Rio or Walla Walla are juicy and mild. Or try Texan 1015 onions if you can find them. They are wonderfully sweet and especially good for French onion soup. If you can't find any of these varieties, use Spanish or red onions.

Clubhouse Chicken

Serves 4

Thanks go to my neighbor Caroline Wolff for passing along her favorite family slow cooker recipe. Everyone loves a clubhouse sandwich, so this combination will please kids and parents alike.

• • •

Tip

A can of condensed soup is used because it holds up well through the long slow-cooking process. Choose a reduced-sodium soup if possible.

- Slow cooker size: 3½ to 6 quart

8	boneless skinless chicken thighs	8
1 tbsp	Dijon mustard	15 mL
4	thin slices Black Forest ham, halved	4
8	slices Swiss cheese	8
1 tsp	dried thyme	5 mL
½ tsp	paprika	2 mL
1	can (10 oz/284 mL) condensed cream of mushroom soup, undiluted	1
½ cup	evaporated milk	125 mL
4	slices bacon, cooked and crumbled	4

1. Lay chicken thighs, smooth side down, between two pieces of waxed paper and pound with a mallet until ¼ inch (5 mm) thick. Spread inside of each thigh with mustard. Place a piece of ham on each thigh. Place a slice of cheese on top of ham. Roll up chicken and secure with a toothpick.
2. Lay chicken rolls in slow cooker stoneware. Sprinkle with thyme and paprika.
3. In a bowl, whisk together soup and milk and pour over chicken.
4. Cover and cook on **Low** for 5 to 6 hours, or until juices run clear when chicken is pierced with a fork.
5. Using a slotted spoon, transfer chicken to a plate and discard toothpicks. Whisk sauce in slow cooker until blended and spoon sauce over each serving. Sprinkle with crumbled bacon.

Basque Chicken

Serves 4

Enjoy the flavors of classic Spanish cooking in this easy-to-make chicken dish.

• • •

Tips

Serve over rice or mashed potatoes.

Cooking times for poultry may be longer for larger slow cookers and/or where there is a relatively high proportion of dark to white meat. For predominantly white-meat dishes, be sure to avoid overcooking.

- **Slow cooker size: 3½ to 6 quart**

¼ cup	all-purpose flour	50 mL
½ tsp	salt	2 mL
¼ tsp	freshly ground black pepper	1 mL
Pinch	cayenne pepper	Pinch
4	chicken legs, separated into thighs and drumsticks, skin removed, if desired	4
2 tbsp	vegetable oil (approx.)	25 mL
2	onions, coarsely chopped	2
8	thin slices prosciutto, trimmed of excess fat and chopped, or shaved Black Forest ham	8
1	can (28 oz/796 mL) diced tomatoes, drained	1
1	red bell pepper, coarsely chopped	1
1	green bell pepper, coarsely chopped	1
12	pitted black olives, halved	12

1. In a heavy plastic bag, combine flour, salt, black pepper and cayenne. In batches, add chicken pieces to flour mixture and toss to coat.
2. In a large skillet, heat half the oil over medium-high heat. Cook chicken pieces in batches, adding more oil as needed, until browned all over. Transfer chicken to slow cooker stoneware. Add onions, prosciutto and tomatoes.
3. Cover and cook on **Low** for 6 to 8 hours or on **High** for 4 to 6 hours, until juices run clear when chicken is pierced with a fork.
4. Add red and green peppers. Cover and cook on **High** for 20 to 25 minutes longer. Serve garnished with black olives.

Chicken Cacciatore

Serves 6 to 8

This Italian specialty is prepared hunter style, which means it is slowly cooked in a tomato sauce seasoned with onions and herbs.

• • •

Tip

I like to serve this over plain spaghetti or noodles, but you can also serve it with roasted potatoes (page 289) and a green salad.

- **Slow cooker size: 3½ to 6 quart**

¼ cup	all-purpose flour	50 mL
½ tsp	salt	2 mL
1 tsp	dried Italian seasoning (see box, page 105)	5 mL
¼ tsp	freshly ground black pepper	1 mL
3 lbs	boneless skinless chicken thighs	1.5 kg
1	onion, chopped	1
8 oz	mushrooms, sliced (about 3 cups/750 mL)	250 g
2	stalks celery, chopped	2
2	cloves garlic, minced	2
1	can (14 oz/398 mL) diced tomatoes, with juices	1
1 cup	pasta sauce or tomato sauce	250 mL
2 tbsp	dry white wine	25 mL
1	bay leaf	1
¼ cup	chopped fresh parsley	50 mL
2 tbsp	freshly grated Parmesan cheese	25 mL

1. In a heavy plastic bag, combine flour, salt, Italian seasoning and pepper. In batches, add chicken pieces to flour mixture and toss to coat. Place chicken in slow cooker stoneware.
2. Add onion, mushrooms, celery, garlic, tomatoes, pasta sauce, wine, bay leaf and parsley to slow cooker.
3. Cover and cook on **Low** for 5 to 7 hours or on **High** for 2½ to 4 hours, until juices run clear when chicken is pierced with a fork. Discard bay leaf. Serve sprinkled with Parmesan cheese.

Tuscan Chicken Legs

Serves 8

A spicy tomato sauce enhances this Italian-inspired recip[illegible]

[illegible] be [illegible] n [illegible] d[illegible] you[illegible] then[illegible] hot w[illegible] then d[illegible]

Add lots of pepper and serve it with a hearty Italian red wine.

Cooking times for poultry may be longer for larger slow cookers and/or where there is a relatively high proportion of dark to white meat. For predominantly white-meat dishes, be sure to avoid overcooking.

- Slow cooker size: 3½ to 6 quart

¼ cup	all-purpose flour	50 mL
½ tsp	salt	2 mL
¼ tsp	freshly ground black pepper	1 mL
8	chicken legs, separated into thighs, and drumsticks, skin removed, if desired	8
2	red onions, sliced	2
6	cloves garlic, halved	6
1	can (19 oz/540 mL) diced tomatoes, with juices	1
1	can (2 oz/56 g) anchovy fillets, drained and chopped	1
3 tbsp	chopped sun-dried tomatoes (see tip, at left)	45 mL
[illegible] tbsp	balsamic vinegar	25 mL
[illegible]	dried Italian seasoning	10 mL
⅓ cup	drained capers	75 mL
½ cup	pitted black olives	125 mL

1. In a heavy plastic bag, combine flour, salt and pepper. In batches, add chicken to flour mixture and toss to coat. Place in slow cooker stoneware. Add onions, garlic, tomatoes (with juices), anchovies, sun-dried tomatoes, vinegar and Italian seasoning.
2. Cover and cook on **Low** for 6 to 8 hours, or until juices run clear when chicken is pierced with a fork.
3. Add capers and olives; cover and cook on **High** for 10 to 15 minutes longer.

Coconut Curry Chicken

Serves 6

This spicy, fragrant stew is traditionally served over steamed rice. Try basmati or jasmine rice for a more authentic taste sensation.

• • •

Tips

Purchase chicken thighs in economical family packs. Divide into meal-sized portions, wrap in plastic wrap and freeze in freezer bags.

Chopped garlic in the jar is a convenient alternative to fresh garlic. It's easy to use and will keep in the refrigerator for up to 6 months.

Canned coconut milk is made from grated and soaked coconut pulp — not, as you might think, from the liquid found inside the coconut. It can be found in the Asian foods section of most supermarkets or Asian food stores. Be sure you don't buy coconut cream, which is often used for making tropical drinks such as piña coladas.

- **Slow cooker size: 3½ to 6 quart**

½ cup	all-purpose flour	125 mL
½ tsp	salt	2 mL
½ tsp	freshly ground black pepper	2 mL
12	skinless chicken thighs	12
1 tbsp	vegetable oil	15 mL
2	onions, chopped	2
4	cloves garlic, minced	4
1 tbsp	curry powder (or 2 tbsp/25 mL mild curry paste)	15 mL
½ cup	chicken stock	125 mL
1	can (14 oz/400 mL) coconut milk	1
4	carrots, peeled and sliced	4
1	can (19 oz/540 mL) chickpeas, drained and rinsed, or 2 cups (500 mL) home-cooked chickpeas (page 146)	1
1 cup	fresh or frozen green peas or snow peas (thawed if frozen)	250 mL L
1	Granny Smith apple, unpeeled, cut into 1-inch (2.5 cm) chunks	1
1 cup	plain yogurt	250 mL
½ cup	cashews	125 mL
¼ cup	shredded sweetened coconut, toasted	50 mL

1. In a heavy plastic bag, combine flour, salt and pepper. In batches, add chicken thighs to flour mixture and toss to coat. Place chicken in slow cooker stoneware, reserving excess flour.
2. In a large nonstick skillet, heat oil over medium-high heat. Add onions, garlic and curry powder. Cook, stirring, for 3 minutes, or until onions are translucent and fragrant. Sprinkle with reserved seasoned flour and cook, stirring, for 1 minute.
3. Stir in stock and coconut milk and bring to a boil. Add carrots and chickpeas. Mix well and pour over chicken in slow cooker.

4. Cover and cook on **Low** for 5 to 7 hours or on **High** for $2\frac{1}{2}$ to 4 hours, until juices run clear when chicken is pierced with a fork, vegetables are tender and curry is bubbling.
5. Stir in green peas, apple and yogurt. Cover and cook on **High** for 15 to 20 minutes longer, or until warmed through. Serve garnished with cashews and coconut.

Toasting Coconut

Spread flaked or shredded coconut on a baking sheet. Toast at 300°F (150°C) for 10 to 12 minutes, or until golden.

Tip

Cooking times for poultry may be longer for larger slow cookers and/or where there is a relatively high proportion of dark to white meat. For predominantly white-meat dishes, be sure to avoid overcooking.

Thai Chicken Thighs

Serves 4

This knockout Asian dish is full of flavor. The fresh cilantro is essential — its distinctive flavor really enhances the chicken.

• • •

Tips

To store fresh gingerroot, peel and place in a jar. Pour over white wine to cover. Use the infused wine to flavor other chicken dishes.

This recipe can easily be doubled for a larger crowd.

Commercially prepared smooth peanut butter is fine for this sauce. But if you want more peanut flavor (and less sugar), use an all-natural peanut butter.

Make Ahead

This dish can be partially assembled up to 24 hours before cooking Refrigerate sauce ingredients and chicken separately. The next day, assemble and cook as directed.

- **Slow cooker size: 3½ to 5 quart**

8	chicken thighs (about 2 lbs/1 kg), skin removed	8
½ cup	chicken stock	125 mL
¼ cup	peanut butter	50 mL
¼ cup	soy sauce	50 mL
2 tbsp	chopped fresh cilantro	25 mL
2 tbsp	freshly squeezed lime juice	25 mL
1	hot chili pepper, seeded and finely chopped (or ½ tsp/2 mL cayenne pepper)	1
2 tsp	minced fresh gingerroot (or 1 tsp/5 mL ground ginger)	10 mL
¼ cup	chopped peanuts or cashews	50 mL
	Chopped fresh cilantro	

1. Place chicken thighs in slow cooker stoneware.
2. In a bowl, combine stock, peanut butter, soy sauce, cilantro, lime juice, chili pepper and ginger. Mix well and pour sauce over chicken.
3. Cover and cook on **Low** for 6 to 8 hours, until juices run clear when chicken is pierced with a fork.
4. Serve garnished with chopped peanuts and additional fresh cilantro.

Chili Peppers

There are over 100 variations of hot peppers, and some are definitely hotter than others. The general rule: the smaller the chili, the bigger the heat.

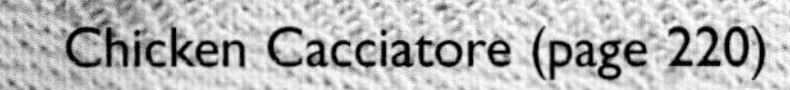

Chicken Cacciatore (page 220)

Coconut Curry Chicken (page 222)

Mother Hubbard's Favorite Shepherd's Pie (page 226)

St. Paddy's Corned Beef and Veggies with Marmalade-Mustard Glaze (page 250)

Coconut Beef Curry (page 262)

Italian Stuffed Peppers (page 277)

Key West Ribs (page 292)

Polynesian Chicken

Slow cooker size: 3½ to 6 quart

	-purpose flour	50 mL
	urry powder	5 mL
	ry mustard, divided	5 mL
	alt	2 mL
	reshly ground black pepper	1 mL
	chicken thighs, skin removed if desired	8
	can (19 oz/540 mL) pineapple pieces, drained, juice reserved	1
	green onions, chopped	4
	soy sauce	50 mL
	dry sherry	25 mL
	packed brown sugar	15 mL
	cornstarch	25 mL
	snow peas, cut in half diagonally	375 mL
	Slivered almonds, toasted	

1. ...heavy plastic bag, combine flour, curry powder, ...p (2 mL) of the mustard, salt and black pepper. In ...hes, add chicken to flour mixture and toss to coat. ...ace in slow cooker stoneware. Add pineapple pieces.
2. In a bowl, combine all but 2 tbsp (25 mL) reserved pineapple juice, green onions, soy sauce, sherry, brown sugar and remaining ½ tsp (2 mL) dry mustard; stir to mix well. Pour over chicken in slow cooker.
3. Cover and cook on **Low** for 6 to 8 hours, until juices run clear when chicken is pierced with a fork.
4. In a bowl, combine cornstarch and remaining pineapple juice; mix well. Pour into slow cooker. Add snow peas. Cover and cook on **High** for 15 to 20 minutes longer, or until sauce has thickened.
5. Serve garnished with slivered almonds.

...meat. For predominantly white-meat dishes, be sure to avoid overcooking.

Make Ahead

To speed up the preparation time, cook the rice in advance and refrigerate or freeze. To reheat, add 1 to 2 tbsp (15 to 25 mL) water or chicken stock and reheat in foil packets in the oven or in a covered microwave-safe dish.

Mother Hubbard's Favorite Shepherd's Pie

Serves 6

Here's a different kind of shepherd's pie — ground chicken and vegetables topped with a buttery yellow squash topping.

• • •

Tip

Always make sure ground meat is fully cooked before adding it to the slow cooker. Cold uncooked ground meat takes too long to come to a safe temperature. (Cooking and draining the meat first also helps eliminate extra fat and the liquid that accumulates during cooking.)

Make Ahead

This pie can be assembled the night before. Follow preparation directions and refrigerate overnight in slow cooker stoneware. The next day, place stoneware in slow cooker and continue cooking as directed.

- Slow cooker size: 3½ to 5 quart

1 tbsp	vegetable oil	15 mL
2 lbs	lean ground chicken	1 kg
2	onions, finely chopped	2
2	cloves garlic, minced	2
1	carrot, peeled and grated	1
1 cup	frozen corn kernels	250 mL
⅔ cup	tomato paste	150 mL
¾ cup	water	175 mL
2 tbsp	dried parsley (or ¼ cup/50 mL fresh)	25 mL
2 tsp	Worcestershire sauce	10 mL
1 tsp	dried thyme	5 mL
1 tsp	paprika	5 mL
1 tsp	salt	5 mL
½ tsp	freshly ground black pepper	2 mL
4 cups	puréed Hubbard squash (see box, opposite)	1 L

1. In a large nonstick skillet, heat oil over medium heat. Add ground chicken and cook, breaking up with a spoon, until no longer pink.
2. Add onions, garlic, carrot and corn; cook for 5 minutes, or until vegetables are tender. Stir in tomato paste, water, parsley, Worcestershire sauce, thyme, paprika, salt and pepper, mixing well. Transfer mixture to slow cooker stoneware and cover with squash purée.
3. Cover and cook on **Low** for 6 to 8 hours or on **High** for 3 to 4 hours, until bubbling and heated through.

To Make Squash Purée

Halve a 3-lb (1.5 kg) Hubbard, acorn or butternut squash, then scoop out seeds and pith. Place flesh side down on microwave-safe plate and cover with plastic wrap. Microwave on High for 8 to 12 minutes, or until tender. Or place in a roasting pan, flesh side up. Pour in enough water to come 1 inch (2.5 cm) up sides of pan. Bake in a 400°F (200°C) oven for 30 to 60 minutes. Let cool. Scoop out flesh and purée in a food processor or mash well with a potato masher. Add 1 tbsp (15 mL) packed brown sugar and 2 tbsp (25 mL) butter or margarine to purée, mixing well.

Tip

Once the fall harvest season rolls around, there are many winter squash varieties to choose from. Choose squash that are heavy for their size.

Cheesy Pesto Pasta

Serves 8 to 10

Round out this deliciously fragrant Italian dish with toasted garlic bread (page 135) and a green salad. For a wonderful splash of color, use rainbow-colored pasta.

• • •

Tips

Pesto can be purchased fresh or bottled in the supermarket.

You can also use ½ cup (125 mL) crumbled goat cheese in place of the last 1½ cups (375 mL) shredded mozzarella.

- **Slow cooker size: 3½ to 6 quart**

4 cups	dried fusilli, penne or other small pasta	1 L
1 tbsp	vegetable oil	15 mL
1 lb	lean ground chicken or turkey	500 g
1	onion, chopped	1
1	can (19 oz/540 mL) Italian-style stewed tomatoes, with juices (see box, page 97)	1
½ cup	basil pesto	125 mL
¼ cup	chopped fresh parsley	50 mL
½ tsp	salt	2 mL
¼ tsp	freshly ground black pepper	1 mL
¼ cup	freshly grated Parmesan cheese	50 mL
3 cups	shredded mozzarella or pre-shredded three-cheese blend, divided	750 mL

1. In a large pot of boiling salted water, cook pasta according to package directions. Drain and return to pot.
2. Meanwhile, in a large nonstick skillet, heat oil over medium-high heat. Add chicken and cook, breaking up with back of a spoon, until no longer pink. Drain any accumulated fat from skillet and stir in onion. Cook, stirring frequently, until softened, about 4 minutes. Add tomatoes, pesto, parsley, salt and pepper. Simmer for 5 minutes.
3. Stir sauce into pasta with Parmesan and half the shredded cheese. Mix well and transfer to lightly greased slow cooker stoneware.
4. Cover and cook on **Low** for 4 to 6 hours or on **High** for 2 to 3 hours, until hot and bubbly.
5. Sprinkle with remaining cheese. Cover and cook on **High** for 15 to 20 minutes longer, or until cheese has melted.

Polenta Tamale Pie

Serves 6 to 8

Ground chicken, salsa and prepackaged polenta are combined in this easy, snappy dish with a Mexican flare.

• • •

Tip

Salsa is Spanish for "sauce." Mexican cuisine includes many raw and cooked salsas based on tomatoes or tomatillos with chilies. Salsa can be chunky or smooth, and it can be spicy, medium or mild. Use your family's favorite.

Make Ahead

This dish can be completely assembled up to 24 hours before cooking. Refrigerate overnight in the slow cooker stoneware. The next day, place stoneware in slow cooker and continue to cook as directed.

- Slow cooker size: 5 to 6 quart

1 tbsp	vegetable oil	15 mL
1 lb	lean ground chicken or turkey	500 g
1 tbsp	chili powder	15 mL
1 tsp	ground cumin	5 mL
1½ cups	salsa	375 mL
1	can (14 oz/398 mL) refried beans	1
2 tbsp	chopped fresh cilantro	25 mL
1	roll (about 1 lb/500 g) prepared polenta, sliced into 20 rounds	1
3 cups	shredded Cheddar cheese, divided	750 mL

1. In a large nonstick skillet, heat oil over medium-high heat. Add chicken and cook, breaking up with back of a spoon, until no longer pink. Add chili powder and cumin, and cook, stirring, for 1 minute. Add salsa and refried beans. Simmer until mixture thickens, about 5 minutes. Stir in cilantro.
2. Place half the polenta slices in bottom of lightly greased slow cooker stoneware. Spoon chicken mixture over polenta. Top with 1½ cups (375 mL) cheese and remaining polenta.
3. Cover and cook on **Low** for 4 to 6 hours, or until heated through and bubbling.
4. Sprinkle with remaining cheese. Cover and cook on **Low** for 10 minutes longer, or until cheese melts.

Polenta

Polenta is a mush made from cornmeal. It is available ready-to-cook and packaged in a plastic wrapper in the refrigerated section or deli department of the supermarket.

Four C's Enchiladas

Serves 4 to 6

The four C's — chicken, chilies, corn and cheese — are the basis for this Mexican specialty consisting of tortillas rolled around a filling and topped with tomato sauce and cheese. Usually cooked shredded meat is used, but I have substituted ground chicken.

• • •

Tip

Tight for time? Look for pre-shredded Mexican blend cheese.

• Slow cooker size: 5 to 6 quart

1 tbsp	vegetable oil	15 mL
1 lb	lean ground chicken	500 g
2 tsp	ground cumin	10 mL
2 tsp	garlic powder	10 mL
½ tsp	dried oregano	2 mL
¼ tsp	hot pepper flakes	1 mL
1	can (4½ oz/127 mL) chopped mild green chilies, including liquid	1
1 cup	fresh or frozen corn kernels (thawed if frozen)	250 mL
1	onion, finely chopped	1
1	can (19 oz/540 mL) tomatoes, drained and chopped, juices reserved	1
8	10-inch (25 cm) flour tortillas	8
2 cups	shredded Cheddar or Monterey Jack cheese, divided	500 mL
1½ cups	salsa	375 mL

1. In a large nonstick skillet, heat oil over medium-high heat. Add chicken and cook, breaking up with back of a spoon, until no longer pink. Add cumin, garlic powder, oregano and hot pepper flakes. Cook, stirring, for 1 to 2 minutes, or until fragrant. Stir in chilies, corn, onion and drained tomatoes. Bring mixture to a boil, reduce heat and simmer for 5 minutes, or until slightly thickened.
2. Pour reserved tomato juices into a large bowl. Dip each tortilla in juices to coat lightly. Spoon chicken mixture over tortillas. Sprinkle each tortilla with about 2 tbsp (25 mL) cheese.
3. Fold tortilla over filling and place in lightly greased slow cooker stoneware, seam side down, in layers if necessary. Top each layer with salsa. Cover and cook on **Low** for 4 to 5 hours, or until hot and bubbling.
4. Sprinkle remaining cheese over salsa. Cover and cook on **High** for 15 to 20 minutes longer, or until cheese melts.

Jamaican Jerk Shredded Chicken Sandwiches

Serves 4 to 6

These sandwiches are great for casual get-togethers. Let guests serve themselves, and round out the menu with a basket of tortilla chips and a tray of raw veggies and dip.

• • •

Tip

There is nothing more Jamaican in flavor than jerk seasoning. The ingredients vary depending on the cook, but it is primarily a combination of hot chilies, thyme, cinnamon, ginger, allspice, ground cloves, fresh garlic and onions. Jerk seasoning is sold in dried or paste form, or as a liquid marinade. If you are using the marinade, use 1⁄4 cup (50 mL) and reduce the chicken stock to 1⁄4 cup (50 mL).

- Slow cooker size: 3 1⁄2 to 6 quart

2 tbsp	Caribbean jerk seasoning powder or paste	25 mL
2 lbs	boneless skinless chicken thighs	1 kg
1	red bell pepper, chopped	1
1	onion, finely chopped	1
1⁄2 cup	chicken stock	125 mL
1⁄4 cup	ketchup	50 mL
1	green bell pepper, chopped	1
2 tbsp	dark rum (optional)	25 mL
6	kaiser rolls, split	6

1. Rub jerk seasoning generously over chicken thighs. Place red pepper and onion in bottom of slow cooker stoneware. Place seasoned thighs over vegetables.
2. In a small bowl, combine stock and ketchup. Pour over chicken.
3. Cover and cook on **Low** for 5 to 7 hours or on **High** for 2 1⁄2 to 4 hours, until juices run clear when chicken is pierced with a fork.
4. Transfer chicken to a bowl and shred by pulling meat apart with two forks. Skim fat from sauce in slow cooker.
5. Return chicken to slow cooker with green pepper and rum, if using, and mix well with sauce. Cover and cook on **High** for 15 to 20 minutes longer, or until pepper has softened slightly.
6. With a slotted spoon, spoon chicken and vegetable mixture into kaiser rolls.

Savory Orange Turkey Breast

Serves 4 to 6

This simple but tasty dish brings out the best in fresh turkey breast, which is widely sold as a separate cut in supermarkets.

Tips

If you prefer dark meat, replace the turkey breast with 2 turkey thighs.

Look for turkey parts after a long holiday weekend, when they can be purchased more economically. Freeze them to have on hand for dishes like this one, or for other recipes.

Cooking times for poultry may be longer for larger slow cookers and/or where there is a relatively high proportion of dark to white meat. For predominantly white-meat dishes, be sure to avoid overcooking.

- Slow cooker size: 5 to 6 quart

1	bone-in turkey breast (2 to 3 lbs/1 to 1.5 kg)	1
½ tsp	dried thyme	2 mL
	Salt and freshly ground black pepper	
1 cup	orange juice	250 mL
1	bay leaf	1

1. Season turkey breast with thyme and salt and pepper to taste. Place in slow cooker stoneware. Add orange juice and bay leaf.
2. Cover and cook on **Low** for 6 to 8 hours, or until a meat thermometer inserted into the thickest part of the breast reads 170°F (77°C). Discard bay leaf before carving.

Turkey Breast with Bulgur and Feta

Serves 6

Most major supermarkets stock small turkey breasts on a regular basis. However, you can always find them around long holiday weekends in the summer, Thanksgiving and Christmas. Pop them in the freezer for later use; they will keep for up to 6 months.

- Slow cooker size: 4 to 6 quart

1	bone-in turkey breast (about 2 to 2½ lbs/1 to 1.25 kg)	1
½ tsp	salt	2 mL
1½ tsp	dried oregano, divided	7 mL
1 cup	uncooked bulgur	250 mL
3 tbsp	freshly squeezed lemon juice	45 mL
¼ tsp	freshly ground black pepper	1 mL
4	green onions, sliced	4
1	clove garlic, minced	1
1	can (10 oz/284 mL) condensed chicken broth, undiluted	1
¼ cup	pitted Kalamata olives (see tip, page 62)	50 mL
¼ cup	crumbled feta cheese	50 mL

1. Sprinkle turkey breast with salt and ½ tsp (2 mL) oregano.
2. In slow cooker stoneware, combine bulgur, lemon juice, pepper, green onions, garlic, broth and remaining 1 tsp (5 mL) oregano. Place turkey breast on top of bulgur mixture.
3. Cover and cook on **Low** for 4 to 8 hours, or until a meat thermometer inserted into the thickest part of the breast reads 170°F (77°C). Remove turkey from slow cooker and let stand for 5 minutes before slicing.
4. Stir olives and feta into bulgur mixture. Serve with turkey.

Bulgur

A staple in Middle Eastern cooking, bulgur, or cracked wheat, is wheat kernels that have been steamed, dried and crushed. It can be coarse, medium or fine and has a tender, chewy texture.

Turkey Tetrazzini

Serves 4 to 6

This quintessential comfort-food dish is perfect for a family meal. All you need to add is a big green salad. Serve it in shallow soup or pasta bowls and sprinkle a little chopped parsley on top for color and added flavor.

• • •

Tips

Use your favorite fresh mushrooms in this stew. Try cremini, shiitakes, cèpes or chanterelles.

A quick way to mix cornstarch with a liquid is to use a jar. Screw the lid on tightly and shake the jar until the mixture is smooth. (This is faster than trying to stir or whisk until all the cornstarch is dissolved.)

- **Slow cooker size: 3½ to 6 quart**

2 lbs	boneless skinless turkey thighs or breasts, cut into 2- by ½-inch (5 by 1 cm) strips	1 kg
1 cup	chicken stock	250 mL
½ cup	dry white wine	125 mL
1	onion, finely chopped	1
2 tbsp	chopped fresh parsley	25 mL
½ tsp	salt	2 mL
¼ tsp	dried thyme	1 mL
¼ tsp	freshly ground black pepper	1 mL
3 tbsp	cornstarch	45 mL
¼ cup	water	50 mL
4 oz	fresh mushrooms, sliced	125 g
8 oz	dried linguine, broken into 2-inch (5 cm) pieces	250 g
½ cup	table (18%) cream	125 mL
½ cup	freshly grated Parmesan cheese, divided	125 mL

1. In slow cooker stoneware, combine turkey, stock, wine, onion, parsley, salt, thyme and pepper.
2. Cover and cook on **Low** for 4 to 5 hours, or until juices run clear when turkey is pierced with a fork.
3. In a bowl or jar, combine cornstarch and water (see tip, at left). Stir into slow cooker along with mushrooms. Cover and cook on **High** for 20 minutes longer.
4. Meanwhile, in a large pot of boiling salted water, cook linguine according to package directions. Drain well.
5. Stir cream, noodles and ¼ cup (50 mL) cheese into slow cooker. Cover and cook on **High** for 5 to 10 minutes longer, or until heated through.
6. Spoon into serving bowls and top with remaining Parmesan.

Spinach Turkey Rolls

Serves 4 to 6

Wow your guests with these sage-infused turkey rolls. If you have fresh sage growing in your garden, substitute 12 to 15 finely chopped leaves for the dried sage.

• • •

Tips

To toast almonds: Spread on a baking sheet and bake in a 350°F (180°C) oven for 5 to 7 minutes, or until golden brown and fragrant.

Prosciutto is an Italian cured ham with a slightly salty flavor. Make sure the deli slices it paper-thin. A good-quality Black Forest ham can be substituted, if you must.

- Slow cooker size: 6 quart

1½ lbs	turkey breast cutlets (about 6)	750 g
1	package (10 oz/300 g) frozen chopped spinach, thawed and squeezed dry	1
2 tbsp	finely chopped fresh parsley	25 mL
¼ cup	dry bread crumbs	50 mL
3 tbsp	freshly grated Parmesan cheese	45 mL
3 tbsp	chopped toasted almonds	45 mL
½ tsp	dried sage, divided	2 mL
½ tsp	freshly ground black pepper, divided	2 mL
6	thin slices prosciutto or ham	6
¼ tsp	salt	1 mL
¼ tsp	paprika	1 mL
¼ cup	dry white wine	50 mL
¾ cup	chicken stock	175 mL
1 tbsp	all-purpose flour	15 mL
2 tbsp	water	25 mL

1. With a mallet, pound turkey cutlets between two sheets of waxed paper until about ¼ inch (1 cm) thick.
2. In a bowl, combine spinach, parsley, bread crumbs, Parmesan, almonds, ¼ tsp (1 mL) sage and ¼ tsp (1 mL) pepper. Mix well.
3. Place a slice of prosciutto on each cutlet. Spoon about ½ cup (125 mL) spinach mixture on top of prosciutto. Starting at short end, roll up each cutlet, encasing filling. Secure rolls with a toothpick. Place rolls in slow cooker stoneware, seam side down, and sprinkle with salt, remaining pepper and paprika. Pour wine and stock around rolls.
4. Cover and cook on **Low** for 3 to 5 hours, or until turkey is tender. Remove rolls from slow cooker and keep warm.
5. In a small bowl, whisk together flour, remaining sage and water. Add to slow cooker and whisk in. Cover and cook on **High** for 10 to 15 minutes, or until thickened.
6. Remove toothpicks and cut turkey rolls into ½-inch (1 cm) slices. Spoon sauce over turkey.

Turkey Mushroom Loaf

Serves 4 to 6

My family would love it if I made this loaf every night of the week. It's a natural with mashed potatoes.

• • •

Variation

To make a fancier version of the sauce in Step 5, sauté 1 cup (250 mL) finely chopped mushrooms in 1 tbsp (15 mL) butter until juices have evaporated; add remaining soup and water as directed and bring to a boil. Stir in 1 tbsp (15 mL) madeira wine and a pinch of thyme.

Make Ahead

Loaf can be assembled 12 hours in advance. Prepare the ingredients in the slow cooker up to the cooking stage and refrigerate in stoneware insert overnight. The next day, place stoneware in slow cooker and cook as directed.

- **Slow cooker size: 3½ to 5 quart**

1½ lbs	ground turkey	750 g
1	can (10 oz/284 mL) cream of mushroom soup	1
⅓ cup	fine dry bread crumbs	75 mL
1	egg, lightly beaten	1
2	green onions, finely chopped	2
½ cup	finely chopped mushrooms	125 mL
1 tbsp	Worcestershire sauce	15 mL
1 tsp	dry mustard	5 mL
¼ tsp	freshly ground black pepper	1 mL
Dash	hot pepper sauce	Dash

Topping

2 tbsp	fine dry bread crumbs	25 mL
1 tbsp	chopped fresh parsley (or 1 tsp/5 mL dried)	15 mL

1. Cut a 2-foot (60 cm) length of foil in half lengthwise. Fold each strip in half lengthwise, forming two long strips. Crisscross the strips in the bottom of the slow cooker, bringing the ends of the foil strips up and clear of the stoneware rim.
2. In a large bowl, combine turkey, half the soup (remainder will be used for sauce in Step 4), bread crumbs, egg, onions, mushrooms, Worcestershire sauce, dry mustard, black pepper and hot pepper sauce; mix well. Press evenly into foil-lined slow cooker stoneware, tucking foil ends under lid.
3. *Topping:* In a bowl, combine bread crumbs and parsley. Sprinkle over loaf.
4. Cover and cook on **Low** for 8 to 10 hours or on **High** for 4 to 6 hours, until a meat thermometer inserted into meatloaf reads 170°F (77°C). Let stand for 15 minutes. Remove lid and grasp ends of foil strips to lift out meatloaf.
5. Heat remaining soup with ¼ cup (50 mL) water and serve alongside loaf.

Tex-Mex Turkey Pancake

Serves 6

Sure, go ahead and use up the Christmas turkey in sandwiches and soups. Or try something a little different like this rice pancake. It's sure to become a family favorite.

• • •

Tip

You can also line the slow cooker with cheesecloth, using enough material to lift out the finished pancake.

• Slow cooker size: 5 to 6 quart

2½ cups	cooked rice (about ¾ cup/175 mL uncooked)	625 mL
2	eggs, lightly beaten	2
2 tbsp	butter, melted	25 mL
2 cups	shredded cooked turkey or chicken	500 mL
1	onion, thinly sliced	1
2 cups	salsa	500 mL
½ cup	sliced black olives	125 mL
1 cup	shredded Cheddar or Monterey Jack cheese	250 mL
¼ cup	chopped fresh cilantro	50 mL

1. Cut a 2-foot (60 cm) length of foil in half lengthwise. Fold each strip in half lengthwise, forming two long strips. Crisscross the strips in the bottom of the slow cooker, bringing the ends of the foil strips up and clear of the stoneware rim.
2. In a bowl, combine rice, eggs and melted butter. Pour into slow cooker. Sprinkle turkey, onion, salsa and olives over rice mixture. (Mixture will be quite liquid.) Tuck foil ends under lid.
3. Cover and cook on **Low** for 3 to 4 hours, or until hot and bubbly.
4. Sprinkle pancake with cheese and cilantro. Cover and cook on **High** for 10 to 15 minutes longer, or until cheese is melted. Turn off slow cooker, remove lid and let stand for 5 minutes.
5. Run knife around edge of pancake. Using foil handles, lift pancake out of slow cooker.

Beef and Veal

Anthony's Big Ragu

Serves 6 to 8

My good friend Anthony Scian, a brilliant computer engineer, loves to cook. He will spend Sundays making a big pot of this sauce so his family can enjoy it during the week. Serve it over hot pasta, sprinkled with grated Parmesan cheese.

• • •

Tips

Anthony's mother taught him two rules for making pasta sauce: never use tomato paste and always add a little butter and vinegar at the end for a smooth, rich flavor.

Make Ahead

This dish can be completely assembled up to 24 hours before cooking. Chill ground meat mixture completely before combining with other sauce ingredients. Refrigerate sauce overnight in slow cooker stoneware. The next day, place stoneware in slow cooker and continue to cook as directed.

• Slow cooker size: 3½ to 6 quart

1 lb	lean ground beef	500 g
½ lb	lean ground pork or turkey	250 g
2	onions, finely chopped	2
4	cloves garlic, minced	4
1	stalk celery, finely chopped	1
1 tbsp	dried Italian seasoning (see box, page 105)	15 mL
1	can (28 oz/796 mL) diced tomatoes, with juices	1
1	carrot, peeled and finely chopped	1
1	red bell pepper, finely chopped	1
8 oz	mushrooms, sliced	250 g
1	can (28 oz/796 mL) pasta sauce	1
3	whole cloves	3
1 tbsp	balsamic vinegar	15 mL
2 tbsp	butter (optional)	25 mL

1. In a large nonstick skillet, over medium-high heat, combine ground beef, ground pork, onions, garlic, celery and Italian seasoning. Cook, breaking up meat with back of a spoon, until vegetables are tender and meat is no longer pink. Drain and transfer to slow cooker stoneware.
2. Add tomatoes, carrot, red pepper, mushrooms, pasta sauce and cloves to slow cooker. Stir to combine.
3. Cover and cook on **Low** for 8 to 10 hours or on **High** for 4 to 6 hours, until hot and bubbling.
4. Stir in vinegar and butter, if using. Cover and cook on **High** for 5 to 10 minutes longer, or until butter is completely melted.

Basic Spaghetti Sauce Italiano

Makes 6 cups (1.5 L)

This is my favorite recipe for spaghetti sauce. It makes enough for a couple of meals. If you have a small amount left over, spoon it over a split baked potato and add a dollop of sour cream for a satisfying quick meal.

• • •

Tip

It is always best to brown ground meat before adding it to the slow cooker. This ensures the meat is completely cooked and reaches the recommended cooked temperature of 150°F (65°C). If you have a good nonstick skillet, you will not need to add any extra fat (from cooking oil) unless you are browning ground turkey or chicken, which is generally very lean.

- Slow cooker size: 3½ to 6 quart

1 tbsp	vegetable oil	15 mL
2 lbs	lean ground beef, turkey or chicken	1 kg
4	cloves garlic, minced	4
2	onions, finely chopped	2
2	stalks celery, finely chopped	2
1 tbsp	dried oregano	15 mL
½ tsp	dried thyme	2 mL
½ tsp	dried basil	2 mL
1	can (28 oz/796 mL) diced tomatoes, with juices	1
1	can (5½ oz/156 mL) tomato paste	1
1	bay leaf	1
1 tbsp	packed brown sugar	15 mL
½ tsp	salt	2 mL
½ tsp	hot pepper flakes (optional)	2 mL
	Salt and freshly ground black pepper	
	Hot cooked spaghetti	

1. In a large skillet, heat oil over medium-high heat. Cook beef, breaking up with back of a spoon, until no longer pink. Add garlic, onions, celery, oregano, thyme and basil. Cook for 2 to 3 minutes, or until vegetables are tender. With a slotted spoon, transfer seasoned meat mixture to slow cooker stoneware.
2. Add tomatoes (with juices), tomato paste, bay leaf, brown sugar, salt and hot pepper flakes, if using, to slow cooker; stir to combine.
3. Cover and cook on **Low** for 8 to 10 hours or on **High** for 4 to 6 hours, until hot and bubbling. Discard bay leaf. Season sauce to taste with salt and black pepper.
4. Serve over hot cooked spaghetti or other pasta.

Chili Spaghetti Pie

Serves 6 to 8

Spaghetti pie originated as a creative use for leftover cooked spaghetti. This pie combines two family favorites — spaghetti and chili.

• • •

Tip

If you can't find Italian-style stewed tomatoes, use regular stewed tomatoes and add ½ tsp (2 mL) dried Italian seasoning or a combination of dried basil, marjoram, oregano and thyme.

- Slow cooker size: 5 to 6 quart

Crust

8 oz	dried spaghetti	250 g
1	egg, lightly beaten	1
¼ cup	butter, melted	50 mL
⅓ cup	freshly grated Parmesan cheese	75 mL
1 tsp	chili powder	5 mL

Filling

1 lb	lean ground beef	500 g
1	onion, finely chopped	1
1	can (14 oz/398 mL) baked beans in tomato sauce	1
1	can (19 oz/540 mL) Italian-style stewed tomatoes, with juices	1
1 tsp	chili powder	5 mL
½ tsp	freshly ground black pepper	2 mL
2 cups	shredded Monterey Jack cheese, divided	500 mL

1. *Crust:* In a pot of boiling salted water, cook spaghetti according to package directions. Drain and rinse well under cold water.
2. In a large bowl, combine egg, melted butter, Parmesan and chili powder. Add cooked spaghetti and toss to coat. Spoon into lightly greased slow cooker stoneware, pushing mixture slightly up sides.
3. *Filling:* In a large nonstick skillet, over medium-high heat, cook ground beef and onion, breaking up meat with back of a spoon, until meat is no longer pink. Drain off any fat. Add beans, tomatoes, chili powder and pepper. Cook, stirring, for 2 minutes, or until thoroughly heated. Stir in 1 cup (250 mL) Monterey Jack cheese. Spoon meat/bean mixture into spaghetti-lined stoneware.

4. Cover and cook on **Low** for 4 to 6 hours, or until hot and bubbling.
5. Sprinkle remaining Monterey Jack cheese over top of pie. Cover and cook on **High** for 20 to 30 minutes longer, or until cheese melts.

Cooking Ground Meat in the Slow Cooker

Always make sure ground meat is fully cooked before adding it to the slow cooker. Cold uncooked ground meat takes too long to come to a safe temperature. (Cooking and draining the meat first also helps eliminate extra fat and the liquid that accumulates during cooking.)

Tip

The beans in this recipe are an excellent source of soluble fiber.

Easy-on-Ya Lasagna

Serves 6 to 8

This easy slow cooker version of lasagna is another contribution from my neighbor Caroline Wolff. It tastes as good as the baked version but is a lot less work.

• • •

Tip

You can substitute mild Italian sausage for the ground beef. Reduce the basil and oregano to 1⁄4 tsp (1 mL) each.

- Slow cooker size: 3½ to 6 quart

8	dried lasagna noodles, broken into bite-sized pieces	8
1½ lbs	lean ground beef	750 g
1	onion, finely chopped	1
2	cloves garlic, minced	2
1	can (28 oz/796 mL) diced tomatoes, with juices	1
2 tbsp	tomato paste	25 mL
2 tsp	granulated sugar	10 mL
2 tbsp	chopped fresh parsley	25 mL
½ tsp	dried basil	2 mL
½ tsp	dried oregano	2 mL
1 cup	creamed cottage cheese	250 mL
2 cups	shredded mozzarella cheese	500 mL
½ tsp	freshly ground black pepper	2 mL
½ cup	freshly grated Parmesan cheese	125 mL

1. In a large pot of boiling salted water, cook noodles for 5 to 7 minutes, or until softened but slightly undercooked. Drain and rinse under cold water.
2. In a large nonstick skillet, over medium-high heat, cook ground beef, onion and garlic, breaking up meat with back of a spoon, until beef is no longer pink. With a slotted spoon, transfer meat mixture to slow cooker stoneware.
3. In a bowl, combine tomatoes, tomato paste, sugar, parsley, basil and oregano. Add to slow cooker along with cottage cheese, mozzarella, pepper and partially cooked noodles. Stir well.
4. Cover and cook on **Low** for 6 to 8 hours or on **High** for 3 to 4 hours, until hot and bubbling.
5. Sprinkle with Parmesan cheese. Cover and cook on **High** for 10 minutes longer, or until cheese has melted.

Homestyle Pot Roast

Serves 6 to 8

I make this pot roast when I want to be reminded of my childhood and the wonderful aromas that greeted me when I walked in the door. I'm sure my children will have similar memories when they get older.

• • •

Tip

Slow cooking helps to tenderize less expensive cuts of meat. Pot roast benefits from a longer cooking on **Low**, but if you're short of time, count on 6 hours of simmering on **High** to produce fork-tender meat.

Make Ahead

This dish can be completely assembled up to 12 hours in advance of cooking. Follow preparation directions and refrigerate overnight in the slow cooker stoneware. The next day, place stoneware in slow cooker and continue cooking as directed.

- Slow cooker size: 3½ to 5 quart

¼ cup	all-purpose flour	50 mL
	Salt and freshly ground black pepper	
1	boneless beef cross rib or rump roast (3 to 4 lbs/1.5 to 2 kg)	1
1 tbsp	vegetable oil	15 mL
2	onions, quartered	2
4	carrots, peeled and sliced	4
4 to 6	potatoes, peeled and quartered	4 to 6
1 cup	beef stock	250 mL
1	can (7½ oz/221 mL) tomato sauce	1
1	clove garlic, minced	1
½ tsp	dried thyme	2 mL
1	bay leaf	1

1. In a bowl, season flour with salt and pepper. Pat meat dry and coat on all sides with seasoned flour.
2. In a large skillet, heat oil over medium-high heat. Add meat and cook, turning with wooden spoons, for 7 to 10 minutes, or until browned on all sides. Transfer meat to slow cooker stoneware.
3. Add onions, carrots, potatoes, stock, tomato sauce, garlic, thyme and bay leaf to slow cooker.
4. Cover and cook on **Low** for 10 to 12 hours or on **High** for 6 to 8 hours, until vegetables and meat are tender.
5. Remove roast, onions, carrots and potatoes, cover and set aside. Discard bay leaf. Tip slow cooker and skim off any excess fat from surface of gravy; season with additional salt and pepper. Pour gravy into sauceboat. Slice roast, arrange on a serving platter and surround with vegetables. Serve with gravy.

Wine-Braised Pot Roast

Serves 6 to 8

Roast beef has to be one of the most popular Sunday dinner entrées. Although traditionally made in the oven, this slow cooker version is delicious. Serve with roasted potatoes (page 289) or mashed potatoes (pages 255 and 303).

• • •

Tip

Browning the meat before it is placed in the slow cooker will give the pot roast an extra-rich flavor and eliminate any additional fat. But if you are pressed for time, you can place it directly in the slow cooker without browning first.

- Slow cooker size: 3½ to 6 quart

1 tbsp	vegetable oil	15 mL
1	boneless beef cross rib or rump roast (3 to 4 lbs/1.5 to 2 kg)	1
4	carrots, peeled and cut into 1-inch (2.5 cm) chunks	4
2	stalks celery, sliced	2
6	cloves garlic, peeled	6
1 cup	dry red wine	250 mL
1	can (10 oz/284 mL) condensed beef consomme, undiluted	1
1 tsp	whole black peppercorns	5 mL
2	bay leaves	2
½ tsp	dried thyme	2 mL

1. In a large skillet, heat oil over medium-high heat. Add roast and cook, turning with wooden spoons, for 7 to 10 minutes, or until browned on all sides. Transfer meat to slow cooker stoneware.
2. Add carrots, celery, garlic, wine, consomme, peppercorns, bay leaves and thyme to slow cooker.
3. Cover and cook on **Low** for 8 to 12 hours or on **High** for 4 to 6 hours, until meat is fork-tender.
4. Remove roast from slow cooker and let stand for 15 minutes before carving. Skim fat from juices and discard bay leaves. To serve, slice beef across the grain. Serve with beef juices and vegetables.

Mediterranean Pot Roast

Serves 6 to 8

I have fond memories of walking into my grandmother's house for Sunday night dinner and being greeted with the tantalizing aroma of a roast braising in the oven. This sophisticated version features tangy sun dried tomatoes and olives and is served with a rich beef juice.

• • •

Tips

Choose a well-marbled roast such as cross rib, blade or rump.

Adding vinegar, apple juice or wine to a pot roast helps tenderize the meat while it simmers.

Make Ahead

This dish can be completely assembled up to 12 hours in advance of cooking. Follow preparation directions and refrigerate overnight in the slow cooker stoneware. The next day, place stoneware in slow cooker and continue cooking as directed.

- Slow cooker size: 3½ to 5 quart

1 tbsp	vegetable oil	15 mL
1 tbsp	dried Italian seasoning	15 mL
1	large clove garlic, minced	1
1	boneless beef cross rib or blade roast (3 to 4 lbs/1.5 to 2 kg)	1
1 tsp	freshly ground black pepper	5 mL
⅓ cup	oil-packed sun-dried tomatoes, drained and chopped	75 mL
½ cup	pitted black olives, halved	125 mL
10 to 12	pearl onions, peeled	10 to 12
½ cup	beef stock	125 mL
1 tbsp	balsamic vinegar	15 mL

1. In a large skillet, heat oil over medium-high heat. Add Italian seasoning and garlic; cook for 1 minute. Sprinkle roast with pepper and place in hot seasoned oil. Cook, turning with wooden spoons, for 7 to 10 minutes, or until browned on all sides. Transfer meat to slow cooker stoneware and sprinkle with sun-dried tomatoes, olives and onions.
2. In a bowl, combine stock and vinegar; pour into slow cooker.
3. Cover and cook on **Low** for 8 to 10 hours or on **High** for 4 to 6 hours, until meat is fork-tender.
4. Remove beef from slow cooker and let stand for 15 minutes before serving. To slice beef, cut across the grain. Serve with beef juice and vegetables.

Orange Sesame Glazed Pot Roast

Serves 6 to 8

This Chinese-inspired roast is a tantalizing blend of sweet and tangy.

• • •

Tips

Slow cooking helps to tenderize less expensive cuts of meat such as pot roasts, which will benefit from longer cooking on low heat. But if you are short of time, cook on **High** for at least 4 hours to produce fork-tender meat.

Browning the meat before it is placed in the slow cooker will give the pot roast an extra-rich flavor and eliminate any additional fat. But if you are pressed for time, you can place it directly in the slow cooker without browning first.

• **Slow cooker size: 3½ to 6 quart**

1 tbsp	vegetable oil	15 mL
1	boneless beef cross rib, blade roast or brisket (3 to 4 lbs/1.5 to 2 kg)	1
½ cup	hoisin sauce	125 mL
1	can (7½ oz/213 mL) tomato sauce	1
¼ cup	cider vinegar	50 mL
2 tsp	grated orange zest	10 mL
¼ cup	freshly squeezed orange juice	50 mL
2 tbsp	grated gingerroot (or 1 tsp/5 mL ground ginger)	25 mL
2 tbsp	sesame oil	25 mL

1. In a large skillet, heat vegetable oil over medium-high heat. Add roast and cook, turning with wooden spoons, for 7 to 10 minutes, or until browned on all sides. Transfer meat to slow cooker stoneware.
2. In a bowl, whisk together hoisin sauce, tomato sauce, vinegar, orange zest, orange juice, ginger and sesame oil. Pour over roast.
3. Cover and cook on **Low** for 8 to 12 hours or on **High** for 4 to 6 hours, until meat is fork-tender.
4. Remove roast from slow cooker and let stand for 15 minutes before carving. Slice beef across the grain and serve with beef juices.

Sesame Oil

Sesame oil is available in pale and dark varieties. Pale sesame oil is usually used for cooking and salad dressings. Dark sesame oil has a much stronger flavor than the pale oil and is usually used as an accent oil, to give a boost of flavor and aroma to a finished dish.

Onion Cranberry Brisket

Serves 8 to 10

If you can't find a brisket roast, a cross rib or blade pot roast will work well, too. Serve with lots of garlic mashed potatoes (page 303) and a green vegetable. Use whole-berry or jellied cranberry sauce. (You may want to melt the cranberry sauce in the microwave first so it mixes smoothly with the other ingredients.)

- Slow cooker size: 5 to 6 quart

1	beef double brisket, boneless cross rib or blade pot roast (3 to 4 lbs/1.5 to 2 kg)	1
1 tbsp	vegetable oil	15 mL
1	can (14 oz/398 mL) cranberry sauce	1
1	envelope (1 ½ oz/40 g) onion soup mix	1
2	cloves garlic, minced	2
¼ cup	water	50 mL
2 tbsp	prepared mustard	25 mL
	Salt and freshly ground black pepper	

1. Cut brisket in half if necessary so it will fit in slow cooker. In a large skillet, heat oil over medium-high heat. Add meat and cook, turning with wooden spoons, for 7 to 10 minutes, or until browned on all sides. Transfer meat to slow cooker stoneware.
2. In a bowl, combine cranberry sauce, onion soup mix, garlic, water and mustard. Mix well and pour over brisket.
3. Cover and cook on **Low** for 10 to 12 hours or on **High** for 6 to 8 hours, until meat is fork-tender. Transfer brisket to a cutting board.
4. Skim any fat from surface of gravy. Season with salt and pepper. Pour gravy into a sauce boat. Slice roast and arrange on a serving platter. Serve with gravy.

St. Paddy's Corned Beef and Veggies with Marmalade-Mustard Glaze

Serves 8 to 10

What better way to celebrate the middle of March than with a succulent corned beef and all the trimmings?

• • •

Tips

Because the cabbage is cooked separately after meat is finished, it doesn't impart its strong flavor to the other vegetables.

I use a large (5- to 6-quart) slow cooker for this recipe. If you have a smaller (3½- to 4-quart) cooker, cut the brisket in pieces to fit.

- Slow cooker size: 5 to 6 quart

4 to 6	potatoes, peeled and quartered	4 to 6
4 to 6	carrots, peeled and cut into 2-inch (5 cm) chunks	4 to 6
2	onions, cut into quarters	2
1	corned beef brisket (about 4 lbs/2 kg)	1
1	bottle (12 oz/341 mL) strong beer	1
2 to 4	whole cloves	2 to 4
1 tsp	whole peppercorns	5 mL
1 tbsp	packed brown sugar	15 mL
	Water	
1	small cabbage, cut into wedges	1

Marmalade Glaze

½ cup	orange marmalade	125 mL
2 tbsp	Dijon mustard	25 mL
2 tbsp	packed brown sugar	25 mL

1. In slow cooker stoneware, combine potatoes, carrots and onions. Add corned beef, beer, cloves, peppercorns and brown sugar. Pour in enough water to cover meat and vegetables.
2. Cover and cook on **Low** for 10 to 12 hours or on **High** for 6 to 8 hours, until meat is fork-tender. Remove meat from cooking liquid and place on baking sheet. Transfer vegetables to a platter and keep warm.

3. Pour cooking liquid into a large pot over medium-high heat. Taste and, if too salty, discard some of the liquid and replace it with fresh water. Repeat until saltiness is to your taste. Secure cabbage wedges with toothpicks and add to cooking liquid. Bring liquid to a boil; reduce heat and simmer for 15 minutes, or until cabbage is tender.
4. *Marmalade glaze:* In a bowl, combine marmalade, mustard and brown sugar. Spoon over corned beef and place under a preheated broiler, 6 inches (15 cm) from heat source. Cook for about 2 to 3 minutes.
5. Thinly slice beef against the grain and place on platter with vegetables. Add cabbage wedges to platter and serve with additional mustard.

Tips

Removing lid of slow cooker releases heat, which will lengthen the cooking time. Do not remove lid until minimum cooking time.

Ginger Beef and Broccoli

Serves 4 to 6

This is just like a stir-fry, only much easier. Serve it with steamed rice (page 163). Stop at your favorite Asian take-out restaurant and pick up an order of egg rolls or pot stickers to accompany this dish. Fortune cookies and green tea complete the meal.

• • •

Tips

You can substitute 2 cups (500 mL) chopped bok choy or kale for the broccoli.

A quick way to mix cornstarch with a liquid is to use a jar. Screw the lid on tightly and shake the jar until the mixture is smooth. (This is faster than trying to stir or whisk until all the cornstarch is dissolved.)

- Slow cooker size: 3½ to 6 quart

1 tbsp	vegetable oil	15 mL
1 tsp	sesame oil (optional)	5 mL
1 lb	outside round or blade beef steak, trimmed and cut into ½-inch (1 cm) cubes	500 g
1 cup	beef stock	250 mL
¼ cup	soy sauce	50 mL
1 tbsp	dry sherry or lemon juice	15 mL
½ tsp	Asian hot chili paste or hot pepper flakes	2 mL
1	small onion, sliced	1
4	cloves garlic, minced	4
2 tbsp	grated gingerroot	25 mL
1	can (8 oz/227 mL) sliced water chestnuts, drained and rinsed	1
1 tbsp	cornstarch	15 mL
2 tbsp	water	25 mL
4	green onions, cut into 1-inch (2.5 cm) pieces	4
2 cups	chopped broccoli	500 mL

1. In a large nonstick skillet, heat vegetable oil and sesame oil, if using, over medium-high heat. Cook beef in batches, stirring, for 5 to 7 minutes, or until browned on all sides. With a slotted spoon, transfer meat to slow cooker stoneware.
2. Add stock, soy sauce, sherry, chili paste, onion, garlic, ginger and water chestnuts to slow cooker; stir to combine.
3. Cover and cook on **Low** for 8 to 10 hours or on **High** for 4 to 6 hours, until beef is tender.
4. In a small bowl or jar, mix together cornstarch and water (see tip, at left). Pour into slow cooker along with green onions and broccoli. Cover and cook on **High** for 15 to 20 minutes longer, or until sauce has thickened and broccoli is tender-crisp.

Mexicali Round Steak

Serves 6

Enjoy this hearty steak with a basket of warmed soft tortillas. Serve with additional salsa and sprinkle with chopped fresh cilantro.

• • •

Tip

Vary the taste of this all-in-one meal by using pinto beans instead of black beans. If you wish, use a pre-shredded cheese blend to save a little time.

- Slow cooker size: 3½ to 6 quart

1½ lbs	outside round beef steak, trimmed	750 g
½ tsp	freshly ground black pepper	2 mL
1 cup	fresh or frozen corn kernels (thawed if frozen)	250 mL
1	can (19 oz/540 mL) black beans, drained and rinsed, or 2 cups (500 mL) home-cooked beans (page 146)	1
½ cup	chopped fresh cilantro	125 mL
2	stalks celery, thinly sliced	2
1	onion, sliced	1
2 cups	salsa	500 mL
½ cup	beef stock	125 mL
1 cup	shredded Cheddar or Monterey Jack cheese (optional)	250 mL

1. Cut steaks into 6 pieces and season with pepper. Place in bottom of slow cooker stoneware. (If using 3½-quart cooker, steaks will have to be layered.)
2. In a bowl, combine corn, beans, cilantro, celery, onion, salsa and stock. Spoon over beef.
3. Cover and cook on **Low** for 8 to 10 hours or on **High** for 4 to 6 hours, until beef is tender.
4. Sprinkle with cheese, if using. Cover and cook on **High** for 15 to 20 minutes longer, or until cheese is melted.

Nancy's Rouladen

Serves 8 to 10

This tasty dish comes courtesy of my friend Nancy Forte. She says it originated in an old church cookbook but has been adapted over the years. She always serves it with mashed potatoes (pages 255 and 303) and a green vegetable. Use garlic-flavored dill pickles if you have them.

• • •

Tip

If the steak slices are large once they have been flattened, cut the rolls in half before adding to the slow cooker. Each roll should be about 4 inches (10 cm) long.

- Slow cooker size: 3½ to 6 quart

2 lbs	rouladen or inside round steak, cut into 8 to 10 slices	1 kg
1 lb	bacon, finely chopped	500 g
8	cloves garlic, minced	8
½ cup	Dijon mustard	125 mL
1	sweet onion, finely chopped	1
1 cup	finely chopped dill pickle	250 mL
2 tbsp	vegetable oil (approx.)	25 mL
	Water	

Gravy

¼ cup	all-purpose flour	50 mL
¼ cup	water	50 mL
1 tbsp	Worcestershire sauce	15 mL
	Salt and freshly ground black pepper	

1. With a mallet, pound steak slices until about ⅛ inch (3 mm) thick. Cut off uneven ends if necessary.
2. In a large nonstick skillet, over medium-high heat, cook bacon, stirring occasionally, for 8 to 10 minutes, or until tender but not crisp. Drain and cool. Discard fat from pan.
3. Lay beef slices on cutting board and rub each with about ½ tsp (2 mL) minced garlic. Spread each slice with a heaping teaspoon (5 mL) Dijon mustard. Sprinkle with cooked bacon, onion and pickle, keeping filling about ½ inch (1 cm) from edge of meat.
4. Starting at narrow end, roll up each slice, encasing filling. Secure each roll with toothpick.
5. Add 1 tbsp (15 mL) oil to skillet and heat over medium-high heat. Add rolls and cook in batches for about 5 minutes, or until browned on all sides, adding more oil as needed. Transfer to slow cooker stoneware, seam side down. Pour in enough water to cover rolls.

6. Cover and cook on **Low** for 8 to 10 hours or on **High** for 4 to 6 hours, until tender. With a slotted spoon, carefully remove rolls to a platter and keep warm.
7. *Gravy:* Strain 2 cups (500 mL) cooking liquid from slow cooker into a saucepan. (Discard remaining liquid.) In a bowl, whisk together flour and water until smooth. Whisk into saucepan. Bring to a boil over high heat, whisking constantly, for 5 to 7 minutes, or until thickened. Add Worcestershire sauce, salt and pepper.
8. Pour sauce over rolls on platter or serve separately in a sauceboat.

Horseradish Mashed Potatoes

Cook and mash 2 lbs (1 kg) peeled potatoes. Stir in 1 cup (250 mL) milk, 2 tbsp (25 mL) butter, 1 clove minced garlic and 2 tbsp (25 mL) creamed horseradish sauce. *Serves 6.*

Variation

Mushroom and Green Pepper Rouladen: Omit dill pickle. After cooking bacon, cook 1 cup (250 mL) finely chopped mushrooms and 1⁄2 cup (125 mL) finely chopped green pepper in bacon drippings. Add to filling when assembling rolls.

Comforting Shredded Beef

Serves 4 to 6

Here's true comfort food at its best. These succulent shreds of juicy roast beef can be served with mashed potatoes or used to make Philly Beef Wraps (see recipe, page 257). Take comfort in the fact that if you have any leftovers, they won't be around for long!

• • •

Tips

Sirloin tip roast is a very lean cut of beef but ideal for shredding in this recipe.

You can omit the brandy, if you wish, but it imparts a rich, dark color to the juice.

Make Ahead

This dish can be completely assembled up to 12 hours in advance of cooking. Follow preparation directions and refrigerate overnight in the slow cooker stoneware. The next day, place stoneware in slow cooker and continue cooking as directed.

- **Slow cooker size: 3½ to 4 quart**

1	sirloin tip roast (3 to 4 lbs/1.5 to 2 kg)	1
	Salt and freshly ground black pepper	
1 tbsp	vegetable oil	15 mL
¼ cup	cognac or brandy (optional)	50 mL
2 cups	beef stock	500 mL
1 cup	red wine	250 mL
2	onions, sliced	2

1. Season roast with salt and pepper. In a large skillet or Dutch oven, heat oil over medium-high heat. Add roast and cook, turning with wooden spoons, for 10 minutes, or until browned on all sides. Pour cognac over meat (if using) and flame with a match. Transfer meat to slow cooker stoneware. Add stock, red wine and onions.
2. Cover and cook on **Low** for 10 to 12 hours or on **High** for 6 to 8 hours, until meat is very tender. (If using a large [4- to 6-quart] slow cooker, meat may not be completely submerged in liquid; turn 2 or 3 times during cooking so exposed edges will not dry out.)
3. Remove meat from juice and let stand for 10 minutes. Using a fork, pull apart roast, following the natural grain of the meat. It should fall apart very easily. Serve with beef juice for dipping.

Philly Beef Wraps

Serves 4 to 6

This is a great way to use up any leftover shredded beef. Just warm it in the sauce and enjoy this no fuss, make-your-own dinner.

• • •

Tips

To serve, set out bowls of cheese, onions and hot pepper rings and let everyone help themselves.

To fill and fold tortillas: Spoon filling onto warm tortilla. Fold over right side of tortilla. Fold bottom of tortilla. Fold left side over and serve.

8	large flour tortillas	8
2 lbs	warm cooked shredded beef (from Comforting Shredded Beef, see recipe, page 256)	1 kg
8	slices provolone or Swiss cheese	8
	Cooked onion slices	
	Pickled hot pepper rings	

1. Wrap tortillas in aluminum foil. Place in 350°F (180°C) oven for 15 to 20 minutes, or until warmed.
2. Spoon shredded beef into center of each warm flour tortilla. Top with cooked onions (from slow cooker), one cheese slice and a few pepper rings. Fold into a package shape. (See tip, at left.)
3. Serve with warm cooking juice for dipping.

Bargain Beef Stroganoff

Serves 4

This stroganoff is delicious and much more economical than the traditional version, which is usually made with filet of beef.

• • •

Tips

Serve with buttered wide egg noodles and a simple green vegetable such as steamed green beans or broccoli. To complete the meal, accompany it with a hearty red wine.

The most flavorful paprika comes from Hungary. It can range from mild to hot. Use whatever suits your taste.

• • •

Variation

Try this recipe with cubes of stewing veal instead of beef.

- Slow cooker size: 3½ to 5 quart

¼ cup	all-purpose flour	50 mL
1 tsp	salt	5 mL
½ tsp	freshly ground black pepper	2 mL
2 lbs	stewing beef, cut into 1-inch (2.5 cm) cubes	1 kg
2 tbsp	vegetable oil (approx.)	25 mL
8 oz	small white button mushrooms, cleaned, or large white mushrooms, quartered (about 2 cups/500 mL)	250 g
2	onions, thinly sliced	2
1½ cups	beef stock	375 mL
3 tbsp	Worcestershire sauce	45 mL
3 tbsp	tomato paste	45 mL
2 tbsp	paprika	25 mL
1½ tbsp	Dijon mustard	20 mL
1 cup	sour cream	250 mL
	Hot cooked egg noodles	

1. In a heavy plastic bag, combine flour, salt and pepper. In batches, add beef to seasoned flour and toss to coat.
2. In a large nonstick skillet, heat half the oil over medium-high heat. Cook beef in batches, adding more oil as needed, until browned all over. With a slotted spoon, transfer beef to slow cooker stoneware. Add mushrooms and onions.
3. In a 2-cup (500 mL) measure, combine beef stock, Worcestershire sauce, tomato paste, paprika and Dijon mustard, mixing well. Pour into slow cooker.
4. Cover and cook on **Low** for 8 to 10 hours or on **High** for 4 to 6 hours, until hot and bubbling. Stir in sour cream and serve over hot noodles.

Oxford Beef with Mushrooms

Serves 4

This delicious stew is similar to Beef Bourguignonne, but with added sweetness from the jam.

• • •

Tips

For a jewel-like appearance, add chopped dried apricots halfway through the cooking.

Browning seasoned meat before it is placed in the slow cooker will give the stew an enhanced rich flavor and eliminate any additional fat. But if you're pressed for time, you can dredge the meat in flour and add it directly to the slow cooker without browning first.

Cooking this stew the day before will give the flavors a chance to mingle and mellow.

- Slow cooker size: 3½ to 5 quart

¼ cup	all-purpose flour	50 mL
1 tsp	salt	5 mL
½ tsp	freshly ground black pepper	2 mL
2 lbs	stewing beef, cut into 1-inch (2.5 cm) pieces	1 kg
2 tbsp	vegetable oil (approx.)	25 mL
1	large onion, sliced	1
2	cloves garlic, minced	2
8 oz	sliced mushrooms	250 g
½ cup	apricot jam	125 mL
½ cup	red wine	125 mL
1 cup	beef stock	250 mL
1	green or red bell pepper, sliced	1

1. In a heavy plastic bag, combine flour, salt and pepper. In batches, add beef to flour mixture and toss to coat.
2. In a large skillet, heat half the oil over medium-high heat. Cook beef in batches, adding more oil as needed, until browned all over. Transfer beef to slow cooker stoneware. Add onion, garlic and mushrooms.
3. In a bowl, combine jam, wine and stock; add to slow cooker, stirring to combine.
4. Cover and cook on **Low** for 8 to 10 hours or on **High** for 4 to 6 hours, until hot and bubbling.
5. Add sliced pepper. Cover and cook on **High** for 15 to 20 minutes longer.

East-West Beef Curry

Serves 6 to 8

Fire up your guests with this stew that combines flavors from two different cuisines.

• • •

Tip

Select lean stewing beef or trim the excess fat from the meat before using. (Trimming may take a little extra time, but the result will be worth it.)

Chopped garlic in the jar is a convenient alternative to fresh garlic. It's easy to use and will keep in the refrigerator for up to 6 months.

Mild green chilies are found in the Mexican foods section of the supermarket. They are sold whole or chopped.

- Slow cooker size: 3½ to 6 quart

2 tbsp	vegetable oil (approx.)	25 mL
2 lbs	stewing beef, cut into 1-inch (2.5 cm) cubes	1 kg
1 tbsp	curry powder	15 mL
1 tbsp	ground coriander	15 mL
1 tsp	ground cumin	5 mL
1 tsp	dry mustard	5 mL
1½ tsp	salt	7 mL
1 tsp	freshly ground black pepper	5 mL
2	onions, sliced	2
1	red bell pepper, chopped	1
2	cloves garlic, minced	2
1 tsp	grated lemon zest	5 mL
1	can (19 oz/540 mL) stewed tomatoes, with juices	1
1	can (4½ oz/127 mL) chopped mild green chilies, including liquid	1
1 cup	beef stock	250 mL
2 tbsp	cider vinegar	25 mL
1 cup	coconut milk	250 mL

1. In a large nonstick skillet, heat half the oil over medium-high heat. Cook beef in batches, adding more oil as needed, until browned all over. Return all meat to skillet.
2. Sprinkle meat with curry powder, coriander, cumin, mustard, salt and pepper. Cook, stirring, for 2 minutes. With a slotted spoon, transfer seasoned meat to slow cooker stoneware.
3. Add onions, red pepper, garlic, lemon zest, tomatoes, green chilies, stock and vinegar to slow cooker. Stir well to combine.

4. Cover and cook on **Low** for 8 to 10 hours or on **High** for 4 to 6 hours, until beef is tender and stew is bubbling.
5. Stir in coconut milk. Cover and cook on **High** for 5 minutes longer, or until warmed through.

Coconut Milk

Canned coconut milk is made from grated and soaked coconut pulp, not (as you might expect) from the liquid inside the coconut. It can be found in the Asian or canned milk section of most supermarkets or in Asian food stores. Make sure you don't buy coconut cream, which is used to make tropical drinks such as piña coladas.

Tip

Serve with steamed basmati rice (page 163), chutney and/or raisins, chopped peanuts and Indian flatbread (naan). For an extra kick, try using fiery Madras curry powder. Curry powder and naan are both available in Indian food shops.

Coconut Beef Curry

Serves 6 to 8

Red curry paste is often available in the Asian food section of the supermarket. It is popular in Indian and Thai dishes and adds a wonderful zing to most recipes. If you can't find it, use curry powder instead.

• • •

Tips

Serve this dish over hot cooked couscous (page 198) or basmati rice (page 163).

Canned coconut milk is made from grated and soaked coconut pulp — not, as you might think, from the liquid found inside the coconut. It can be found in the Asian foods section of most supermarkets or Asian food stores. Be sure you don't buy coconut cream, which is often used for making tropical drinks such as piña coladas.

- Slow cooker size: 3½ to 5 quart

2 tbsp	vegetable oil (approx.)	25 mL
2 lbs	stewing beef, cut into ¼-inch (0.5 cm) strips	1 kg
2	onions, sliced	2
2	cloves garlic, minced	2
2 tbsp	paprika	25 mL
2 tbsp	ground cumin	25 mL
1 tsp	ground cinnamon	5 mL
2 tsp	red curry paste (or 1 tbsp/15 mL curry powder)	10 mL
4	potatoes, peeled and chopped	4
1	bag (1 lb/500 g) baby carrots	1
2 tbsp	tomato paste	25 mL
1	can (14 oz/398 mL) coconut milk	1
½ cup	water	125 mL
1 tsp	salt	5 mL
	Chopped fresh cilantro	

1. In a large nonstick skillet, heat half the oil over medium-high heat. Cook beef in batches, adding more oil as needed, until browned all over. Return all meat to skillet.
2. Add onions, garlic, paprika, cumin, cinnamon and curry paste (or curry powder). Sauté for 2 minutes, or until fragrant. With a slotted spoon, transfer mixture to slow cooker. Add potatoes and carrots.
3. In a small bowl, combine tomato paste, coconut milk, water and salt; mix well. Add to slow cooker; stir to combine with meat and vegetables.
4. Cover and cook on **Low** for 8 to 10 hours or on **High** for 4 to 6 hours, until vegetables are tender and stew is bubbling. Serve sprinkled with cilantro.

Gooey Glazed Beef Ribs

Serves 6

A zipped-up sauce slathered over a peppery rub makes these ribs a great summertime treat. No need to stand over a hot barbecue to get great-tasting ribs. Your kitchen can stay cool while the slow cooker does all the work.

• • •

Tip

Beef short ribs are a perfect cut of beef for the slow cooker. However, they are high in fat, so broil them first to reduce the fat.

- Slow cooker size: 5 to 6 quart

3 to 4 lbs	beef short ribs or braising ribs	1.5 to 2 kg
1 tsp	freshly ground black pepper	5 mL
6	cloves garlic, minced	6
1 cup	ketchup	250 mL
½ cup	water	125 mL
½ cup	maple syrup	125 mL
2 tbsp	Worcestershire sauce	25 mL
1 tbsp	Dijon mustard	15 mL

1. Position a broiler rack 6 inches (15 cm) from heat source and preheat broiler. Place ribs on a foil-lined baking sheet or broiler pan and sprinkle with pepper. Broil, turning often, for 10 to 15 minutes, or until browned on both sides. Transfer to a paper towel–lined plate to drain.
2. In a bowl, combine garlic, ketchup, water, maple syrup, Worcestershire sauce and mustard. Place ribs in slow cooker stoneware and pour sauce over ribs.
3. Cover and cook on **Low** for 8 to 12 hours or on **High** for 4 to 6 hours, until tender. Skim any fat from surface of sauce before serving.

Lumberjack Ribs

Serves 6

Beef braising ribs or short ribs are meaty bones about 4 to 6 inches (10 to 15 cm) long. Slow cooking makes them extremely flavorful and tender. But beware — these ribs require the hearty appetite of a hungry lumberjack! Horseradish is a must-have with these meaty morsels.

• • •

Tips

When purchasing short ribs, allow 2 servings for each 1 lb (500 g) of meat.

Broiling ribs allows them to brown and removes excess fat.

Chopped garlic in the jar is a convenient alternative to fresh garlic. It's easy to use and will keep in the refrigerator for up to 6 months.

- **Slow cooker size: 5 to 6 quart**

3 lbs	beef short ribs or braising ribs	1.5 kg
	Freshly ground black pepper	
1	can (19 oz/540 mL) Italian-style stewed tomatoes, coarsely chopped	1
2 cups	carrots, finely chopped	500 mL
2	onions, thinly sliced	2
8	cloves garlic, minced	8
½ cup	chopped fresh parsley (or ¼ cup/50 mL dried)	125 mL
2 tbsp	tomato paste	25 mL
2 tbsp	red wine vinegar	25 mL
2 tbsp	packed brown sugar	25 mL
2 tsp	salt	10 mL
½ tsp	dry mustard	2 mL
1 tbsp	grated gingerroot (or 1 tsp/5 mL ground ginger)	15 mL
1	bottle (12 oz/341 mL) beer	1
2 tbsp	prepared horseradish	25 mL

1. Position a broiler rack 6 inches (15 cm) from heat source and preheat broiler. Place ribs on foil-lined broiler pan or baking sheet and sprinkle liberally with pepper. Broil, turning often, for 10 to 15 minutes or until browned on all sides. Transfer to a paper towel–lined plate to drain.
2. In a bowl, combine tomatoes, carrots, onions, garlic, parsley, tomato paste, vinegar, brown sugar, salt, dry mustard and ginger, mixing well to combine. Place half the vegetable mixture in slow cooker stoneware, lay ribs on top and spoon over remaining vegetable mixture. Pour beer over vegetables and meat.

3. Cover and cook on **Low** for 8 to 10 hours or on **High** for 4 to 6 hours, until ribs are tender. Transfer meat to a platter and keep warm.
4. Skim fat from the surface of cooking liquid and add horseradish; stir to combine. Transfer mixture, in batches, to a blender or food processor and process until smooth. Pour sauce over ribs and serve immediately.

Italian-Style Tomatoes

In place of one 19-oz (540 mL) can Italian-style stewed tomatoes, use regular stewed tomatoes and add ½ tsp (2 mL) dried Italian herb seasoning or a combination of dried basil, marjoram, thyme and oregano.

Tip

Tired of opening a whole can of tomato paste when all you need is a small amount? Look for the squeeze tubes of tomato paste sold in most supermarkets.

Classic Homestyle Meatloaf

Serves 6 to 8

Everyone loves an old-fashioned meatloaf. Serve with mashed potatoes (pages 255 and 303).

• • •

Tip

You can also line the slow cooker with cheesecloth, using enough material to lift out the finished meatloaf.

- **Slow cooker size: 3½ to 6 quart**

1	large onion, finely chopped	1
2	stalks celery, finely chopped	2
1	carrot, peeled and shredded	1
1	egg, lightly beaten	1
1½ lbs	lean ground beef	750 g
1 cup	dry bread crumbs	250 mL
½ cup	ketchup	125 mL
1 tbsp	garlic powder	15 mL
¾ tsp	dried thyme	4 mL
¾ tsp	salt	4 mL
¾ tsp	freshly ground black pepper	4 mL

1. Cut a 2-foot (60 cm) length of foil in half lengthwise. Fold each strip in half lengthwise, forming two long strips. Crisscross the strips in the bottom of the slow cooker, bringing the ends of the foil strips up and clear of the stoneware rim.
2. In a large bowl, combine onion, celery, carrot, egg, beef, bread crumbs, ketchup, garlic powder, thyme, salt and pepper. Using your hands, blend meat mixture well. Press evenly into foil-lined slow cooker stoneware, tucking foil ends under lid.
3. Cover and cook on **Low** for 8 to 10 hours or on **High** for 4 to 6 hours, or until a meat thermometer inserted into meatloaf reads 170°F (77°C). Remove lid and grasp ends of foil strips to lift out meatloaf.

Magnificent Meatloaf

Serves 4 to 6

I am convinced there is no better way to cook meatloaf than in a slow cooker. Slow cooking helps keep it juicy and moist, and makes for easy cutting too.

• • •

Tip

This loaf can be made with 2 lbs (1 kg) ground beef (instead of the beef and pork) or you can use 1 lb (500 g) beef and substitute ground chicken or turkey for the ground pork.

- Slow cooker size: 3½ to 6 quart

1 lb	lean ground beef	500 g
1 lb	lean ground pork	500 g
4	green onions, finely chopped	4
1	package (10 oz/300 g) frozen chopped spinach, thawed and drained	1
¾ cup	fine dry bread crumbs	175 mL
½ cup	freshly grated Parmesan cheese	125 mL
¼ cup	chili sauce	50 mL
2	eggs, lightly beaten	2
¼ cup	finely chopped parsley (or 2 tbsp/25 mL dried)	50 mL
2 tsp	salt	10 mL
½ tsp	ground nutmeg	2 mL
¼ tsp	freshly ground black pepper	1 mL
	Chopped fresh parsley	

1. Cut a 2-foot (60 cm) length of foil in half lengthwise. Fold each strip in half lengthwise, forming two long strips. Crisscross the strips in the bottom of the slow cooker, bringing the ends of the foil strips up and clear of the stoneware rim.
2. In a large bowl, combine beef and pork, mixing well. In a separate bowl, combine green onions, spinach, bread crumbs, cheese, chili sauce, eggs, parsley, salt, nutmeg and pepper. Add to meat and mix well. Press evenly into foil-lined slow cooker stoneware, tucking foil ends under lid.
3. Cover and cook on **Low** for 8 to 10 hours or on **High** for 4 to 6 hours, or until a meat thermometer inserted into meatloaf reads 170°F (77°C). Remove lid and grasp ends of foil strips to lift out meatloaf. Serve sprinkled with parsley.

Stuffed Mexican Meatloaf

Serves 4 to 6

This family favorite is like an all-in-one taco dish. Serve with a corn and bean salad over shredded lettuce, with additional salsa on the side.

• • •

Tips

For an extra kick, substitute Monterey Jack or a nacho cheese blend in place of the Cheddar.

You can also line the slow cooker with cheesecloth, using enough material to lift out the finished meatloaf.

- Slow cooker size: 3½ to 6 quart

2 lbs	lean ground beef	1 kg
1	can (7½ oz/213 mL) tomato sauce	1
2 tbsp	taco seasoning mix	25 mL
⅓ cup	finely chopped green bell pepper	75 mL
⅓ cup	finely chopped onion	75 mL
⅔ cup	crushed tortilla chips, divided	150 mL
1	egg, lightly beaten	1
2 cups	shredded Cheddar cheese, divided	500 mL
½ cup	sour cream	125 mL
1	tomato, sliced	1
2 tbsp	chopped fresh cilantro	25 mL

1. Cut a 2-foot (60 cm) length of foil in half lengthwise. Fold each strip in half lengthwise, forming two long strips. Crisscross the strips in the bottom of the slow cooker, bringing the ends of the foil strips up and clear of the stoneware rim.
2. In a large bowl, combine beef, tomato sauce, taco seasoning mix, green pepper, onion, ½ cup (125 mL) tortilla chips and egg. Mix well.
3. In a separate bowl, combine 1½ cups (375 mL) cheese and sour cream.
4. Press half the meat mixture evenly into foil-lined slow cooker stoneware, making a well in center of loaf. Spoon sour cream mixture into well. Top with remaining meat mixture. Tuck foil ends under lid.
5. Cover and cook on **Low** for 8 to 10 hours or on **High** for 4 to 6 hours, or until a meat thermometer inserted into meatloaf reads 170°F (77°C).
6. Sprinkle remaining cheese over top of loaf and garnish with remaining tortilla chops, tomato slices and cilantro. Cover and cook on **High** for 5 to 10 minutes longer, or until cheese is melted. Remove lid and grasp ends of foil strips to lift out meatloaf.

Three-Cheese Meatloaf

Serves 4 to 6

If you can't imagine serving meatloaf to guests, try this one. With all the cheese, even the kids will love it! Make sure you serve it hot so the cheese still bubbles.

• • •

Tip

You can also line the slow cooker with cheesecloth, using enough material to lift out the finished meatloaf.

- Slow cooker size: 3½ to 5 quart

2 lbs	lean ground beef	1 kg
1	large onion, finely chopped	1
½	green bell pepper, finely chopped	½
½ cup	fine dry bread crumbs	125 mL
1 tsp	salt	5 mL
½ tsp	freshly ground black pepper	2 mL
½ tsp	paprika	2 mL
2	eggs, lightly beaten	2
¼ cup	milk	50 mL
1 tsp	dried Italian seasoning	5 mL
⅓ cup	diced mozzarella cheese (½-inch/1 cm cubes)	75 mL
⅓ cup	diced Swiss cheese (½-inch/1 cm cubes)	75 mL
½ cup	freshly grated Parmesan cheese	125 mL

1. Cut a 2-foot (60 cm) length of foil in half lengthwise. Fold each strip in half lengthwise, forming two long strips. Crisscross the strips in the bottom of the slow cooker, bringing the ends of the foil strips up and clear of the stoneware rim.
2. In a large bowl, combine beef, onion, green pepper, bread crumbs, salt, pepper and paprika, mixing well. In a small bowl, combine eggs and milk; stir into meat mixture. Add Italian seasoning, mozzarella, Swiss and Parmesan cheeses. Using your hands, blend meat mixture well. Press evenly into foil-lined slow cooker stoneware, tucking foil ends under lid.
3. Cover and cook on **Low** for 8 to 10 hours or on **High** for 4 to 6 hours, or until a meat thermometer inserted into meatloaf reads 170°F (77°C) and cheese is bubbling. Remove lid and grasp ends of foil strips to lift out meatloaf. Serve immediately.

Easy Cabbage Roll Casserole

Serves 6 to 8

While everyone enjoys the great taste of cabbage rolls, they're a lot of work to make. This recipe is an easy alternative with the same great taste.

• • •

Tip

To grease slow cooker stoneware, use a vegetable nonstick spray. Or use cake pan grease, which is available in specialty cake-decorating or bulk-food stores.

Make Ahead

This dish can be completely assembled up to 12 hours in advance of cooking. Follow preparation directions and refrigerate overnight in the slow cooker stoneware. The next day, place stoneware in slow cooker and continue cooking as directed.

- Slow cooker size: 3½ to 5 quart

1½ lbs	lean ground beef or turkey	750 g
2	onions, finely chopped	2
1	clove garlic, minced	1
1 tsp	salt	5 mL
¼ tsp	freshly ground black pepper	1 mL
1	can (7½ oz/221 mL) tomato sauce	1
1 cup	water	250 mL
1	can (10 oz/284 mL) condensed tomato soup, undiluted	1
½ cup	long-grain rice	125 mL
4 cups	shredded cabbage	1 L
⅓ cup	tomato juice or water	75 mL
	Sour cream	

1. In a large nonstick skillet, over medium-high heat, cook ground beef, onions, garlic, salt and pepper, breaking up meat with back of a spoon, until no longer pink. Drain off any excess fat. Return to heat and add tomato sauce, water and half the can of tomato soup, mixing well. Add rice, stirring to combine.
2. Place half the meat mixture in lightly greased slow cooker stoneware, then half the cabbage. Top with remaining meat mixture and remaining cabbage.
3. In a bowl, combine remaining tomato soup with tomato juice, mixing well. Pour into slow cooker.
4. Cover and cook on **Low** for 8 to 10 hours or on **High** for 4 to 6 hours, until bubbling and heated through. Serve with sour cream.

Cheeseburger Sloppy Joes

Serves 4 to 6

This dish is a great choice for those nights when everyone is coming and going at different times, since you can leave it simmering in the slow cooker and people can help themselves.

• • •

Tip

Serve over toasted kaiser rolls or whole wheat toast and add a tossed green salad for a delicious meal.

- **Slow cooker size: 3½ to 5 quart**

2 lbs	lean ground beef or turkey	1 kg
1	onion, finely chopped	1
2	stalks celery, finely chopped	2
1	can (10 oz/284mL) condensed tomato soup, undiluted	1
¼ cup	water	50 mL
2 tbsp	tomato paste	25 mL
1 tbsp	Worcestershire sauce	15 mL
2 tsp	dried Italian seasoning	10 mL
1 cup	diced Cheddar cheese (½-inch/1 cm cubes)	250 mL
	Salt and freshly ground black pepper	
4 to 6	kaiser buns, split and toasted	4 to 6

1. In a large nonstick skillet, over medium-high heat, cook ground beef, breaking up with back of a spoon, until no longer pink. With a slotted spoon, transfer meat to slow cooker.
2. Add onion, celery, tomato soup, water, tomato paste, Worcestershire sauce and Italian seasoning to slow cooker; stir to combine.
3. Cover and cook on **Low** for 6 to 10 hours or on **High** for 3 to 4 hours, until hot and bubbling.
4. Reduce heat to **Low**. Add cheese cubes. Cover and cook for 10 to 15 minutes longer, or until cheese melts. Season to taste with salt and pepper.
5. Spoon mixture over half a kaiser bun and top with the other half.

Tortilla Stack

Serves 4 to 6

Enchiladas are a Mexican specialty consisting of tortillas rolled around a meat, vegetable or cheese filling. The tortillas are heated and topped with tomato sauce and cheese. I have simplified things a bit in this recipe, where the tortillas are simply layered with seasoned meat filling, beans, cheese and sour cream.

• • •

Tips

You can substitute 1½ cups (375 mL) shredded cooked chicken for the ground beef.

Pickled jalapeños can be found in the Mexican food section of the supermarket.

- Slow cooker size: 5 to 6 quart

1½ lbs	lean ground beef	750 g
1	onion, finely chopped	1
4	cloves garlic, minced	4
4 tsp	chili powder	20 mL
½ tsp	dried oregano	2 mL
¼ tsp	salt	1 mL
Pinch	cayenne pepper	Pinch
1	can (19 oz/540 mL) red kidney or black beans, drained and rinsed, or 2 cups (500 mL) home-cooked beans (page 146)	1
1 cup	fresh or frozen corn kernels (thawed if frozen)	250 mL
1 cup	salsa, divided	250 mL
4	10-inch (25 cm) corn or flour tortillas	4
1 cup	shredded Cheddar cheese, divided	250 mL
2 tbsp	pickled jalapeño slices	25 mL
½ cup	sour cream	125 mL

1. In a large nonstick skillet, over medium-high heat, cook ground beef, onion and garlic, breaking up meat with back of a spoon, until meat is no longer pink. Add chili powder, oregano, salt and cayenne and cook, stirring, for 2 minutes.
2. In a bowl, mash kidney beans. Stir in corn and ¼ cup (50 mL) salsa.
3. Lay one tortilla in bottom of lightly greased slow cooker stoneware. Spread one-third of beef mixture over tortilla, then one-third of salsa/bean mixture, one-quarter of cheese and one-third of jalapeño slices. Repeat layers twice. Top with remaining tortilla and spread remaining salsa over top.

4. Cover and cook on **High** for 2 to 3 hours, or until heated through.
5. Spread sour cream over tortillas and sprinkle with remaining cheese. Cover and cook on **High** for 15 minutes longer, or until cheese melts.
6. Let stand for 10 minutes before serving. Remove from slow cooker with a spatula and slice.

Frozen Vegetables

In general, you should defrost frozen vegetables before adding them to the slow cooker. Adding them while still frozen will bring down the cooking temperature of the dish. Defrost overnight in the refrigerator or rinse under cold running water to separate; drain well.

Tip

Serve this casserole with sliced fresh tomatoes or a green salad tossed with radishes and orange segments.

Beef and Bean Burritos

Serves 4 to 6

Looking for a hot and hearty meal to please the whole family? Here's just the recipe. All you need is a crisp salad for a complete dinner.

Make Ahead

This dish can be completely assembled up to 24 hours before cooking. Cook ground beef mixture and cool completely before assembling dish. Refrigerate overnight in the slow cooker stoneware. The next day, place stoneware in slow cooker and continue to cook as directed. You can also cook the entire filling ahead, refrigerate overnight and assemble the burritos the next day. Refrigerate until ready to bake.

- **Slow cooker size: 3½ to 6 quart**

2 lbs	lean ground beef	1 kg
1	onion, finely chopped	1
2	cloves garlic, minced	2
1 tbsp	chili powder	15 mL
1 tsp	ground cumin	5 mL
1	can (14 oz/398 mL) tomato sauce	1
1 cup	salsa	250 mL
1	can (19 oz/540 mL) pinto or Romano beans, drained and rinsed, or 2 cups (500 mL) home-cooked beans (page 146)	1
1 cup	fresh or frozen corn kernels (thawed if frozen)	250 mL
10 to 12	10-inch (25 cm) flour tortillas	10 to 12
1 cup	shredded Cheddar cheese	250 mL

1. In a large nonstick skillet, over medium-high heat, cook ground beef, onion, garlic, chili powder and cumin, breaking up meat with back of a spoon, until meat is no longer pink. Drain off all fat and transfer meat to slow cooker stoneware.
2. Add tomato sauce, salsa, beans and corn to slow cooker; stir to combine.
3. Cover and cook on **Low** for 6 to 10 hours or on **High** for 3 to 4 hours, until hot and bubbling.
4. Divide meat mixture evenly among tortillas and roll up burrito style. Arrange in a 13- by 9-inch (3 L) baking dish. Sprinkle with shredded Cheddar.
5. Cover with foil and bake in a preheated 350°F (180°C) oven for 20 minutes, or until burritos are slightly browned.

Barbecued Beef Sandwiches

Serves 8

Hot sandwiches don't come any easier. Just combine the sauce ingredients and pour over the meat in the slow cooker. Be sure to toast the sandwich buns to help keep them from getting soggy. You can also serve the beef on its own as a roast.

• • •

Tips

Do not use diet cola in this recipe. It will impart a strange aftertaste.

Liquid smoke is exactly that — liquid mixed with smoke. Brushed on or stirred into food, it lends a smoky, hickory flavor to dishes. Look for it in the condiment aisle of the supermarket.

- Slow cooker size: 3½ to 6 quart

1	boneless beef cross rib or blade roast (3 to 4 lbs/1.5 to 2 kg)	1
1 tsp	salt	5 mL
½ tsp	freshly ground black pepper	2 mL
1 tbsp	vegetable oil	15 mL
2 cups	ketchup	500 mL
1	can (12 oz/355 mL) cola	1
¼ cup	Worcestershire sauce	50 mL
2 tbsp	prepared mustard	25 mL
2 tbsp	liquid smoke	25 mL
¼ tsp	hot pepper sauce (or 1 jalapeño pepper, seeded and finely chopped)	1 mL
8	kaiser buns, toasted	8

1. Season roast on all sides with salt and pepper. In a large skillet, heat oil over medium-high heat. Add meat and cook, turning with wooden spoons, for 7 to 10 minutes, or until browned on all sides. Transfer meat to slow cooker stoneware.
2. In a bowl, combine ketchup, cola, Worcestershire sauce, prepared mustard, liquid smoke and hot pepper sauce. Pour sauce over roast.
3. Cover and cook on **Low** for 10 to 12 hours or on **High** for 4 to 6 hours, until meat is fork-tender.
4. Remove meat from slow cooker and let stand for 10 minutes before carving. Skim fat from sauce. Place meat on a kaiser bun, add 1 tbsp (15 mL) sauce and cover with remaining half of bun. Serve with additional sauce for dipping.

Texas-Style Barbecued Brisket Sandwiches

Serves 6 to 8

Brisket, a less tender cut of beef, is extremely well suited to slow cooking. This down-home favorite recipe uses hickory-flavored barbecue sauce which adds a rich, smoky flavor. It is best cooked long and slow.

• • •

Tip

Serve this perfect picnic fare with Best-Ever Baked Beans (see recipe, page 167), which can be made the day before and eaten cold.

- Slow cooker size: 3½ to 5 quart

1	brisket point roast (about 3 lbs/1.5 kg), well-trimmed	1
½ cup	ketchup	125 mL
¼ cup	water	50 mL
¼ cup	liquid honey	50 mL
¼ cup	red wine vinegar	50 mL
2 tbsp	packed brown sugar	25 mL
2 tbsp	hot pepper sauce (or 1 tsp/5 mL hot pepper flakes)	25 mL
2 tbsp	hickory-flavored barbecue sauce	25 mL
1 tbsp	Worcestershire sauce	15 mL
1 tbsp	Dijon mustard	15 mL
1 tbsp	soy sauce	15 mL
2	cloves garlic, minced	2
1	onion, finely chopped	1
8	kaiser buns, split	8

1. Place brisket in slow cooker stoneware. (If meat is too large for your slow cooker, cut crosswise into 2 or 3 chunks.)
2. In a large bowl or glass measure, combine ketchup, water, honey, vinegar, brown sugar, hot pepper sauce, barbecue sauce, Worcestershire sauce, Dijon mustard, soy sauce, garlic and onion. Mix well and pour over brisket.
3. Cover and cook on **Low** for 8 to 10 hours, until meat is very tender.
4. Remove meat from slow cooker and let stand for 10 minutes before carving. Using a sharp knife, slice meat across the grain into thin slices. Place meat on one kaiser half, add 1 tbsp (25 mL) sauce and cover with other kaiser half. Serve with additional sauce for dipping.

Italian Stuffed Peppers

Serves 6

Stuffed peppers are a classic slow cooker meal. They are quick and easy to prepare, and this recipe will be a welcome addition to your family's repertoire. It is best to use an oval slow cooker so that the peppers fit in one layer.

• • •

Tips

Cutting a hole in the bottom of the peppers allows moisture and steam to penetrate, promoting even cooking.

You can substitute ground turkey or chicken for the veal, but increase the pepper to ½ tsp (2 mL).

- Slow cooker size: 6 quart

6	small to medium red, yellow and/or green bell peppers, tops removed, cored and seeded	6
1 lb	lean ground veal	500 g
1½ cups	cooked rice (about ½ cup/125 mL uncooked)	375 mL
2	eggs, lightly beaten	2
2	cloves garlic, minced	2
⅓ cup	freshly grated Parmesan cheese	75 mL
2 tbsp	finely chopped fresh parsley	25 mL
½ tsp	salt	2 mL
¼ tsp	freshly ground black pepper	1 mL
1 cup	tomato sauce or pasta sauce	250 mL

1. Cut a small hole in the bottom of each pepper.
2. In a bowl, combine veal, rice, eggs, garlic, Parmesan, parsley, salt and pepper. Spoon meat mixture into peppers. Do not pack down.
3. Stand peppers upright in slow cooker stoneware. Spoon tomato sauce evenly over top of each stuffed pepper.
4. Cover and cook on **Low** for 4 to 5 hours, or until peppers are tender and a meat thermometer inserted into the center of a pepper reads 170°F (77°C).

Osso Buco with Lemon Gremolata

Serves 6 to 8

This classic Italian dish is perfect for the slow cooker. It needs long slow, all-day cooking — just what you need for easy entertaining. Your guests will be greeted with a tantalizing aroma when they walk through the door!

• • •

Tip

I recommend you use a large (5- to 6-quart) slow cooker to make this recipe. For a smaller (2½- to 4-quart) slow cooker, reduce ingredients by half and use a 19-oz (540 mL) can of tomatoes.

- Slow cooker size: 5 to 6 quart

8	thick slices veal shank, each tied with string	8
	Salt and freshly ground black pepper	
	All-purpose flour	
2 tbsp	olive oil	25 mL
2 tbsp	butter	25 mL
2	onions, finely chopped	2
2	carrots, peeled and finely chopped	2
1	stalk celery, finely chopped	1
6	large cloves garlic, minced	6
1 cup	dry white wine	250 mL
¾ cup	chicken or beef stock	175 mL
1	can (28 oz/796 mL) diced tomatoes, drained	1
2	fresh basil leaves (or ½ tsp/2 mL dried)	2
2	fresh thyme sprigs (or ½ tsp/2 mL dried)	2
¼ cup	chopped fresh parsley (or 2 tbsp/25 mL dried)	50 mL
2	bay leaves	2

Gremolata

1 tbsp	grated lemon zest	15 mL
1	clove garlic, minced	1
¼ cup	chopped fresh parsley	50 mL

1. Lightly sprinkle veal shanks on both sides with salt and pepper. Coat on both sides with flour, shaking off the excess.
2. In a large skillet, heat olive oil over medium-high heat. Add veal and cook until browned on both sides. Transfer veal to slow cooker stoneware. Pour off any excess fat from skillet.

3. Return skillet to medium heat and melt butter. Add onions, carrots, celery and garlic. Sauté for 5 minutes or until vegetables are softened. Add wine, stock, tomatoes, basil, thyme, parsley and bay leaves; stir to combine. Spoon over veal in slow cooker.
4. Cover and cook on **Low** for 8 to 12 hours or on **High** for 5 to 7 hours, basting occasionally. (If cooking on **High**, heat can be reduced to **Low** once meat has cooked the recommended length of time. The slow cooker will keep meat warm until ready to serve.) Discard bay leaves. Season to taste with salt and pepper.
5. *Gremolata:* In a bowl, combine lemon zest, garlic and parsley.
6. When shanks are tender, remove strings and transfer to a warm platter. Spoon sauce over meat and sprinkle with gremolata garnish.

Tip

Veal shanks are readily available in the fresh meat section of the supermarket. It's important to secure them with butcher's twine so they won't fall apart while cooking. Ask the butcher to do this for you — it will save you some extra work at home.

Pork and Lamb

Roast Pork with Two Potatoes

Serves 6

This simple roast is delicately flavored with the licorice accent of fennel, making it an easy but elegant dish for entertaining.

• • •

Tips

Yellow flesh potatoes such as Yukon Gold look great next to the bright orange color of the sweet potatoes.

There are three basic types of pork roast — loin, leg and shoulder. While loin roasts are very lean and tender, they are not the best for slow cooking. A boneless shoulder butt roast is ideal — it has some marbling and is less tender, which makes it perfect for all-day, moist-heat cooking.

- **Slow cooker size: 3½ to 6 quart**

2	sweet potatoes, peeled and cut into ½-inch (1 cm) cubes	2
2	potatoes, peeled and cut into ½-inch (1 cm) cubes	2
2 tsp	fennel seeds	10 mL
1 tsp	dried oregano	5 mL
1 tsp	paprika	5 mL
½ tsp	garlic powder	2 mL
½ tsp	salt	2 mL
¼ tsp	freshly ground black pepper	1 mL
1	boneless pork loin rib end or shoulder butt roast (2 to 3 lbs/1 to 1.5 kg), trimmed of excess fat	1
1 cup	chicken stock	250 mL

1. Place all potatoes in bottom of slow cooker stoneware.
2. With a mortar and pestle or with a rolling pin on a cutting board, crush fennel seeds. In a small bowl, combine crushed fennel seeds, oregano, paprika, garlic powder, salt and pepper. Rub into pork roast. Place seasoned roast on potatoes. Pour stock around meat and vegetables.
3. Cover and cook on **Low** for 10 to 12 hours or on **High** for 5 to 6 hours, until pork and potatoes are tender.
4. To serve, transfer roast to a cutting board and cover loosely with foil. Let stand for 15 minutes before carving. Slice roast and serve with potatoes.

Roast Pork with Tangy Cranberry Sauce

Serves 6 to 8

If you can't find dried cranberries, use raisins instead. The resulting sauce will be sweeter (and less tangy) but equally delicious.

Make Ahead

This recipe can be assembled 12 to 24 hours in advance. Prepare the ingredients in the slow cooker up to the cooking stage (without adding cornstarch and remaining ¼ cup/50 mL cranberry juice) and refrigerate in stoneware insert overnight. The next day, place stoneware in slow cooker and continue cooking as directed.

- Slow cooker size: 3½ to 5 quart

1	boneless pork shoulder butt roast (2 to 3 lbs/1 to 1.5 kg), trimmed of excess fat	1
1 cup	dried cranberries	250 mL
½ cup	chicken stock	125 mL
½ cup	cranberry juice cocktail	125 mL
	Grated zest of ½ orange	
1 tsp	ground ginger	5 mL
2 tbsp	cornstarch	25 mL
	Salt and freshly ground black pepper	

1. Place roast in slow cooker stoneware.
2. In a bowl, combine cranberries, stock, ¼ cup (50 mL) cranberry juice, orange zest and ginger, mixing well. Pour over roast.
3. Cover and cook on **Low** for 6 to 10 hours or on **High** for 3 to 4 hours, until meat is tender.
4. Remove roast from slow cooker. Cover with foil to keep warm. Pour juices from slow cooker into a medium saucepan and skim off any accumulated fat.
5. In a small saucepan, combine cornstarch with remaining ¼ cup (50 mL) cranberry juice, stirring well to dissolve any lumps. Over medium-high heat, bring mixture to a boil, stirring constantly until thickened. Season to taste with salt and pepper and serve with roast pork.

Sweet-and-Sour Pork

Serves 4 to 6

Traditional sweet-and-sour pork is made with deep-fried pork pieces cooked in a sweet-tangy sauce. Ground ginger flavors the sauce in this lean and easy one-pot version.

• • •

Tip

Serve over steamed rice (page 163) or rice (cellophane) noodles. To prepare noodles, place in a large bowl of hot water. Soak for about 5 minutes to soften. As soon as noodles are tender, drain in a colander and set aside. Before serving, stir-fry in hot oil for 5 minutes, or until heated through.

- Slow cooker size: 3½ to 6 quart

2 tbsp	vegetable oil (approx.)	25 mL
2 lbs	boneless pork shoulder butt roast, trimmed of excess fat, cut into 1-inch (2.5 cm) cubes	1 kg
1 tsp	ground ginger	5 mL
½ tsp	dry mustard	2 mL
1	can (14 oz/398 mL) unsweetened pineapple tidbits, with juices	1
3 tbsp	packed brown sugar	45 mL
¼ cup	white vinegar	50 mL
3 tbsp	soy sauce	45 mL
1	red bell pepper, coarsely chopped	1
3 tbsp	water	45 mL
2 tbsp	cornstarch	25 mL
1 cup	snow peas, cut in half	250 mL

1. In a large nonstick skillet, heat oil over medium-high heat. Cook pork in batches, adding more oil as needed, until browned all over. Return all pork to skillet. Add ginger and dry mustard and cook, stirring, for 2 minutes. Transfer meat to slow cooker stoneware.
2. Add pineapple, brown sugar, vinegar and soy sauce to slow cooker; stir to combine.
3. Cover and cook on **Low** for 6 to 8 hours or on **High** for 3 to 4 hours, until pork is tender.
4. Stir in red pepper. Cover and cook on **High** for 20 minutes longer.
6. In a small bowl or jar, combine water and cornstarch (see tip, page 285). Stir into pork along with snow peas. Cover and cook on **High** for 10 minutes longer, or until sauce thickens and vegetables are tender-crisp.

Honey and Spice Glazed Pork Chops

Serves 4

The best chops to buy for the slow cooker are thick-cut loin chops from the rib end or shoulder butt chops. Avoid center-cut loin chops as they will cook too quickly and dry out.

• • •

Tip

A quick way to mix cornstarch with a liquid is to use a jar. Screw the lid on tightly and shake the jar until the mixture is smooth. (This is faster than trying to stir or whisk until all the cornstarch is dissolved.)

- Slow cooker size: 3½ to 6 quart

¼ cup	liquid honey	50 mL
2 tbsp	Dijon mustard	25 mL
½ tsp	ground ginger	2 mL
¼ tsp	ground cinnamon	1 mL
Pinch	ground cloves	Pinch
1 tbsp	vegetable oil	15 mL
4	pork loin rib end chops or shoulder butt chops, 1 inch (2.5 cm) thick, trimmed of excess fat	4
½ tsp	salt	2 mL
¼ tsp	freshly ground black pepper	1 mL
2 tbsp	cornstarch	25 mL
2 tbsp	water	25 mL

1. In a small bowl, combine honey, Dijon mustard, ginger, cinnamon and cloves.
2. In a large nonstick skillet, heat oil over medium-high heat. Sprinkle chops with salt and pepper and cook in batches for about 5 minutes per side, or until browned.
3. Transfer chops to slow cooker stoneware. Pour honey-mustard sauce mixture over chops.
4. Cover and cook loin rib end chops on **Low** for 4 to 5 hours or on **High** for 2 to 3 hours, until pork is tender. (Shoulder butt chops should cook on **Low** for 6 to 8 hours or on **High** for 3 to 4 hours.) With a slotted spoon, remove pork to a platter. Cover to keep warm.
5. In a small bowl or jar, combine cornstarch and water (see tip, at left). Stir into sauce in slow cooker. Cover and cook on **High** for 15 to 20 minutes, or until thickened. Pour over pork chops and serve.

Pork Chops with Creamy Mustard Sauce

Serves 4 to 6

This simple dish owes its origins to French country cooking. The creamy mustard sauce goes well with the tender, juicy pork chops.

• • •

Tip

Parsnips are a wonderful winter vegetable that resemble white carrots. (At least that's the description I give my vegetable-wary children when they ask, "What's that?") Parsnips have a slightly sweet flavor and make a delicious addition to many soups and stews.

- **Slow cooker size: 3½ to 6 quart**

2	large carrots, peeled and sliced	2
2	parsnips, peeled and sliced	2
1	small shallot, finely chopped	1
2 tbsp	all-purpose flour	25 mL
1 tsp	salt	5 mL
½ tsp	freshly ground black pepper	2 mL
1 tbsp	vegetable oil	15 mL
4 to 6	boneless pork loin rib end chops, 1 inch (2.5 cm) thick, trimmed of excess fat	4 to 6
¾ cup	dry white wine or undiluted condensed chicken broth	175 mL
1	large onion, sliced	1
¼ cup	whipping (35%) cream or evaporated milk	50 mL
1 tbsp	Dijon mustard	15 mL

1. Place carrots, parsnips and shallot in slow cooker stoneware. Sprinkle with flour, salt and pepper and toss to coat.
2. In a large nonstick skillet, heat oil over medium-high heat. Add pork chops in batches and cook for 5 minutes per side, or until browned. Remove pork chops and drain on a paper towel–lined plate to remove any excess oil.
3. Pour wine into skillet and bring to a boil, scraping up any browned bits.
4. Place browned pork on top of vegetables in slow cooker and lay onion slices on top of meat. Pour in wine mixture.

5. Cover and cook on **Low** for 4 to 5 hours or on **High** for 2 to 3 hours, until meat is tender.
6. With a slotted spoon, remove pork chops and vegetables from slow cooker and keep warm. Skim fat from juices.
7. In a small bowl, combine cream and mustard. Stir into juices in slow cooker. Cover and cook on **High** for 5 minutes, or until slightly thickened.
8. For a thicker sauce, transfer to a saucepan and bring to a boil. Cook gently for about 5 minutes, or until desired consistency. Serve sauce with pork chops.

Roasted Potatoes

Scrub 2 lbs (1 kg) potatoes and cut in chunks. Toss with 2 tbsp (25 mL) vegetable or olive oil, ½ tsp (2 mL) salt and ¼ tsp (1 mL) black pepper. Place in a greased baking dish and roast in a preheated 425°F (220°C) oven for 50 to 60 minutes, or until tender and golden brown. Turn once during cooking. *Makes 4 to 6 servings.*

Tip

Removing lid of slow cooker releases heat, which will lengthen the cooking time. Do not remove lid until minimum cooking time.

Pork Chops with Curried Apple Onion Sauce

Serves 4

The curry flavor goes well with the pork and fruit in this dish.

• • •

Tips

You can substitute 1/4 cup (50 mL) evaporated milk for the cream. Freeze leftover evaporated milk in ice cube trays to make it easy to add small amounts to pasta sauces and soups.

If you wish, you can purée the sauce in a blender or food processor (or use an immersion blender) before spooning it over the pork chops.

- Slow cooker size: 5 to 6 quart

1 tbsp	curry powder	15 mL
1 tsp	dried thyme	5 mL
1 tsp	dried marjoram	5 mL
4	pork loin rib end chops or shoulder butt chops, 1 inch (2.5 cm) thick, trimmed of excess fat	4
1 tbsp	vegetable oil	15 mL
1	large onion, thinly sliced	1
3	cloves garlic, minced	3
1	apple, peeled and chopped	1
1/2 cup	chicken stock	125 mL
1/2 cup	dry white wine	125 mL
2 tbsp	honey mustard	25 mL
1/4 cup	whipping (35%) cream	50 mL
	Salt and freshly ground black pepper	

1. In a bowl, combine curry powder, thyme and marjoram. Rub both sides of pork chops with spice mixture.
2. In a large nonstick skillet, heat oil over medium-high heat. Add pork chops in batches and cook for 5 minutes per side, or until browned. Remove to a plate.
3. Add onion, garlic and apple to drippings in skillet. Cook, stirring, for 2 minutes. Transfer to slow cooker stoneware. Place reserved pork chops over onion mixture. Pour in stock and wine.
4. Cover and cook loin rib end chops on **Low** for 4 to 5 hours or on **High** for 2 to 3 hours, or until pork is tender. (Shoulder butt chops should cook on **Low** for 6 to 8 hours or on **High** for 3 to 4 hours.) Remove pork to a platter and cover loosely with foil to keep warm.
5. Stir honey mustard and cream into sauce. Season with salt and pepper. Spoon sauce over pork chops and serve.